Excel

PRELIMINARY

ENGINEERING STUDIES

Get the Results You Want!

T0360066

PETER METCALFE & ROGER METCALFE

PASCAL
PRESS

© 2006 Peter Metcalfe, Roger Metcalfe and Pascal Press
Reprinted 2009
Revised for HSC syllabus changes 2014
Reprinted 2015, 2019, 2022

ISBN 978 1 74125 456 3

Pascal Press
PO Box 250
Glebe NSW 2037
(02) 8585 4050
www.pascalpress.com.au

Publisher: Vivienne Joannou
Project editor: Mark Dixon
Edited by Ian Rohr
Reviewed by Neil Faulkner
Typeset by Peter Metcalfe
Cover by DiZign Pty Ltd
Printed by Vivar Printing/Green Giant Press

Note to students
All care has been taken in the preparation of this study guide, but please check with your
teacher or the NSW Education Standards Authority about the exact requirements of the
course you are studying as these can change from year to year.

The validity and appropriateness of the internet addresses (URLs) in this book were
checked at the time of publication. Due to the dynamic nature of the internet, the publisher
cannot accept responsibility for the continued validity or content of these web addresses.

PREFACE

We live in a world surrounded by the products of engineering and yet in the minds of many, what engineering is, what an engineer does, and who can call themselves an engineer is unclear.

An inquiry undertaken by the Australian Senate into the shortage of engineering and related employment skills published in July 2012 noted that there was:

'… a sense among witnesses and submitters that the role of engineers was not well understood by the broader population. Indeed the committee itself was enlightened to hear of the wide scope of work and many challenges facing engineers on a day to day basis across Australia.'

These problems of clarity relate largely to the broad range of activities undertaken under the heading of Engineering and the historical origins of the terms engineering and engineer. According to Engineers Australia:

'Engineering is the profession in which advanced knowledge of mathematics, science and technology are combined with the principles of management and deployed in the practical application and management of technology and associated human, physical and financial resources for the creation and operation of products, processes and systems, and community works and services, in the fulfilment of commercial or societal needs.'

A professional engineer is therefore a person who possesses the training and abilities to perform these functions, with the essential prerequisite being professional engineering qualifications, usually involving a Bachelor of Engineering degree as a minimum requirement. Engineering Studies Stage 6 is directed toward providing students with an appreciation of the skills, knowledge and understanding associated with a study of engineering, its practices and associated methodologies, along with the role of a professional engineer.

The rationale of the Engineering Studies syllabus sums up the need for future engineers and the continued study of engineering through the statement:

'In the 21st century, engineering will continue to be directed towards developing insight and understanding to the provision of infrastructure, goods and services needed for industry and the community.'

© 2011 NSW Education Standards Authority

ACKNOWLEDGEMENTS

The authors would like to thank Bureau Veritas Australia Pty Ltd for permission to reproduce several documents for the purpose of illustrating engineering reports.

Peter Metcalfe
Roger Metcalfe
June 2014

TABLE OF CONTENTS

INTRODUCTION TO ENGINEERING STUDIES

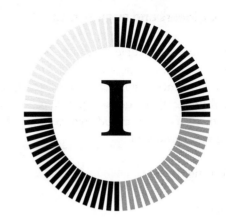

CONTENTS

COURSE ORGANISATION

The Engineering Studies Stage 6 syllabus comprises a Preliminary course made up of four compulsory modules (three application modules and one focus module), and an HSC course made up of four compulsory modules (two application modules and two focus modules).

Engineering application module 1
Engineering fundamentals

Engineering application module 2
Engineered products

Engineering application module 3
Braking systems

Engineering focus module 4
Biomedical engineering

The HSC modules are:

Engineering application module 1
Civil structures

Engineering application module 2
Personal and public transport

Engineering focus module 3
Aeronautical engineering

Engineering focus module 4
Telecommunications engineering

© 2011 NSW Education Standards Authority

KEY TERMS AND CONCEPTS

Account	Evaluate
Analyse	Examine
Apply	Explain
Appreciate	Extract
Assess	Extrapolate
Calculate	Identify
Clarify	Interpret
Classify	Investigate
Compare	Justify
Construct	Outline
Contrast	Predict
Critically	Propose
Deduce	Recall
Define	Recommend
Demonstrate	Recount
Describe	Summarise
Discuss	Synthesise
Distinguish	

I.1 Scope of the profession

Types of engineers and engineering

Engineering involves people working as individuals and as part of a team, pooling their knowledge of mathematics, science and technology to generate creative and practical solutions to problems. There are many categories of engineers and engineering, but most fit into four main groups of:

- chemical engineering
- civil engineering
- mechanical engineering
- electrical engineering.

Engineering ethics

New and developing technological capabilities confront engineers with ethical problems regularly. The 21st century promises to bring enormous ethical challenges such as electronic piracy, genetic and defence technologies.

Like other professions, engineering has specialised knowledge, the privilege of self-regulation, and a responsibility to the public and the environment.

Professional codes or codes of ethics are guidelines developed by professional associations to assist members with the decision-making process. Ethical codes, like technical codes, respond to the problems that engineers commonly encounter. At each stage of their ongoing development, codes represent the consensus of a particular community of engineering professionals. These standards go beyond common morality and interpret responses to specific details within an occupational setting. As an example, almost all engineering codes would include the fundamental canon 'engineers shall act in professional matters for each employer or client as faithful agents' (a canon being a set of rules). Codes of ethics would encompass such issues as confidentiality and conflict of interest.

Avoiding injury (financial or physical) to the employer or client is a requirement specific to the conditions of practice, but are codes hierarchical? That is, are some canons more important than others? For example, is the client's financial well-being more important than the safety of the end user or is the environment

an even greater responsibility? Ethical and technical standards are part of and expressions of the expertise of engineers. Nevertheless, there are many 'grey areas' that can challenge engineers as they struggle to behave in an ethical and moral manner. When there is conflict between these guidelines, an engineer must use appropriate philosophical models and standards to make ethical decisions.

Some of the questions engineers pose as a test within their ethical framework are outlined below.

- Can we do it?
- Should we do it?
- Just because it is legal, is it right?
- If we do it, can we control it?
- Are we willing to be accountable for it?
- Would we be proud to publicly claim the work as ours?
- Is the most economic decision the best decision?

Engineers understand that these codes are crucial to their safety and the safety of others and consequently safety is the foremost ethical consideration of all engineers. In the end, handling ethical dilemmas, making ethical decisions and finally being accountable are all-important elements of being a professional.

Standards and engineering

A standard is a published document which sets out agreed-upon specifications and guidelines for the performance, operation or composition of an object, process or system. These specifications are designed to ensure that a material, product, method or service is fit for its purpose and safely and consistently performs the way it was intended.

Regulatory agencies create standards that provide a means of sharing measures, generate commonality of language and have legal standing. Engineers of all persuasions need to consult the appropriate standards when developing solutions to engineering briefs.

I.2 Engineering mechanics

Mathematics

Trigonometry is an indispensable tool in physics, engineering and all the applied sciences. There are a few rules to follow in elementary trigonometry that will allow students to solve the problems presented in this text and at examination level. The word trigonometry is derived from the Greek language and means the 'measurement of triangle.' A triangle in which one angle is 90° is called a right-angled triangle. The side opposite to the right angle is called the hypotenuse and the remaining sides are called the legs of the triangle.

Associated with the angle Φ are three lengths: the hypotenuse, the opposite side, and the adjacent side (Figure I.2.1). Trigonometric functions of the angle Φ are defined as ratios of the sides of a right-angled triangle.

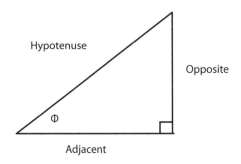

Figure I.2.1 Right-angled triangle

The following trigonometric relationships are the ones most commonly used.

$$\text{Sin } \Phi = \frac{\text{opposite}}{\text{hypotenuse}}$$

$$\text{Cos } \Phi = \frac{\text{adjacent}}{\text{hypotenuse}}$$

$$\text{Tan } \Phi = \frac{\text{opposite}}{\text{adjacent}}$$

Trigonometry may be used to solve both unknown angles and lengths. Along with trigonometry, Pythagoras' theorem is used to solve unknown quantities (both angles and lengths) within right-angled triangles.

Pythagoras stated his theorem as 'the sum of the squares of two sides of a right-angled triangle equals the square of the hypotenuse', or:

$$a^2 + b^2 = c^2$$

Figure I.2.2 shows the relationship between the sides of a right-angled triangle.

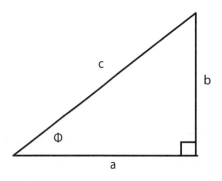

Figure I.2.2 Pythagorean triangle

Worked example

Using the data supplied in Figure I.2.3, find the length of side 'a' given the length of the other two sides in the triangle shown.

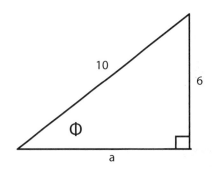

Figure I.2.3 Sample of Pythagorean triangle

Using Pythagoras' theorem:

$$a^2 + b^2 = c^2$$

$$a^2 + 6^2 = 10^2$$

Length of side a = $\sqrt{64}$ or a = 8

Using trigonometry the angle Φ may also be found:

$$\sin\Phi = \frac{6}{10}$$

$$\sin\Phi = 0.6$$

$$\Phi = \sin^{-1} 0.6$$

$$\Phi = 64.35°$$

I.3 Engineering units

SI units

This book will deal with a host of composite units: newtons, joules, watts, pascals, etc. These units are all expressible in terms of the fundamental SI units. The International System of Units, universally abbreviated to SI (from the French Le Système International d'Unités), is the modern metric system of measurement. Conversion of units will be a frequent necessity for the student of engineering studies. Historically SI is founded on seven base quantities assumed to be mutually independent, which are detailed below in Table I.3.1 The Engineering Studies syllabus concerns itself with these seven but employs degrees centigrade °C as the unit for temperature.

Base quantity	Name	Symbol
Length	metre	m
Mass	kilogram	kg
Time	second	s
Electric current	ampere	A
Thermodynamic temperature	kelvin	K
Potential difference	volt	V
Electrical resistance	ohm	Ω

Figure I.3.1 SI base units

Note: the basic measure of temperature, celsius or centigrade (°C), is used more commonly than the thermodynamic temperature measured in kelvin (K), yet both have the same temperature gradients. Water freezes at 273.15 °K which is 0 °C. Engineering and scientific communities switch between kelvin and celsius as the situation requires.

Note: the kilogram is the only SI unit with a prefix as part of its name and symbol. Because multiple prefixes may not be used, in the case of the kilogram the prefix names are used with the unit name 'gram' and the prefix symbols are used with the unit symbol 'g.' With this exception, any SI prefix may be used with any SI unit.

Prefixes

SI prefixes are used to form decimal multiples and submultiples of SI units. The most commonly occurring prefixes are given in Table I.3.2.

Factor	Name	Symbol
10^9	giga	G
10^6	mega	M
10^3	kilo	k
10^{-2}	centi	c
10^{-3}	milli	m
10^{-6}	micro	μ
10^{-9}	nano	n

Figure I.3.2 SI prefixes

SI derived units

Derived quantities are defined in terms of the seven base quantities via a system of equations (see Figure I.3.3).

Quantity	Relationship	Symbol
Area	square metre	m^2
Volume	cubic metre	m^3
Velocity	metres/second	ms^{-1}
Acceleration	metres/second squared	ms^2
Force	Newton = kilogram etres/second squared	N
Moment	newton metre	Nm
Work and energy	Joule = kilogram metres squared/second squared	J
Stress and pressure	Pascal = newtons/metre squared	Pa
Power	Watt = joules/second	W

Figure I.3.3 Derived quantities, names and symbols

I.4 Communication

Engineering reports

'In the engineering profession, an Engineering Report contributes to effective management, communication, decision-making and teamwork by providing a synthesis of the various elements that are relevant to a given project. The report can be developed by individuals or collaboratively as a team.

An Engineering Report can be developed for a new project that involves the synthesis of a new design, or it can be prepared as a result of the analysis of an existing engineering application. Engineering Reports may be related to individual components, complex engineered products or engineered systems.'

© 2011 Board of Studies NSW

Within Engineering Studies, students will be required to write a number of reports. These reports will need to follow the format of an engineering report. Part of the documentation process is the acknowledgement in print of all sources used in compiling the report. This recognition is referred to as referencing or citation and allows the report writer to:

- substantiate information upon which the report is based

- inform readers of other sources of information related to the topic

- avoid charges of plagiarism

- demonstrate breadth of research undertaken.

Referencing occurs as citations within the text and as a list under a separate heading at the end of the document. Styles of referencing vary depending on the discipline but whatever style is adopted consistency is required. Widely used referencing styles include Harvard, APA and Physics Review.

Engineering reports often follow a particular format and most include:

- an executive summary

- an introduction to the purpose of the report

- appropriate research

- analysis/synthesis of related issues

- conclusions and/or recommendations

- references in the form of in-text citations and a bibliography.

Graphical communication

Graphical communication is a way of exchanging information through the use of graphic elements and words. This approach may be used to communicate, partially or completely, ideas, data, concepts, etc.

There is a range of techniques available for use and selection of the correct technique is based upon the end use of the information being communicated. Graphic styles include:

- perspective

- orthographic

- infographic

- tables and charts

- pictorial (oblique, isometric and planometric).

I.5 Glossary

Account	Account for, state reasons for, report on; give an account of, narrate a series of events or transactions
Analyse	Identify components and the relationship between them; draw out and relate implications
Apply	Use, utilise, employ in a particular situation
Appreciate	Make a judgement about the value of
Assess	Make a judgement of value, quality, outcomes, results or size
Calculate	Ascertain/determine from given facts, figures or information
Clarify	Make clear or plain
Classify	Arrange or include in classes/categories
Compare	Show how things are similar or different
Construct	Make, build, put together items or arguments
Contrast	Show how things are different or opposite
Critically	Add a degree or level of accuracy, depth, knowledge and understanding, logic, questioning, reflection and quality to (analyse/evaluate)
Deduce	Draw conclusions
Define	State meaning and identify essential qualities
Demonstrate	Show by example
Describe	Provide characteristics and features
Discuss	Identify issues and provide points for and/or against
Distinguish	Recognise or note/indicate as being distinct or different from; note differences between
Evaluate	Make a judgement based on criteria; determine the value of
Examine	Inquire into
Explain	Relate cause and effect; make the relationships between things evident; provide why and/or how
Extract	Choose relevant and/or appropriate details
Extrapolate	Infer from what is known
Identify	Recognise and name

Interpret	Draw meaning from
Investigate	Plan, inquire into and draw conclusions about
Justify	Support an argument or conclusion
Outline	Sketch in general terms, indicate the main features of
Predict	Suggest what may happen based on available information
Propose	Put forward (for example, a point of view, idea, argument, suggestion) for consideration or action
Recall	Present remembered ideas, facts or experiences
Recommend	Provide reasons in favour
Recount	Retell a series of events
Summarise	Express, concisely, the relevant details
Synthesise	Put together various elements to make a whole

© 2011 Board of Studies, Teaching and Educational Standards NSW

ENGINEERING FUNDAMENTALS

CONTENTS

STUDENT OUTCOMES

A student:

- explains the relationship between properties, structure, uses and applications of materials in engineering.

- describes the types of materials, components and processes and explains their implications for engineering development.

- uses mathematical, scientific and graphical methods to solve problems of engineering practice.

- applies graphics as a communication tool.

- describes developments in technology and their impact on engineering products.

- describes the influence of technological change on engineering and its effect on people.

- identifies the social, environmental and cultural implications of technological change in engineering.

© 2011 Board of Studies, Teaching and Educational Standards NSW

KEY TERMS AND CONCEPTS

Amorphous	Lever
Austenite	Mass
Atomic bonding	Metal
Bonds	Non-ferrous
Brass	Pearlite
Bronze	Polymer
Cementite	Pulley
Ceramic	Scalar
Concrete	Screw
Composites	Steel
Crystal	Stiffness
Density	Timber
Ductility	Thermoplastic
Ferrous	Thermoset
Fulcrum	Toughness
Hardness	Vector

1.1 Areas of engineering practice

Nature and range of the work of engineers

Engineering is intimately entwined with an understanding and application of mathematics and science. It should be remembered, however, that materials have been extracted, transported and shaped into useful devices for centuries. Indeed all seven of the wonders of the ancient world had been constructed before the birth of Archimedes.

These achievements in design and construction were made without the scientific understanding of mechanics, hydraulics or thermodynamics that are today taken for granted. Construction was accomplished through the use of general 'rules of thumb' developed in some cases over centuries, along with simple tools and the organisation of an unlimited supply of labour.

Over the centuries, human knowledge has grown through the efforts of many individuals mostly unknown to history, undertaking work that today world be recognised as that of a scientist or an engineer. The word 'engineer' has its roots in Latin words *ingenaire* (to design or devise) and *ingenium* (cleverness) and began to appear in the 13th century. A list of notables from the past may include those listed below.

- Archimedes
- Leonardo da Vinci
- Michael Faraday
- Robert Hooke
- William Thomson (Lord Kelvin)
- Nikola Tesla
- Alfred Nobel
- Guglielmo Marconi

The term scientist dates only from 1833 when William Whewell coined the term from the Latin *scientia* or knowledge, to describe those active in the pursuit of what had previously been known as natural philosophy. Increasing specialisation in both engineering and science has resulted in the role of the scientist being defined in terms of searching for knowledge of nature, while engineers apply this knowledge to solve practical problems. While the different focus in training results in quite diverse fields of activity, many projects will find people with either engineering or science qualifications working together and in many instances performing the same work.

Further reading

MacIlwain, C, 'Scientists vs engineers: this time it's financial', *Nature*, vol. 467, p. 885, October 2010, www.nature.com/news/2010/101020/full/467885a.html

Petroski, H, 'Engineering is not science: and confusing the two keeps us from solving the problems of the world', *EEE Spectrum*, November 2010, www.spectrum.ieee.org/at-work/tech-careers/engineering-is-not-science

1.2 Historical and societal influences

Historical developments of engineering

As civilisation transitioned from the Stone Age hunter gatherer (10 000 BCE) to the agrarian economy of the Copper Age (3000 BCE) the need for technological developments that supported food production, housing, transport and defence became increasingly important. This period saw the development of irrigation, the plough, wheel and axle, and water wheel. As civilisation progressed from the Copper Age, so too did the reliance on engineering to support population expansion and trade. Machines were able to harness the power of flowing water and wind to supplement human and animal labour.

With this change came an increasing specialisation of skills within the workforce in which artisans with their specialised knowledge in stone masonry, carpentry, metalwork, etc, became the builders and innovators of the civilisation. These artisans were the first engineers. Training was through an apprenticeship model in which a young student laboured for the master artisan while he received training and gained in skill. The engineering of ancient Egypt, Greece and in turn Rome led to the rise of skilled engineering leaders in the design and construction of engineering works such as Imhotep, Archimedes, Hero of Alexandria and Vitruvius. Ancient Rome in particular relied on the development of machines for mining and the military to maintain growth of the empire.

The Renaissance in Europe, spanning the period from the 14th to the 17th century, led to a dramatic increase in engineering innovation with luminaries such as Leonardo da Vinci and Filippo Brunelleschi. The Renaissance saw the introduction of drawings rather than scale models as the means of communicating design information.

It wasn't until the Industrial Revolution of the mid-18th century, however, that the machine began to change society and the lives of the populace in a fundamental way. Steam power replaced the need to locate machinery near flowing rivers.

Up until this period the model for engineering training remained largely unchanged. However, the 18th century saw the appearance in Europe of the first professional schools in engineering offered by universities. These courses were primarily concerned with military engineering, to facilitate the establishment of roads, bridges and fortifications. In a similar vein, the first engineering school in the USA was established by the US Military Academy at West Point in 1802. This is perhaps not surprising given that the word 'engineering' is derived from the word engine which originally referred to engines of war such as the catapult.

The first school of engineering in Australia did not commence until 1858 at the University of Melbourne, but was nevertheless one of the first in the world to train engineers for the public sector. The term civil engineer was coined to distinguish such courses from those of military engineering. The names of some famous engineers are provided below.

- James Watt (1736–1819)

- Richard Trevithick (1771–1833)

- Nicolas Carnot (1796–1832)

- AGM Michell (1870–1959)

- Werner von Braun (1912–1977)

- James Dyson (1947–)

- Steve Wozniak (1950–)

Effect of engineering innovation on people's lives

For centuries the fundamental role of engineering has been to create devices and processes that benefit society, and in this engineering has played a significant role in the development of civilisation. The impact of engineering can be seen in the simple act of providing water for drinking and irrigation. Simple machines such as the lever were used over 4000 years ago to create the shâdûf (or shadoof), a device used to draw water from a river to aid irrigation, while wheel and axle systems were employed to draw water from wells. These devices assisted in the supply and distribution of water from a local source. The development of aqueducts from about 300 BCE by the engineers of ancient Rome allowed water from natural springs to be transported relatively long distances from its source to supply their cities and could therefore support a larger population and economic activity. Today, we take for granted the supply of clean water to millions of people, distributed widely by modern, largely unseen reticulated water systems drawn from large dams.

The security of water supplies to today's population centres has become possible only through engineering advances that have allowed the building of large stable dams. These dams have not only provided security of drinking water, they have also extended the amount of land that could be irrigated while providing flood mitigation along with the provision of 'clean' power through hydroelectricity.

The impacts of engineering are not however wholly positive and many negative impacts, both foreseen and unforeseen, may attend engineering activities. While the damming of rivers can bring many advantages it can also lead to the forced relocation of populations along with the loss of cultural heritage sites, degradation of ecosystems and potential loss of biodiversity.

The development of vessels capable of ocean voyages greatly increased trade and employment from the rise of economies of scale. Such travel however also led to the spread of diseases and the introduction of flora and fauna to ecosystems unprepared for their intrusion. The development of the internal combustion engine and modern road systems allowed greater mobility and the replacement of horse-drawn transport that had been choking city streets in the late 1800s with effluent, but has led to CO_2 emissions that are believed, at least in part, to be contributing to climate change.

Positive and negative consequences can be found for most engineering developments and it is for this reason that environmental impacts, as far as they can be ascertained, are routinely included along with evaluations of safety and cost in developing an engineering solution.

1.3 Engineering mechanics

Mass and force

Mass

The mass of an object is a measure of the amount of matter that it contains. Mass is therefore an intrinsic property of an object and does not vary. The unit of mass within the SI system is the kilogram (kg). As with all measures, the kilogram is an arbitrarily derived quantity that must be capable of accurate determination in disparate locations. In the 18th century when its standardisation was initially undertaken, the kilogram was defined as one litre of water at 40 °C. Problems with adjustments for the mass of any container and difficulties in the measurement of the volume of water led to the adoption of a platinum-iridium (Pt-Ir) alloy cylinder as the reference standard. The international prototype kilogram is held at the International Bureau of Weights and Measures in Sevres, France. Replicas of this standard, known as secondary standards, are held by the appropriate authority in each country. In Australia, the kilogram replica No. 44 is held at the National Measurement Laboratory within the CSIRO division of Telecommunications and Industry. From this standard a set of auxiliary standards are produced for use by laboratories and industry.

Force

While mass is a property inherent to an object, weight is not. Weight is a force and represents the mass of an object under the influence of acceleration due to gravity. Because of this, weight can vary depending on the amount to which gravity varies.

Sir Isaac Newton found that a relationship existed between the forces acting on an object and its acceleration. This has come to be known as Newton's second law of motion.

The net force acting on an object is directly proportional to the acceleration of the object. It also acts in the same direction:

$$F_{net} \propto a$$

The constant of proportionality was subsequently defined as the mass of the object, thus,

$$F_{net} = m\,a$$

The units of force are kg m/s^2 since acceleration is measured in metres per second per second (m/s^2). In honour of Newton's achievements, the units of force were named after him as the newton and are abbreviated as a capital N.

All matter is accelerated by the force of gravity. On Earth, the acceleration due to gravity (g) varies slightly from place to place but is approximately 9.8 m/s^2. This means that if an object is dropped from rest, at the end of one second it will have travelled 9.8 m. That is, it will have reached a velocity of 9.8 m/s. At the end of the next second, it will have increased its velocity by another 9.8 m/s to a value of 19.6 m/s. Acceleration has therefore been 9.8 metres per second per second.

To assist with calculation, a value of 10 m/s^2 is often accepted and recommended for acceleration due to gravity on Earth. The value expected to be used in any calculation will usually be stated in the question. If it is not, the value used in answering the question should be stated. As mentioned previously weight is a force and represents the mass of an object accelerated under the influence of gravity.

An object of 5 kg mass sitting on a table and assuming acceleration due to gravity is 10 m/s^2 has a weight of 50 N. If the mass is not moving down through the table, the table is said to be exerting a matching reactive force against the object as shown in Figure 1.3.1.

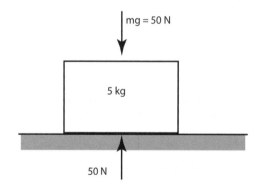

Figure 1.3.1 Reactive forces

The net force on the object is zero and it does not move. An object can be acted upon by many forces of various magnitude and direction of course, but it is only the net force that is of interest in determining the movement of an object. If the object shown above is exposed to a sideways force of 20 N on a frictionless surface as represented in Figure 1.3.2, the net force is 20 N acting to the right.

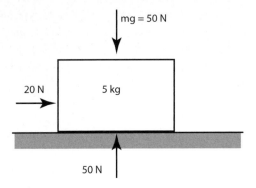

Figure 1.3.2 Net force without friction

Using Newton's equation, the acceleration can be calculated:

$$F = m\,a$$

Rearranging for a,

$$a = F / m$$

$$= 20 \div 5$$

$$= 4 \text{ m/s}^2$$

If the surface is not frictionless, a force due to friction will oppose movement of the object and the net force will be reduced appropriately.

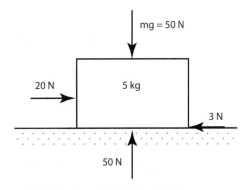

Figure 1.3.3 Net force including friction

The net force in Figure 1.3.3 is 17 N, acting to the right. Friction will be discussed in more detail in Chapter 3, Braking systems.

Scalar and vector quantities

The terms scalar and vector quantities are referred to regularly in engineering. A scalar quantity is any measure that consists of a magnitude only. The value of scalar quantities might be found on a measuring scale such as temperature, mass or speed.

A vector quantity by way of comparison possesses not only a magnitude but also a direction, such as force, displacement and velocity. An arrow is often used to indicate the direction of movement of a vector quantity. For example, if a car was to travel from Sydney to Brisbane such a journey could be illustrated diagrammatically as shown in Figure 1.3.4.

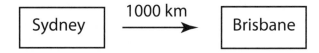

Figure 1.3.4 Simple vector diagram

In this instance, in travelling from Sydney to Brisbane a displacement of 1000 km has occurred in the direction of Brisbane. This displacement could also be represented as shown in Figure 1.3.5.

Sydney   Brisbane = 1000 km

Figure 1.3.5 Displacement vector

More generally, the displacement from point A to point B can be represented as shown in Figure 1.3.6.

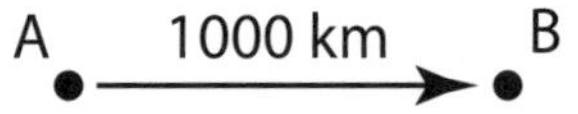

A   1000 km   B   or $\overrightarrow{AB}$ = 1000 km

Figure 1.3.6 Vector representation

It is easy to see that a journey from point to point can be represented by a number of displacement vectors. In Figure 1.3.7, a journey starting at A has proceeded to the final destination D after stopping at several locations along the way. It can be seen from this figure that although the distance travelled (a scalar quantity) to arrive at point D was 23 km the resultant displacement (a vector quantity) from A to D is only 11 km.

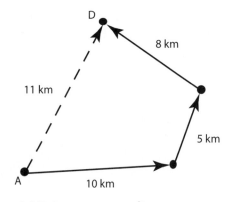

Figure 1.3.7 Journey vector diagram

Note that the arrows are arranged in a head-to-tail (or tip-to-tail) pattern. By using the head-to-tail technique, problems involving vector quantities, drawn to scale, can be solved relatively easily and quickly by graphical means.

The final solution, joining the starting-point with the end-point to complete a vector polygon, is termed the resultant. The resultant force as shown in Figure 1.3.7 has the opposite sense to the preceding vector.

The same technique is used to determine the resultant vector when a number of vectors act on a single point (concurrent) as shown in the example in Figure 1.3.8.

Worked example

Determine graphically the resultant force acting on the object shown in Figure 1.3.8.

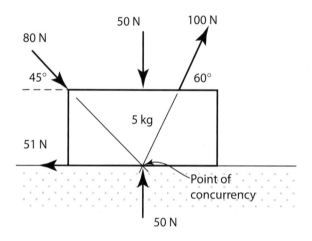

Figure 1.3.8 Concurrent forces

To solve the problem, the forces are organised as arrows (to scale) in a tip-to-tail arrangement as shown in Figure 1.3.9. The order in which the arrows are arranged within the diagram is not particularly important but clarity may favour one arrangement over others. This type of diagram is called a force polygon. A closed polygon represents a force system in equilibrium.

The magnitude and angle of the resultant force can now be measured directly from the diagram using a rule and protractor.

A force of 63 N acting at an angle of 28° is indicated.

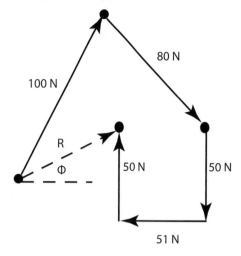

Figure 1.3.9 Force polygon

Because of inaccuracies in drawing and measurement, the answer obtained by the graphical method described will not be exact, but rather a good approximation. A more accurate although time consuming method of determining the resultant vector would be to solve analytically by resolving each vector into its x and y co-ordinates.

$$+\uparrow \Sigma\, y = 100 \sin 60° - 80 \sin 45° + 50 - 50$$
$$= 100 \times 0.866 - 80 \times 0.707$$
$$= 86.6 - 56.57$$
$$= 30.03 \text{ N} \uparrow$$

$$+\rightarrow \Sigma\, x = 100 \cos 60° - 51 + 80 \cos 45°$$
$$= 100 \times 0.5 - 51 + 80 \times 0.707$$
$$= 50 - 51 + 56.56$$
$$= 55.56 \text{ N} \rightarrow$$

Therefore, the resultant could be represented as shown below.

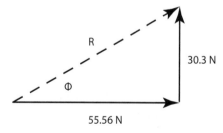

Figure 1.3.10 Resultant

$$\tan \Phi = 30.03 \div 55.56$$
$$= 0.54$$

$$\Phi = \tan^{-1} 0.54$$
$$= 28.37°$$

By Pythagoras:

$$R = \sqrt{(30.03)^2 + (55.56)^2}$$

$$= \sqrt{3988.7}$$

$$= 63.16 \text{ N}$$

Simple machines

All of today's complicated machines are based on six simple machines. These six machines consist of:

- gears

- levers

- screws

- inclined plane

- wheel and axle

- pulley systems.

The value of simple machines comes in the mechanical advantage (MA) they provide. In simple terms this means simple machines help us to do work with less effort. Mechanical advantage is a dimensionless figure generated through application of the formula:

$$\text{Mechanical advantage} = \frac{\text{Load}}{\text{Effort}}$$

Since both the load and effort are measured in newtons they cancel each other out. Mathematically the formula may be shown as:

$$MA = \frac{L}{E}$$

The other measure associated with simple machines is the velocity ratio (VR) which is the relationship between the distance the effort moves relative to the distance the load moves or:

$$\text{Velocity ratio} = \frac{\text{distance effort travels}}{\text{distance load travels}}$$

Again, since both the figures in this equation have common units they cancel out to produce a dimensionless result. Mathematically the formula may be shown as:

$$VR = \frac{d_E}{d_L}$$

Efficiency (η) is another consideration to take into account when dealing with simple machines. It is expressed as the relationship between mechanical advantage and velocity ratio and may be shown as a decimal or as a percentage.

$$\text{Efficiency} = \frac{\text{mechanical advantage}}{\text{velocity ratio}}$$

Mathematically the formula may be shown as:

$$\eta = \frac{MA}{VR}$$

Levers

One of the simplest and most widely used machines is the lever. The lever consists of a rigid beam that is arranged on a support about which it can turn. This support is known as the pivot point or fulcrum. Levers are made up of three components, including:

- effort

- fulcrum (a lever's balance point)

- load.

The effectiveness or mechanical advantage of individual levers is based on the relationship between distance of the effort (force) and load (force) from the fulcrum.

With the use of a lever, objects can be raised or lowered with greater ease than might be possible without such assistance. By assisting in lifting or lowering a load the lever is said to give a mechanical advantage to our effort. That is, a lever can be used to magnify our effort and allow a load to be lifted with greater ease or speed than would otherwise be the case.

Orders of levers

The mechanical advantage obtained by a lever depends on the relative positions of the fulcrum, load and effort. There are three basic categories of levers based on the arrangement of these elements. A lever is therefore variously described as a first, second or third order (or class) lever. An example of the general arrangement of each class of levers is shown in Figure 1.3.11.

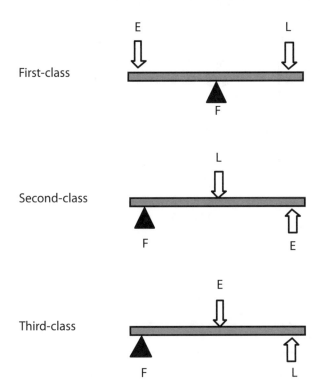

Figure 1.3.11 Schematic representation of the three categories of a lever

The easiest way of remembering the designation of levers into the three classes is to remember the element in the centre by the anagram FLE.

E	F	L	first-class
F	L	E	second-class
F	E	L	third-class

Although levers have been in use since before recorded history, the name of one person is most associated with the lever: the Greek engineer and mathematician Archimedes. It was Archimedes who gave a mathematical description to the lever. He is recorded as saying in 230 BCE 'Give me a lever long enough and a place to stand and I will move the world'.

Archimedes showed that the distance the effort and load were situated from the fulcrum was important and affected the effort required to move or balance a load. The distance from the fulcrum for any force on a lever is called the lever arm. More specifically, when considering the distance of the effort from the fulcrum, the distance is known as the effort arm and similarly the distance of the load from the fulcrum is known as the load arm. The load and effort each represent forces moving the lever around the fulcrum and this turning action is known as

a moment or the torque (τ). The lever arm is therefore sometimes described as the moment arm or torque arm. Archimedes found that for equilibrium to be obtained, that is, for the sum of the moments about the fulcrum to be zero, the product of the distance from the fulcrum and the opposing forces applied (load and effort) must be equivalent.

$$\Sigma \text{ Moments} = 0 \ \text{ or } \ \Sigma M = 0$$

$$(\text{effort} \times \text{effort arm}) - (\text{load} \times \text{load arm}) = 0$$

In the example of a first-class lever represented by a see-saw shown in Figure 1.3.12, two children of equal weight sit on opposite sides and at the same distance from the fulcrum. This situation is also represented in Figure 1.3.12 as a force diagram. Because the children are of equal weight and distance from the fulcrum the moments about the fulcrum cancel each other and the system is balanced or is said to be in equilibrium.

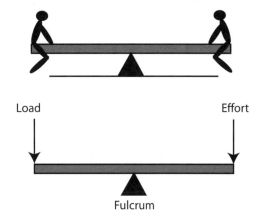

Figure 1.3.12 Schematic of a first-class lever, and the associated force diagram

First-class levers

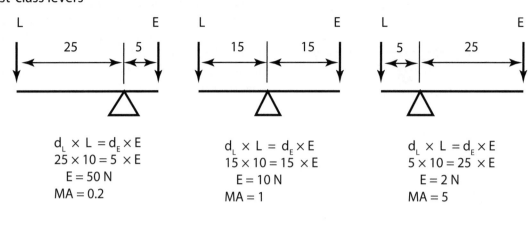

$d_L \times L = d_E \times E$
$25 \times 10 = 5 \times E$
$E = 50\text{ N}$
$MA = 0.2$

$d_L \times L = d_E \times E$
$15 \times 10 = 15 \times E$
$E = 10\text{ N}$
$MA = 1$

$d_L \times L = d_E \times E$
$5 \times 10 = 25 \times E$
$E = 2\text{ N}$
$MA = 5$

Second-class levers

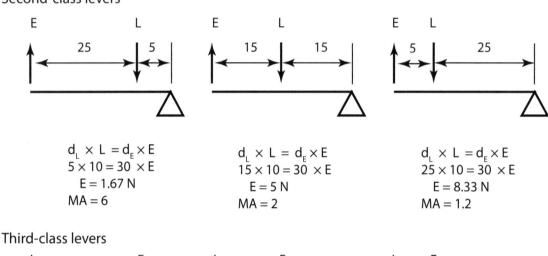

$d_L \times L = d_E \times E$
$5 \times 10 = 30 \times E$
$E = 1.67\text{ N}$
$MA = 6$

$d_L \times L = d_E \times E$
$15 \times 10 = 30 \times E$
$E = 5\text{ N}$
$MA = 2$

$d_L \times L = d_E \times E$
$25 \times 10 = 30 \times E$
$E = 8.33\text{ N}$
$MA = 1.2$

Third-class levers

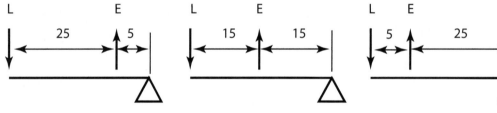

$d_L \times L = d_E \times E$
$30 \times 10 = 5 \times E$
$E = 60\text{ N}$
$MA = 0.2$

$d_L \times L = d_E \times E$
$30 \times 10 = 15 \times E$
$E = 20\text{ N}$
$MA = 0.5$

$d_L \times L = d_E \times E$
$30 \times 10 = 25 \times E$
$E = 12\text{ N}$
$MA = 0.83$

Figure 1.3.13 Calculations from the various lever classes

Most first and second-class levers would be expected to provide a VR > 1, although VR < 1 for a first class lever is possible. In this arrangement, a diminution of effort results in a magnification of movement and since the load is made to move a greater distance than the effort in the same time, a greater velocity is achieved.

Mechanical advantage varies for each class of lever depending on the relative position of the load, effort and fulcrum. Assuming the load of 10 N in each of the cases presented in Figure 1.3.13 remains the same, the effort required to maintain equilibrium can be calculated. From this the following may be determined.

- MA advantage of a first-class lever can vary from force multiplier to force reducer.

- Second-class levers act as force multipliers because the load is always between the fulcrum and the effort.

- Third-class levers are always force reducers because the effort is always between the fulcrum and the load.

Worked example 1

In the example shown in Figure 1.3.14 a child and an adult sit on either side of the seesaw. If the child has a mass of 40 kg and is sitting 3 m from the fulcrum, where would the adult need to sit to balance the seesaw if the adult has a mass of 90 kg?

In the first part of the solution the mass of the seesaw occupants must be converted into a force acting on the lever. This is accomplished by simply multiplying the respective masses by acceleration due to gravity $(g) = 10$ m/s^2. The child's weight therefore becomes:

$$40 \text{ kg} \times 10 \text{ m/s}^2 = 400 \text{ kgm/s}^2 \text{ or } 400 \text{ N}$$

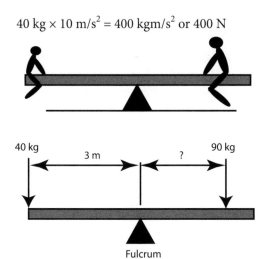

Figure 1.3.14 Schematic of a first-class lever

Similarly, the adult's weight becomes:

$$90 \text{ kg} \times 10\text{m/s}^2 = 900 \text{ kgm/s}^2 \text{ or } 900 \text{ N}$$

$$\Sigma \text{ moments} = 0$$

$$(\text{effort} \times \text{effort arm}) - (\text{load} \times \text{load arm}) = 0$$

$$(900 \times EA) - (400 \times 3) = 0$$

$$900 \text{ EA} = 1200$$

$$EA = 1.33 \text{ m}$$

Therefore, in order to balance the child the adult would need to move to within 1.33 m of the fulcrum.

Worked example 2

A second-class lever, represented by a wheel barrow, is shown in Figure 1.3.15.

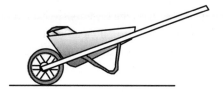

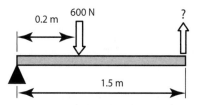

Figure 1.3.15 Schematic of a second-class lever

What effort is required to hold a load of 60 kg if the centre of gravity of the load is 200 mm from the wheel hub (the fulcrum) and the handle has a length of 1.5 m? Assume all forces are acting normal to the lever.

$$\Sigma \text{ moments} = 0$$

$$(\text{effort} \times \text{effort arm}) - (\text{load} \times \text{load arm}) = 0$$

$$(E \times 1.5) - (600 \times 0.2) = 0$$

$$1.5E = 120$$

$$E = 80 \text{ N}$$

Therefore, because of the longer lever arm of the wheel barrow, only a relatively small effort (80 N) is required to move the 60 kg load.

Note also that a mechanical disadvantage exists in using a third-class lever. That is, a greater effort must be supplied than the load being balanced.

The law of levers can therefore be simply stated as:

> In a simple lever, effort applied at right angles to the lever, multiplied by the effort arm equals the load times the load arm.

Effective lever arm

Giovanni Batista Benedetti (1500s) recognised that the forces on a lever did not always act normal to the lever but could act at an oblique angle. Under such conditions, the calculation of equilibrium moments about the fulcrum could not use the simple lever arm distance used when the force acted normal to the lever. He found, however, that the forces could be resolved graphically such that a new position on the lever existed at which the force could be said to be acting normal to the lever. The lever arm at which the force was acting obliquely could then be rearranged to be acting normal to a new position from the fulcrum known as the effective lever arm.

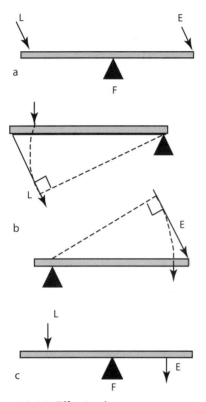

Figure 1.3.16 Effective lever arm

In the simple example shown in Figure 1.3.16a both the effort and load are shown to be operating obliquely to the lever. The effective lever arm is obtained by projecting the line of force until a position is reached that a line normal to the force line can be drawn that will intersect with the fulcrum point, as shown in Figure 1.3.16b. The length of this line is the length of the effective lever arm. By taking this length as the radius of a circle centred on the fulcrum the original diagram can be redrawn with the forces shown to be acting normal to the lever, as indicated in Figure 1.3.16c. The effective lever arm shown in Figure 1.3.16 can also be obtained analytically.

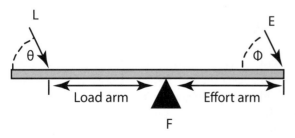

Figure 1.3.17 Analytical problem solving

Determining the effective load arm analytically, the line of force is again projected until a position is reached that a line normal to the force line can be drawn that will intersect with the fulcrum point as shown in Figure 1.3.18.

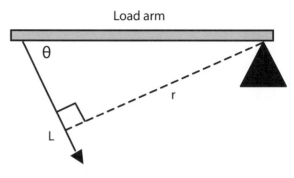

Figure 1.3.18 Projecting line of action (load)

Using trigonometry, the effective length of the lever arm (LA) is r where:

$$r = LA \sin \theta$$

Similarly for the effort arm EA in Figure 1.3.19:

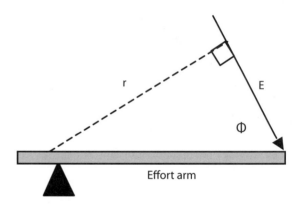

Figure 1.3.19 Projecting line of action (effort)

Using trigonometry, the effective length of the effort arm EA is r where:

$$r = EA \sin \Phi.$$

Worked example 1

Consider the first-class lever shown in Figure 1.3.20, in which a crowbar is being used to raise the edge of a 50 kg object. The length of the crowbar handle is 3 m. The heel of the crowbar is 100 mm. What is the effective lever arm and effort required to hold the load as indicated if $\theta = 50°$? Ignore the weight of the crowbar.

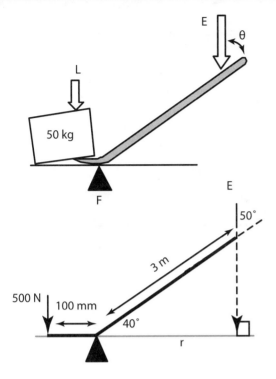

Figure 1.3.20 First-class lever

The effective lever arm for effort is:

$$r = EA \sin \theta$$
$$= 3 \sin 50$$
$$= 2.12 \text{ m}$$

$$\Sigma \text{ moments} = 0$$

$$(\text{effort} \times \text{effort arm}) - (\text{load} \times \text{load arm}) = 0$$

$$(E \times 2.12) - (500 \times 0.1) = 0$$
$$E = 50 \div 2.12$$
$$E = 23.58 \text{ N}$$

Therefore, an effort of 23.58 N was applied at an angle of 50° to the lever, 3 m from the fulcrum. Because it was applied at an oblique angle to the fulcrum the full benefit of the lever had not been realised, even though a significant advantage was gained. In effect, it was as if the effort had been applied normal to the lever, at a distance of 2.12 m from the fulcrum. A similar process can analytically determine the effective effort or load by resolving the applied force into its horizontal and vertical components relative to the lever arm.

Worked example 2

Consider a similar situation to the previous example in which a first-class lever shown in Figure 1.3.21 is being used to raise the edge of a 50 kg object. The length of

the crowbar handle is 3 m. The heel of the crowbar is 100 mm. What is the effective load being applied at 3 m and actual effort required to hold the load as indicated if $\theta = 50°$? Ignore the weight of the crowbar.

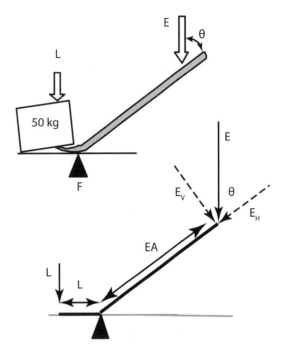

Figure 1.3.21 Lever problem

where: $E_H = E \cos\theta$, and

$$E_V = E \sin\theta$$

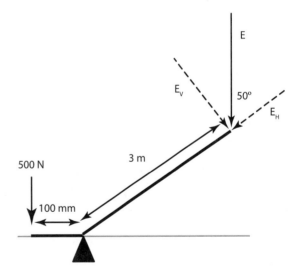

Figure 1.3.22 First-class lever problem solution

$$E_V = E \sin\theta$$
$$= E \sin50$$
$$= 0.766 E$$

Since Σ moments = 0

(effort × effort arm) – (load × load arm) = 0

$(E_V \times 3) - (500 \times 0.10) = 0$

$(0.766\ E \times 3) - 50 = 0$

$E = 50 \div 2.298$

$= 21.76\ N$

Since $E_V = E\sin\theta$

$= 21.76 \times 0.766$

$= 16.67\ N$

Therefore, an effort of 21.76 N was applied at an angle of 50° to the lever and 3 m from the fulcrum as shown in Figure 1.3.22.

Because it was applied at an oblique angle to the fulcrum the full benefit of the force had not been realised. In effect, it was as if an effort of only 16.66 N normal to the lever had been applied.

Note that a horizontal component E_H is present and can be considered to be resisted by an equal and opposite force at the fulcrum.

Inclined plane

The inclined plane allows objects to be raised by gradually sliding them up a ramp. Note that the same amount of work is done whether using a larger force to lift the load vertically over a small distance, such as a step, or using a lesser force to raise the load gradually by travelling a longer path.

In Figure 1.3.23 a 38 kg lawnmower is pushed up an inclined plane at a constant velocity. Calculate the force required (F) to perform this task (ignoring friction).

The free body diagram in Figure 1.3.23 shows the force opposing motion down the plane as mg sinθ, where θ is the angle of the incline. This force is calculated by resolving the force exerted by the mower under the influence of gravity into components relative to the incline. As with all inclined planes the larger the angle of the incline the greater the force opposing motion up the plane.

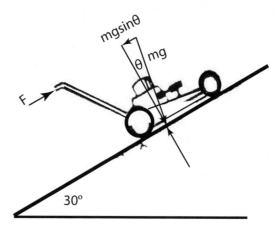

Figure 1.3.23 Inclined plane free body diagram

$F_{down} = mg\sin\theta$

$= (38 \times 10) \times \sin 30°$

$= 190\ N$

Thus the force down the plane and therefore the balancing force required to push the lawnmower up the plane at a constant velocity (and maintain equilibrium) must be equal (190 N) but of opposing sense. Thus the force pushing the mower up the plane at a constant velocity is 190 N.

Note: conditions for equilibrium would also exist if the mower were stationary but just on the point of moving.

Screws

The screw thread also represents an inclined plane: in this instance a helical path is followed around a central axis. In this manifestation the incline allows precise control of movement when used in metering devices or resistance to extraction when used as a fastener.

An example of a thread used to gain a mechanical advantage is seen in the deck height adjuster from a 1950s 'Victa 18' shown in Figure 1.3.24.

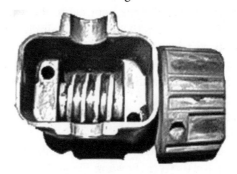

Figure 1.3.24 Threaded height adjuster

Employing a pitch of 6 mm against an input knob of 50 mm in diameter, the device produces a velocity ratio of 26 derived from the calculation below.

Note: the pitch of the thread is the amount the load travels through for every rotation of the shaft, which in this case is driven by the knob through the application of the effort. Because both the effort knob and the screw thread are on the same shaft, one rotation of the knob causes the thread to move forward the distance of the thread pitch:

$$VR = \frac{d_E}{d_L}$$

$$= \frac{\pi D}{6}$$

$$= \frac{\pi \times 50}{6}$$

$$= 26.1799$$

Wheel and axle

This device is simply a pulley fixed to an axle around which a rope is attached (Figure 1.3.25). The wheel and shaft must move together to be a simple machine. The variation in size between the pulley and axle allows the effort to travel further than the load for each revolution, thus providing a mechanical advantage. Sometimes the effort pulley may have a lever arm or crank attached to even further improve the mechanical advantage.

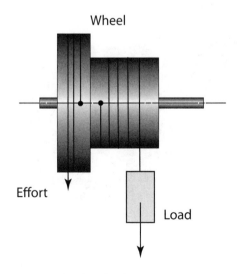

Figure 1.3.25 Wheel and axle

Worked example

A garden hose wound onto a car rim (Figure 1.3.26) uses the principle of a wheel and axle. Calculate the initial effort required to turn the rim if the resisting force from the hose is 42 N.

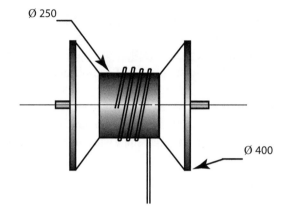

Figure 1.3.26 Garden hose roll

When the efficiency of a machine is not quoted it is assumed to be 100%. When a machine is 100% efficient then the velocity ratio and the mechanical advantage are equal:

$$VR = \frac{d_E}{d_L}$$

In these situations the constants (π) may be ignored when calculating the distance travelled by the effort and load because they cancel each other out. In this case we are simply able to compare the relative diameters:

$$VR = 400 \div 250$$

$$VR = 1.6$$

As stated earlier in this situation MA = VR such that:

$$MA = 1.6$$

$$MA = \frac{L}{E} = 1.6$$

$$1.6 = 42 \div E$$

$$\text{therefore effort} = 42 \div 1.6$$

$$= 26.25 \text{ N}$$

Pulley systems

Single pulleys alone offer no mechanical advantage but do change the direction of the effort relative to the load i.e. a downward force translated through a single pulley causes upward movement.

The combination of fixed pulleys and movable pulleys in a system is known as a block and tackle. The velocity ratio of such a pulley system is easily calculated by counting the number of ropes supporting the lower block.

Graphically, the pulleys are shown laid out next to each other and of different sizes. In practice each pulley block is mounted on a single shaft with pulleys all of the same size.

Worked example

Using the system shown in Figure 1.3.27 calculate the maximum load that can be lifted if the effort employed is 85 N and the overall efficiency is 75%.

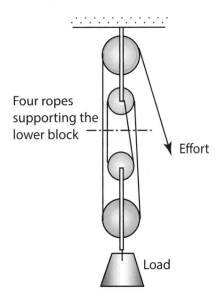

Figure 1.3.27 Block and tackle

In the example provided in Figure 1.3.27 for instance, the number of ropes supporting the lower block is four (4). Note the rope to which effort is being applied is ignored because in this case it is not directly supporting the load.

This equates with a velocity ratio of four. The mechanical advantage can be determined in conjunction with the efficiency using the equation MA/VR = η (efficiency).

$$\text{Efficiency} = \frac{MA}{VR}$$

$$0.75 = \frac{MA}{4}$$

$$MA = 3$$

$$MA = \frac{\text{Load}}{\text{Effort}}$$

$$3 = \frac{\text{Load}}{85}$$

Load = 3 × 85 = 255 N maximum load

Gears

Like pulleys and belts, gears can be used to change the speed of rotating axles. There are however major differences between pulley systems and gears. With a pair of gears the input axle and output axle rotate in opposite directions whereas in a belt and pulley system, the input and output axles rotate in the same direction.

The second major difference is that pulleys cannot transmit as much force as gears. Pulleys translate movement through the friction between pulley and belt while gears rely on the precise meshing of teeth (Figure 1.3.28).

Figure 1.3.28 Meshing gears

Rather than drawing complex gears (including individual teeth) gears are often represented by circles or concentric circles of various sizes (Figure 1.3.29).

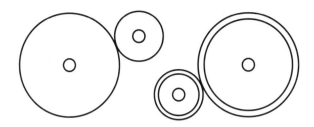

Figure 1.3.29 Gear representation

Gears are not only able to increase speed and change the direction of motion but may also be configured to increase torque or turning forces.

When two gears are meshed, as in Figure 1.3.28, they act in the same way as levers. Each gear tooth acts like a lever with the fulcrum at the centre of the gear. The longer the lever is, the greater the force that is applied to the shaft of the follower. Increasing the number of teeth may increase a gear's lever action.

The simple gear train shown in Figure 1.3.30 shows two meshed gears of differing size. The result of gear A making one revolution (clockwise) will be gear B making four revolutions (anticlockwise). This occurs due to the fact that it takes gear B four revolutions to match the travel of the 60 teeth moved through one revolution of gear A.

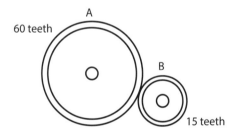

Figure 1.3.30 Simple gear train

Simple gear train

To calculate velocity ratios of gears the following formulae may be applied. One is based on the number of gear teeth while the other is based on gear wheel speeds.

$$VR = \frac{\text{number of teeth on the driven gear}}{\text{number of teeth on the driving gear}}$$

$$VR = 15 \div 60 = 1 \div 4 \text{ or } 0.25$$

An alternative approach to using teeth is to use revolutions or speed of the gears as indicated in the following sample calculation.

$$VR = \frac{\text{speed of driving gear}}{\text{speed of driven gear}}$$

$$VR = 1 \text{ revolution}/4 \text{ revolutions}$$

$$= 1 \div 4 \text{ or } 0.25$$

In these circumstances, the gearing configuration is designed to increase speed. If the system were reconfigured with the 15 tooth gear as the driver, the effect would be one of reducing speed but providing a velocity ratio of four (and a mechanical advantage up to four, depending on the efficiency of the system).

Gears and chain drives were often employed on early push mowers. They allowed the land or rear roller to be connected to the cutting reel and at the same time increased the cutting speed of the attached blades. In the sample gear train shown in Figure 1.3.31 every single revolution of roller A results in 30 revolutions of roller C.

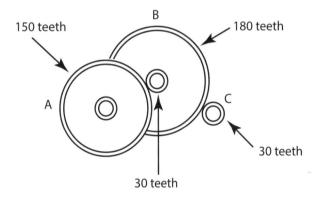

Figure 1.3.31 Gear train

The calculation for the gear train shown in Figure 1.3.31 would appear as follows.

One revolution of gear A (150 teeth) causes five revolutions of gear B (30 teeth), i.e. 150 ÷ 30.

Five revolutions of gear B (180 teeth), causes 900 teeth to mesh with gear C (30 teeth), ending in 30 revolutions of gear C i.e. 900 ÷ 30.

1.4 Engineering materials

Classification of materials

Material classification can be undertaken using a number of criteria. One of the most common is to classify materials into the categories of metal or non-metal as shown in Figure 1.4.1.

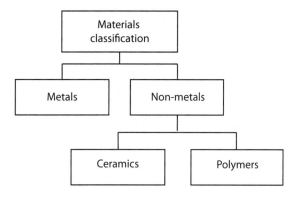

Figure 1.4.1 *Classification of materials into metals and non-metals*

Each of these groups can of course be divided into a number of significant sub-groups, which in turn can be divided into finer categories (Figure 1.4.2).

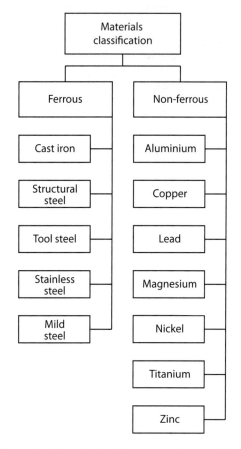

Figure 1.4.2 *Sub-classifications of materials*

Other common classifications include:

- natural and artificial

- transparent, translucent and opaque

- crystalline and non-crystalline

- organic and inorganic

- solid, liquid and gas.

Material properties can also be used as a useful means of classifying materials. Such classifications could relate to properties such as conductivity as indicated in Figure 1.4.3.

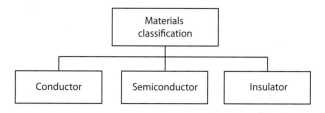

Figure 1.4.3 *Classification of materials based on conductivity*

Many other methods of classification are possible and depend on the purpose for which classification is undertaken.

If the health effects of ingesting various materials in dust form are the criteria, the materials may be divided into toxic or non-toxic. Resistance to corrosion within a specific environment may require the classification of materials into generic categories of excellent, good, fair and poor.

Properties of materials

Physical and mechanical properties

Density

Density is a measure of the quantity of mass per unit volume. The SI units for measuring density are kilograms per cubic metre or kg/m^3. Density is important in relation to product weight and size (e.g. for portability). Motor vehicle and aircraft components are often required to be as low in density as possible to reduce overall weight and improve efficiencies.

Hardness

Hardness refers to the resistance of a material to scratching or abrasion. It may also refer to resistance to indentation, penetration or cutting. The number of definitions for hardness indicates that hardness may not be a fundamental property of a material, but rather a composite one including yield strength, work hardening, true tensile strength, modulus of elasticity, and so on.

Hardness is routinely used as an indication of material condition. As a general guide, the greater the hardness of a material, the greater resistance it has to deformation and wear. As might be expected, a variety of tests have been developed to measure hardness. These tests fall into three broad groups, consisting of:

- scratch hardness (e.g. Mohs, Bierbaum, Pencil)

- static indentation hardness (e.g. Brinell, Rockwell, Vickers, Knoop, Janka, Durometer)

- dynamic hardness (Scleroscope, Leeb).

Hardness is important when resistance to scratching or penetration is required. It is often used as a quality tool to confirm conformance to a standard. Bearing surfaces such as those in motor vehicle brake systems are specifically designed considering hardness and extreme temperature properties. Even rubber-based braking systems in bicycles take into account the hardness of the brake block material.

Tensile strength

Tensile strength is a measure of a material's resistance to plastic deformation from a tensile or stretching type load. When the tensile strength of a material is quoted it is the maximum tensile strength known as the ultimate tensile strength (ultimate tensile stress). This is one of the most often quoted mechanical properties for a material. The ultimate tensile strength (UTS) represents the maximum applied tensile load that a material can sustain, divided by the material's original cross-sectional area. The tensile strength is therefore typically measured in kN/mm^2 or megapascals (MPa). On the engineering stress-strain curve the tensile strength is represented by that position where the maximum stress is achieved.

Tensile strength is important when selecting materials for ropes and cables, e.g. in an elevator. Although these devices are actually purchased based on a breaking strength of the rope, the tensile strength of the individual wires making up the rope is a critical factor.

Stiffness

Stiffness is the resistance of an elastic body to deflection by an applied force. There are several measures of material stiffness depending on the stress state imposed. These include the modulus of elasticity (also known as Young's modulus), the shear modulus (also known as the modulus of rigidity), and the Bulk modulus.

The most commonly quoted measure is the modulus of elasticity or Young's modulus which is a measure of stiffness when a body is subjected to axial tensile or compressive stresses and is visible on the stress-strain diagram as a straight line. The angle of the line (gradient) indicates the relative stiffness of the material, such that a stiff material will have a high Young's modulus. Young's modulus is represented by the capital letter E and typically is expressed in gigapascals (GPa).

Stiffness is important when maintaining shape is critical to performance e.g. an aircraft wing.

Toughness

Toughness is the ability of a material to resist the propagation of cracks. A material's stress-strain curve can be used to give an indication of the overall toughness of the material. The area under the stress-strain curve, within the plastic range, is a measure of a material's toughness. The greater the area under the graph, the tougher the material, and the greater the amount of energy required to cause it to fail.

A commonly employed method of testing the toughness of a material is to measure its resistance to impact. A number of standard tests are available, such as the Izod impact test or the Charpy impact test for metals.

In these tests, a test piece of standardised dimensions is obtained from the material to be evaluated and a notch machined into the surface to a 'V' or 'U' profile. The sample is subsequently fractured by impact with a pendulum and the swing height the pendulum attains following the sample fracture is used as a measure of the energy absorbed. Metals that are tough will generally undergo a ductile fracture in which plastic deformation occurs during crack propagation. Ductile fractures typically exhibit dull fibrous surfaces with obvious plastic deformation.

The more plastic deformation required to advance the crack, the more energy required and hence a tougher material. Low toughness metals will generally fracture in a brittle manner in which the crack is able to propagate without the absorption of additional energy. Little work is done in brittle fracture and hence the material fails catastrophically. Brittle fractures are usually characterised by bright crystalline features with no evidence of plastic deformation.

The toughness of a material will vary depending on the temperature. If tested at elevated temperatures, a material will show ductile fracture behaviour and consequently may be considered to have good toughness. If tested at low temperature the same material may fracture in a brittle manner and may be considered to have poor toughness.

Toughness is required when materials are subjected to impact or must remain operational even when containing cracks, e.g. military equipment must be capable of resisting sudden impacts and have a rate of crack growth slow enough to allow detection and repair.

Ductility

Ductility is the ability of a material to undergo plastic deformation by extrusion or the application of tensile forces. Ductility should not be confused with the related concept of malleability, which is the ability of a material to be shaped plastically, generally by compressive forces.

The amount of cold work that individual metals can withstand without failure therefore depends on their ductility. Materials that are unable to undergo plastic deformation without failing are described as being brittle. Both elongation and reduction of area determined from the stress-strain curve are measures of ductility. Ductility is specified when metals are drawn, e.g. electrical wires.

Structure of materials

Atomic structure

Our modern concept of the atom begins with John Dalton (1766–1844). Dalton proposed that all matter was composed of small indivisible and indestructible particles he called atoms. In his concept of the atom the elements were composed of atoms of unique size and shape.

Later discoveries of the electron (by Joseph Thomson in 1897) and the nucleus (by Ernest Rutherford in 1911) showed that the atom was divisible into smaller sub-atomic particles. The Rutherford concept of atomic structure was close to that of today, consisting mostly of empty space with a positive nucleus surrounded by the negatively charged electron, as illustrated in Figure 1.4.4.

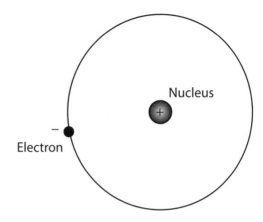

Figure 1.4.4 Rutherford model of the atomic structure

The positive charge of the nucleus arises from the presence of nuclear particles called protons. The number of protons in the nucleus is used to designate the atomic number of an element, sometimes represented by the capital letter 'Z'.

The number of protons present determines the number of electrons orbiting the nucleus, such that the electrical charges are balanced resulting in an overall charge of zero.

Niels Bohr modified the Rutherford model in 1913 by proposing that the electrons orbiting the nucleus could only occupy certain energy levels. These energy levels formed discrete shells or rings around the nucleus much like a sub-microscopic version of the solar system.

Within the nucleus is a second particle known as the neutron, discovered by the British physicist James Chadwick in 1932. The neutron carries no charge and therefore does not affect the balance of charges between the protons and electrons but is significant in explaining radioactivity. The modern electron cloud model of the atom explains that the exact location of the electron within its energy shell cannot be determined but describes a probability cloud defining its location, as illustrated in Figure 1.4.5.

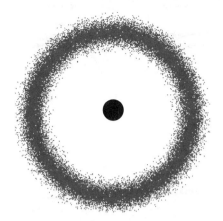

Figure 1.4.5 Electron cloud model

Electrons first fill the lowest energy levels surrounding the nucleus before filling outer, higher energy shells. The first shell, closest to the nucleus, can contain only two electrons before it is complete. Subsequent shells can contain up to $2n^2$ electrons (where n is the shell number) as indicated in Figure 1.4.6, provided that the outermost shell contains a maximum of eight electrons.

It is the outer electron shell that determines the chemical reactivity of the atom and is known as the valence shell. The Periodic Table arranges the elements in order of atomic number in such a way that the elements within each column contain the same number of valence electrons.

This last rule means that a lower shell may remain unfilled before the outer valency shell begins to fill (see Figure 1.4.7).

Note for example the element potassium. With nineteen electrons, the first and second shells are complete leaving nine electrons to be placed in a shell. The third shell can take up to eighteen electrons, but if all nine of the available electrons were placed in the third shell the rule that the outer shell can have only up to eight electrons would be violated. Therefore one electron moves into the fourth shell.

Shell	Electrons allowed per shell ($2n^2$)
1	2
2	8
3	18
4	32
5	50

Figure 1.4.6 Electron cloud model

Element	Atomic No.	Electron/Shell
Hydrogen	1	1
Helium	2	2
Lithium	3	2-1
Neon	10	2-8
Sodium	11	2-8-1
Argon	18	2-8-8
Potassium	19	2-8-8-1
Calcium	20	2-8-8-2
Copper	29	2-8-18-1

Figure 1.4.7 Electrons per shell for various elements

Within each shell, because there are interactions between the electrons present, there are sub-levels of energy or a hierarchy of energy levels known as orbitals.

Bonding

The atom is able to join or bond with other atoms in a number of ways. The form of bonding undertaken depends on the number of valence electrons present. The primary methods of bonding are ionic, covalent and metallic bonds.

Ionic bonds

Ionic bonding occurs between metals (in Groups 1A and IIA) and non-metals (in groups VIA and VIIA). These groups have a valance shell that contains only one or two electrons (in the case of the metals), or are short of completion by one or two electrons (as is the case for the non-metals).

The metal loses (or transfers) an electron(s) and the non-metal gains an electron(s). Following this transaction the metal atom contains more protons in its nucleus than orbiting electrons and therefore has a positive charge. The non-metal, having gained an electron, has more orbiting electrons than there are protons in its nucleus and therefore has a negative charge. In other words a positive and negative ion has been created. These ions, having opposite charges, are attracted to each other, forming an ionic bond held together by electrostatic attraction.

The bonding between the two elements sodium and chlorine to form sodium chloride (NaCl) is a typical example of ionic bonding, illustrated in Figure 1.4.8 using electron dot (or Lewis) notation.

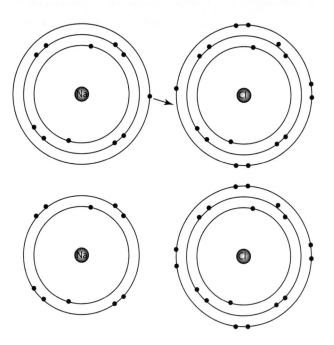

Figure 1.4.8 Ionic bonding of NaCl by the transfer of an electron from Na to Cl

Note that on bonding the outer shells of both participants are complete. Ionic solids typically have the following properties:

- brittle

- transparent

- moderate hardness

- high melting point/boiling point

- form crystal lattices not molecules

- non-conductors of heat or electricity (insulators) when solid

- electrical conductors when dissolved in solution allowing ions freedom to move.

Covalent bonds

Covalent bonding occurs between non-metals and between metals and non-metals. It is the strongest of the chemical bonds. A covalent bond results in the valence electrons being shared in order to complete the outer shells, as shown in Figure 1.4.9.

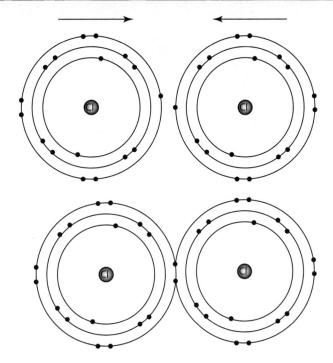

Figure 1.4.9 Covalent bonding of chlorine through the sharing of an electron to complete outer valence shells

Water (H_2O) is another example of a covalently bonded molecule. In this instance, two hydrogen atoms are needed to complete the outer valence shell of oxygen, as shown in Figure 1.4.10.

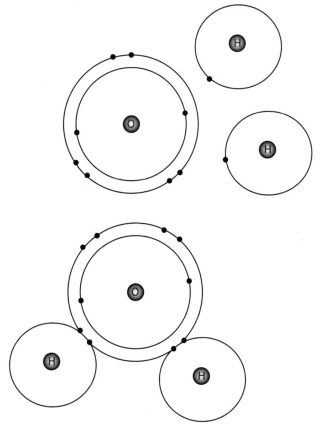

Figure 1.4.10 Covalent bonding of water (H_2O)

Covalently bonded materials typically have mixed properties, including that they may:

- be soft (graphite)

- be hard (diamond)

- have a high or low MP

- be insulators (diamond)

- have metallic lustre (FeS_2).

Metallic bonds

Metals are typically characterised as the atoms being arranged in a regular lattice, as illustrated in Figure 1.4.11. A number of models have been proposed to explain the properties of a metal in terms of its bonding. The most familiar of these is the 'free electron' or 'electron sea' model. This view of metallic bonding proposed a regular lattice of positive atomic nuclei with the outer valence electrons available to move freely (see Figure 1.4.11). Because the valence electrons can move freely among the nuclei, these free electrons are described as being in an electron sea.

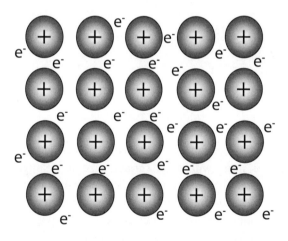

Figure 1.4.11 Free electron model of metallic bonding

These free valence electrons are essentially shared by all of the positive ions making up the metallic lattice, in such a way that electrical neutrality is maintained. It is the non-localised and non-directional nature of metallic bonding that gives metals their tolerance to defects and their malleability.

The ability of the electrons to move freely through the lattice accounts for the conductivity of metals. In metallic bonding, single atomic orbitals no longer exist

but are replaced by energy bands. These bands overlap, making several energy levels available to the valence electrons. The availability of these unoccupied energy levels for valence electrons to move into can be used to explain both the superior conductivity of metals and the relative conductivity between the metals.

Metallic solids typically have the following properties:

- metallic lustre

- malleable

- usually solid at room temperature

- conductors of heat and electricity.

Van der Waals bonding

Van der Waals bonding is a weak secondary bond that is often found joining molecules together. They arise from dipole attraction between those molecules that have an uneven charge distribution, such that a negative and positive pole exists. A common example of such a dipole is water in which the covalent bonding to form H_2O results in a 'bent' molecule (see Figure 1.4.12). This bending results in the formation of an electric dipole. Because these bonds are weak, solids constructed by van der Waals bonding are typically soft and have a low melting point. Van der Waals bonding is particularly important in the structure of polymers.

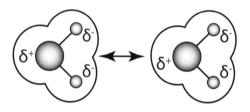

Figure 1.4.12 Model of van der Waals bonding between two water molecules

Crystalline and non-crystalline structures

The primary difference between a crystalline structure and a non-crystalline structure is whether there is long range order on the atomic scale.

Crystalline solids possess a regular, repetitive structure known as a lattice. The lattice is constructed by the 3D repetition of a small arrangement of points known as the unit cell. Each point represents the position of one or more atoms.

In 1840, the French scientist Auguste Bravais demonstrated that only 14 types of unit cell formed a crystal. These Bravais lattices are divided between six crystal systems, consisting of:

- isometric

- hexagonal

- tetragonal

- orthorhombic

- monoclinic

- triclinic.

Within the isometric system, for example, are the simple cubic, face centred cubic and body centred cubic variations.

All ionic solids (such as NaCl) and most covalent solids (such as diamond and quartz) are crystalline.

Non-crystalline or amorphous solids are those solids that do not exhibit long-range order although short-range order may be present.

Pure ionic solids do not form non-crystalline solids. Covalent solids however may form as either crystalline or non-crystalline forms depending on the presence or otherwise of impurities capable of hindering crystallisation.

Impurities in the form of Na_2O and CaO are added to quartz (SiO_2) to create the amorphous solid known as window glass.

While metals are usually crystalline, a non-crystalline or amorphous structure can be obtained if cooling from the molten state is so rapid that the atoms are not able to arrange themselves into the crystalline lattice.

Metals

Ferrous metals including mild steels

Metals can be divided into two broad groups: ferrous and non-ferrous.

Ferrous metals are those based on the metallic element iron (Fe). The two most common of these are steel and cast iron, distinguished primarily by the percentage of carbon present.

Although iron is the fourth most abundant element in the Earth's crust, it was not until approximately 2000 BCE that the Iron Age is believed to have begun, somewhere in Asia Minor. In its natural form iron is found as an oxide Fe_2O_3 (hematite) and relatively high temperatures are required to reduce it to elemental iron (approximately 1540 °C). Early furnace technology was incapable of achieving such temperatures and the initial discovery of metallic iron was most certainly accidental. It is speculated that iron ore was reduced sufficiently in the early furnaces to form a spongy mass that was found to be capable of plastic deformation when hot. This form of reduction was the primary means of iron production in Europe for centuries. Useful items were formed by hammering operations, leading to the material being called wrought iron. An example of a wrought iron microstructure is presented in Figure 1.4.13.

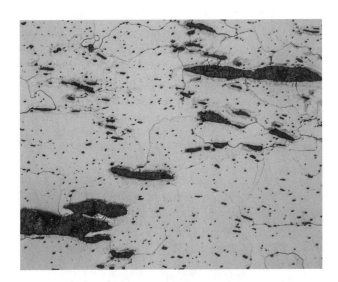

Figure 1.4.13 Wrought iron microstructure

Note the high volume of inclusions (dark) within the structure along with their variable size and elongated appearance. The inclusions consist of non-metallic slag entrained in the iron during reduction of the ore. This slag constituent of the structure represents regions of weakness. The slag particles are broken up and elongated during the working of the material. The process of plastic deformation used, however, resulted in variation in the degree of deformation of both the slag inclusions and the iron matrix throughout the material, resulting in variable properties.

In China, more advanced furnace technology allowed higher temperatures to be achieved. In addition, the influence of carbon as a means of lowering the melting point of iron had been discovered, allowing the complete melting and subsequent casting of iron. Cast iron was therefore used extensively in China from about 400 BCE.

Iron is principally found in one of two basic crystal structures: face centred cubic (FCC) or body centred cubic (BCC). These structures are represented in Figure 1.4.14. Both structures have an iron (Fe) atom at each corner of a unit cube. The BCC structure also has an atom at the centre of the cube body, hence the name body centred cubic. The FCC structure, rather than an atom at the centre of the cube, has an atom at the centre of each of the cube faces, hence the name face centred cubic.

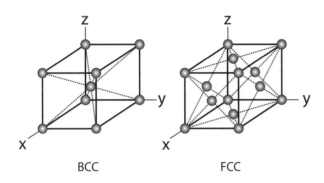

Figure 1.4.14 Basic crystal structures of iron-based alloys

When considering iron, the face centred cubic (FCC) phase is often designated as austenite, and the body centred cubic (BCC) often designated as ferrite. The form in which it is found depends on temperature and the influence of alloy additions maintained in solution.

At room temperature, unalloyed iron is BCC and in the form designated as alpha (α) ferrite. On heating, the structure changes from BCC to FCC and is known as gamma (γ) austenite. With further heating the structure again changes to BCC, designated as delta (δ) iron.

The most common addition to iron is carbon and a phase diagram of the sort illustrated in Figure 1.4.15 typically represents the variation in phases present with increasing carbon content. This diagram is often presented, as in the present instance, as an iron–iron carbide diagram as iron carbide represents the most common form in which carbon will be present.

The equilibrium diagram, representing the lowest energy situation, would be an iron–carbon diagram. This diagram, varies only marginally from the iron–iron carbide diagram, requires long periods at all temperatures to achieve and is of little commercial relevance.

The equilibrium diagram allows the identification of phases present for a given composition at a given temperature under conditions of equilibrium heating

and cooling. Because only two elements are shown, iron (Fe) and carbon (C), this is a binary phase diagram.

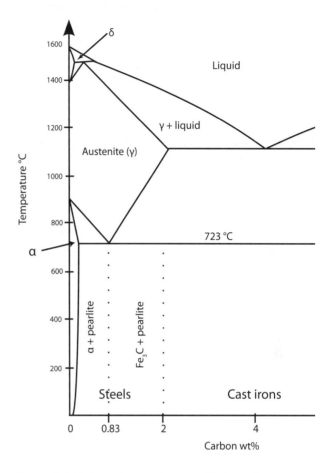

Figure 1.4.15 Iron–iron carbon equilibrium diagram

Carbon additions up to approximately 2.2% represent a group of alloys that come under the general category of steel. The properties of this alloy are affected by the amount of carbon present and the addition of any other alloying elements. Through appropriate alloying and heat-treatment a wide range of mechanical properties can be obtained.

Steels of low carbon content generally exhibit high ductility and relatively low hardness and tensile strength. These steels typically exhibit a matrix structure with a high proportion of ferrite and relatively little pearlite. Pearlite is a composite structure of parallel layers of ferrite and cementite. Cementite is the name given to iron carbide with the general formula Fe_3C.

As the carbon content increases the proportion of pearlite in the matrix increases until at a carbon level of approximately 0.83wt% the matrix is fully pearlitic. With increasing levels of carbon free cementite begins to appear.

Among the most commonly referred to classes of steel is a group of plain carbon steels known as 'mild steel', which typically have a carbon content of 0.15wt% to 0.30wt% carbon. The category of plain carbon refers to the fact that there are no other special alloy additions. Mild steels typically used in the as-rolled condition and exhibit a tensile strength of up to 500 MPa with good weldability, suiting them to structural applications such as I-beams, channels and angles.

Non-ferrous metals including copper, brass, bronze and aluminium

The classification of all metals as ferrous or non-ferrous reflects the importance of the ferrous metals, such as steel, to our civilisation rather than any commonality of properties between the non-ferrous metals. Only the more commonly used non-ferrous metals are examined briefly here. Some basic data for these materials compared with iron are presented in Figure 1.4.16.

Metal	Density kg/m^3	Melting point °C	Structure
Aluminium	2.7×10^3	660	FCC
Iron	7.9×10^3	1535	BCC
Copper	8.9×10^3	1083	FCC

Figure 1.4.16 Non-ferrous metal data

Aluminium and its alloys

Aluminium is obtained by the electrolysis of bauxite and is therefore an intensive user of electricity. Recycling programs for scrap aluminium, however, significantly reduce the energy requirements of reprocessing.

Pure aluminium has a low density at 2.7×10^3 kg/m^3 making it useful for weight reduction applications where strength is not important. When strength is required, alloying with elements such as Si, Mg, Cu and Zn can significantly improve mechanical properties. The good strength–to–weight ratio has resulted in the extensive use of aluminium alloys in the aerospace industry.

Aluminium is non-magnetic and exhibits high thermal and electrical conductivity while its high reactivity results in the formation of a tight adherent oxide surface film leading to excellent corrosion resistance.

Copper and its alloys

Pure copper has high thermal conductivity combined with good corrosion resistance and ductility. These are properties important in copper's extensive early use in household equipment such as cooking pots and irons. Today, the high electrical conductivity of copper has led to its major use in electrical wiring. Pure copper has a density of 8.93×10^3 kg/m^3.

The major alloying alloys in copper are Zn, Sn, Al, Pb, Ni and Fe.

Brass

Brass is an alloy of copper and up to 43% zinc. Brasses with a zinc content of up to 35% consist of a single phase alpha (α) structure. Alloying brass with zinc results in an increase in strength and ductility and a decrease in electrical conductivity. Cartridge brass (70%Cu/30%Zn) is a common alloy within this group. The addition of zinc over approximately 35% results in the introduction of a second phase known as beta (β), leading to a duplex alpha-beta (α + β) structure and a further increase in strength although ductility decreases. A commonly used example of this group is 60/40 brass.

Bronze

Bronze is a term generally applied to an alloy of copper and up to 10% tin. More specifically these alloys are referred to as tin bronze, alloys of copper and up to 10% aluminium are known as aluminium bronzes and alloys of copper and up to 5% silicon are known as silicon bronzes. Bronze finds extensive use as a casting material for bearings, pumps and valves due to its excellent castability, strength and corrosion resistance.

Basic forming processes suitable for materials

Casting

Casting is a very economical process for mass production. Objects may be produced quickly to high tolerances using a wide range of materials. It is less economical for one-off production. In casting, material in liquid form is poured into a mould and allowed to solidify before it is removed from the mould. Defects such as porosity and inclusions also require careful monitoring. Solidified castings represent a reproduction of the cavity of the mould. The mould may be manufactured from any number of materials such as wood, resin, plaster, sand or metal depending on the temperature of the material to be poured into it and requirements for reusability. Sand cast metal objects require post machining and cast objects, although good in compression, are often quite weak in tension.

The advantages of casting include:

- complex and hollow shapes with smooth section changes possible

- applicable to small or large product runs

- large or small products possible

- since castings are produced on a batch-specific basis chemistries can generally be made to order.

There are three basic categories of casting operations determined by the type of mould employed. These are:

- sand casting

- permanent moulding

- die casting.

Sand casting

Sand casting is the oldest of the casting methods and involves the production of a temporary mould produced, as the name implies, from sand. A mixture of sand and various binding agents are poured into a box containing a half pattern of the casting. After the moulding sand sets, the pattern is removed and the cavity surface is painted with a refractory slurry. The final mould is subsequently constructed by joining the individual parts (Figure 1.4.17). The top half of the mould is known as the cope while the bottom half is the drag.

Intricate and hollow shapes are created by the incorporation of appropriately formed internal shapes, also made of sand, known as 'cores'.

Provision is made during the moulding process for metal entry into the mould by way of a 'sprue', 'runners' and 'in-gates' and the 'feeding' of the casting during cooling to solidification using 'risers'.

Castings solidify first at those positions where heat removal is greatest. These positions generally correspond with positions where the molten metal comes into contact with the mould. Solidification therefore usually proceeds from the outer surface toward the casting's interior. During the solidification process the casting contracts and the molten centre 'feeds' the growing front of solidifying metal. If extra molten metal is not supplied, the last part of the cavity to solidify will have insufficient metal to be completely solid and a shrinkage cavity will result. To avoid this situation reservoirs of molten metal are often provided by the incorporation of 'risers' into the mould. Risers are designed to be the last part of the casting to solidify and act to feed molten metal into the casting. If correctly designed, any shrinkage is contained completely within the risers, which are removed during the fettling or clean-up stage.

Heat from the casting gradually degrades the binding agent and the mould crumbles, allowing easy removal or 'knock-out' of the casting.

Because these castings are relatively large, the grain size can also be large, leading to lower strength. Grain size is controlled by adjusting casting temperature, solidification rate and through the addition of grain-refining elements.

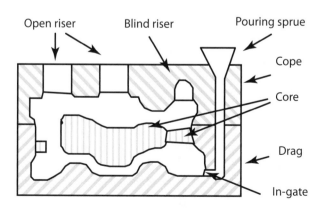

Figure 1.4.17 Schematic diagram of a sand mould

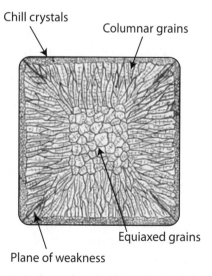

Figure 1.4.18 Cross-section through a casting

Figure 1.4.18 shows a representation of potential grain-size variation through a sand casting.

Features of sand casting include:

- low pattern costs

- relatively large grain size

- cooling rate relatively slow

- easily made design changes

- relatively poor as-cast surface finish

- low cost when only small number of castings required

- relatively high inclusion content can lead to low ductility

- casting size and weight only limited by availability of molten metal

- no limit to cast metal composition, subject to restrictions of melting fluidity and soundness.

Investment casting

Investment casting (also known as lost wax and precision casting) represents a sub-set of sand casting and is used extensively for the production of precision components. While the process is one of the oldest known to humankind it is still used today for its dimensional accuracy and fine surface finish along with its ability to create castings of great complexity.

In the lost wax casting process a permanent mould or die often made of metal is used to produce an expendable wax pattern. The pattern may then be incorporated into an assembly with similar patterns, and attached to a wax feeding system. The whole assembly is subsequently dipped into a ceramic slurry to build up a coating. Fine sand is then added to form a strong shell and the assembly allowed to dry. The dry assembly is then placed in a mould flask and surrounded by a coarser sand/slurry mixture and dried. This coarser sand/slurry backing is technically known as the 'investment'. After setting, the mould is gently heated to melt the wax pattern, leaving a smooth mould cavity behind. In the final stage of production metal is cast into the mould to form the part. Controlled breakdown of the sand/binder mixture from exposure to the temperature of the solidifying metal allows the solidified casting to be

easily removed from the mould for fettling. During the fettling operation the casting is separated from the metal feeder system of sprue, runners and in-gates. Features of investment casting include:

- freedom of design

- production of thin sections and sharp detail

- allowance for pattern removal not required

- near net shape production

- high surface finish possible

- high dimensional accuracy

- no joint lines present

- no limit to cast metal composition, subject to restrictions of melting fluidity and soundness

- die design changes costly

- high initial die costs.

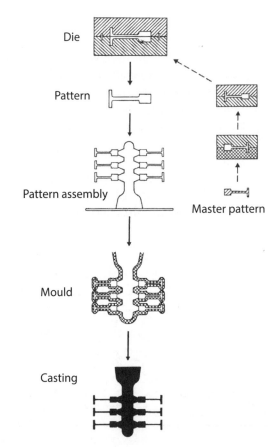

Figure 1.4.19 Lost wax process, image from Beeley, PR and Smart, RF (1995), Investment casting

Permanent moulding

Permanent mould casting, sometimes known as gravity die casting, uses a metal mould, often made of steel or grey iron, composed of two or more parts. This process is similar to sand casting with the exception that the mould can be used many times. Features of permanent mould casting include:

- costly design changes

- improved casting tolerances

- casting weight and size limited

- fewer defects than sand casting

- low cost when a high number of castings required

- improved surface finish compared to sand casting

- higher production rate compared to sand casting

- lower space requirements compared to sand casting

- high initial die costs although cheaper than pressure die casting

- improved mechanical properties resulting from faster cooling rate and smaller grain size compared to sand casting

- limited range of metals that can be cast compared to sand casting in order to avoid early deterioration of the mould surface.

Items produced by permanent moulding include exhaust manifolds and train brake discs. Metals typically cast by this method include but are not limited to aluminium, magnesium, zinc and copper alloys in addition to grey iron.

Die casting

Die casting, (also known as pressure die casting) involves the injection of molten metal under pressure into a metal die or mould. The technique is particularly suitable for small thin-walled high production items. Due to the rapid cooling rate grain size is usually very fine although internal porosity is often high. Features of die casting include:

- high initial die costs

- surface finish very fine

- design changes are costly

- casting weight limited to relatively small items

- low cost when a high number of castings required

- limited to aluminium based and lower melting point alloys.

Rolling

The rolling process is possibly the most extensively used technique for the plastic deformation of metals. In its simplest form metal is introduced to the gap formed between two rolls as shown in Figure 1.4.20. Roll separation is adjusted so that it is slightly smaller than the material thickness entering the rolls. As the material passes between the rolls the material thickness is reduced and the length increases with little lateral movement or 'spread'.

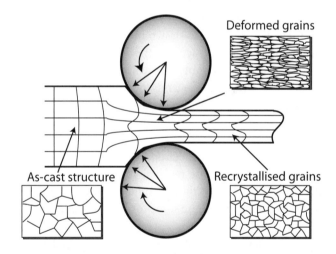

Figure 1.4.20 Hot rolling

Material usually passes through a sequence of roll stands to achieve a simple standard size and shape. Products include squares, slabs, plates, beams, rods, rails, channels and angles.

Hot rolling

As hot rolling is performed above the recrystallisation temperature, recrystallisation occurs concurrently with deformation. The benefits of this are that internal stresses are eliminated, avoiding work hardening, and grain size is reduced. Because the product may undergo a number of deformation and recrystallisation sequences before the rolling process is concluded, mechanical properties are considerably enhanced.

Advantages of hot rolling include:

- the break up of as-cast dendritic structure

- recrystallisation of grains that reduces final austenite grain size

- reorientation of dendrites and inclusions to improve ductility in the rolling direction.

Cold rolling

When a metal is deformed below its recrystallisation temperature, it is said to be cold worked. The strength, machinability, dimensional accuracy, and surface finish of the metal are improved by cold work. Since cold work is normally performed at room temperature, there is no oxidation or scaling problem as seen with hot working.

Larger forces are required to perform cold working operations than hot working. Since there is no recrystallisation occurring, metal grains will be significantly distorted, as shown in Figure 1.4.21. Grain distortion can lead to fracture if the ductility of the metal is exceeded. The amount of cold work that individual metals can withstand depends on their ductility. The higher the ductility of the metal, the more it can be deformed during cold working operations.

Because there is strain hardening occurring during cold work, there will be residual stresses set up inside the metal. To remove these residual stresses, the cold worked metal may require some form of heat treatment.

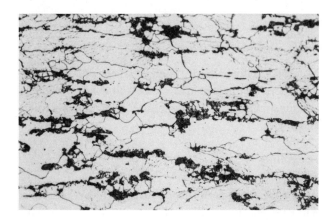

Figure 1.4.21 Photomicrograph of a low carbon, cold rolled steel plate exhibiting grain distortion

Extruding

Extrusion is a process where a material, usually in simple billet form, is placed in a container and subsequently forced to pass through an opening at one end under plastic flow. The shape of the opening through which the extruded material passes determines the shape of the extrusion. Extrusion can be undertaken as either a direct or indirect process, as illustrated in Figure 1.4.22.

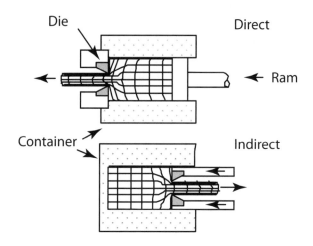

Figure 1.4.22 Direct and indirect extrusion

Lubrication must be applied between the container and billet surfaces to reduce friction when using direct extrusion. Frictional forces increase the load required for extrusion as well as producing shear stresses at the billet surface that can lead to tearing. The hot extrusion of steel and nickel alloys is undertaken using molten glass as the lubricant. The use of the indirect method eliminates frictional forces between the container walls and the billet, reducing the possibility of tearing of the metal surface due to high shear stresses.

Advantages of extrusion include:

- good surface quality

- high dimensional accuracy

- billet to final shape manufacturing

- allowing manufacture of complex shapes, including tubes.

Disadvantages of extrusion include:

- dedicated tooling

- expensive equipment.

Cutting

A wide range of technologies can be classified as cutting, ranging from mechanical separating processes to high temperature processes in which separation is achieved by localised melting. The essential issues relate to material chemistry, dimensions, wastage, quality of finish, and issues of distorting and surface damage. Mechanical cutting processes commonly include:

- shearing (tin snips to rolling mill hot shears)

- sawing (hand saws to rolling mill hot saws)

- abrasion (water jet cutting).

Thermal processes commonly include:

- oxy-acetylene cutting

- plasma cutting

- laser cutting

- electric discharge wire cutting.

Joining

Fusion

Fusing or fusion involves the joining of materials through the process of melting, mixing and solidification. The base materials alone may be locally fused or an additional filler material may be added to the site to provide bulk and reinforcement. Fusion techniques include but are not limited to manual metal arc, metal inert gas, tungsten inert gas, friction, laser, electron beam, electro resistance, plastic and spot welding. The technique chosen for fusing materials is dependent on the materials to be joined, their thickness and the load specifications of the design. The process may or may not involve the addition of pressure.

Fusing or welding is a permanent process. Disassembly of welded items requires breaking the join and most probably the product itself. Manufacturers require specialised equipment, skilled tradesmen and specially prepared environments for welding.

Soldering and brazing

Soldering and brazing are similar operations and involve the joining of two or more parts by melting a filler metal with a heat source. The molten filler metal flows into the joint and, on solidifying, holds the parts together. The heat source for soldering is usually a hot 'iron' while brazing is accomplished with the aid of an oxyacetylene or propane torch.

The primary difference between the processes is the temperature at which the filler metal solidifies. Soldering uses filler metals with solidification temperatures <500 °C (e.g. Pb, Sn, Sb, etc) while brazing uses alloys with solidification temperatures >500 °C (e.g. Cu, Ni etc). The primary requirement of these processes is that the surfaces to be joined are free of oxides, so that the filler metal can 'wet' the surface. Fluxes designed to remove oxides from the surface are used to provide a clean joint while some diffusion occurs across the boundary between the filler metal and parent metal.

Mechanical fasteners

Fastening or joining materials mechanically through the use of techniques such as screws, rivets, bolts, pins, clips, nails, press-studs and snaps has been in common use for hundreds of years. Archimedes is credited with the invention of the screw thread in the 3rd century BCE although the screw form at that time was employed to raise water. The first recorded use of a screw as a method of joining was in the mid-15th century (joining armour and construction of firearms). At this time each screw was individually fashioned. Lathes were later designed to cut the thread form but it was not until 1841 that Joseph Whitworth proposed the introduction of standard fastener sizes to the Institution of Civil Engineers.

The major advantages associated with the use of fasteners is that they are quick and easy to use, dissimilar materials may be joined and they allow for quick and easy assembly or disassembly of product components. However, most require a hole to be drilled into the materials to be joined. This requires additional design considerations, including materials selection, weakening or stress raising and disruption to an otherwise smooth surface. Both screws and nails rely on physical interaction with the material being joined. Nails remain in place by the pressure of the surrounding fibres. Removal requires frictional contact forces to be overcome.

Screws derive their fixation strength from a mechanical bond in which pull-out requires the shearing of material contained between the threads. As a screw is driven into an assembly, the joint is placed in compression when the head of the screw meets the surface.

Adhesives

Adhesives are materials that act as bonding agents between surfaces. To meet the technical definition it must flow at the time of application. Adhesion to surfaces is generally considered to be through the interaction of van der Waals forces or polar forces. Adhesives, depending on their bonding action, may allow for the separation of parts with little or no damage to the original surfaces. They are commonly used to join thin or dissimilar materials and do not employ heat, which may cause distortion or damage. Some adhesives, composed of metallic flakes, are even electrically conductive, cure at room temperature and cause no damage to heat-sensitive componentry. Mechanisms for adhesion include absorption, electrostatic attraction and diffusion. Most adhesives exhibit a combination of these.

Fabricating

Fabrication relates to the general manufacture of parts or products using a range of cutting, machining, forming and joining processes.

Polymers

A polymer (or plastic) consists of giant molecules composed of repeating units known as 'mers' or monomers. These units joined together form a chain of many-mers or a poly-mers. The basic unit of any polymer is the carbon atom, which forms the backbone of the polymer chain. The monomer ethylene C_2H_4 is shown in Figure 1.4.23.

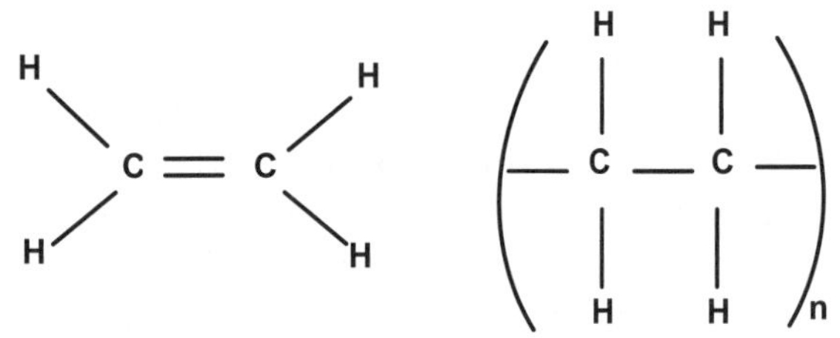

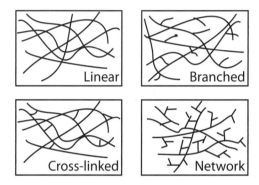

Ethylene   Polyethylene

Figure 1.4.23 The monomer ethylene consisting of two carbon and four hydrogen atoms

Multiple linking of ethylene monomers results in the formation of polyethylene. Through the substitution of other elements with an hydrogen atom, polymers of differing properties are obtained. Replacement of a hydrogen atom for a chlorine results in polyvinyl chloride (PVC) as shown in Figure 1.4.24.

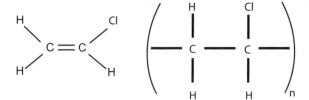

Figure 1.4.24 Monomer of PVC

When two different monomers are joined the product is known as a copolymer and the process described as copolymerisation. This process can be used to soften polymers by adding a monomer of lower molecular weight, also called a plasticiser.

The structure of these giant molecules can be classified into four basic groups depending on the number of linkages between the molecules. Figure 1.4.25 shows various structural types listed from weakest to strongest.

Figure 1.4.25 Structural classification of polymers

Polymers can also be divided into two basic groups based on their response to temperature. These are thermosetting or thermoplastic. Linear polymers are the thermoplastics while the three-dimensional structure of the network group defines the thermosets.

Thermo softening polymers

Also known as thermoplastics, these materials become plastic at elevated temperatures, allowing formation by a number of processes. Thermo softening polymers consist of carbon atoms arranged in a single chain from which there may be many branches. Each chain is joined to its neighbour by van der Waals forces, which weaken on heating, allowing the material to become fluid. Because of their linear structure they can be drawn into fibres e.g. nylon. The characteristics of thermoplastics are:

- ductile

- easily fabricated

- easily drawn into fibres

- freely injected into a mould

- easily remelted and remoulded.

When thermoplastics are heated the weak bonds between chains are broken, allowing the molecular chains to move past each other. In this state the thermoplastic can be plastically formed into a new shape. On cooling, the weak bonds between chains are re-established and the material stays in the new shape to which it was formed.

Because thermoplastics allow numerous cycles of heating and reforming into various shapes without deterioration these plastics are well suited to recycling. Common thermoplastics are polyvinyl chloride (PVC), perspex, polytetrafluoroethene (PTFE) and nylon.

Thermosetting polymers

Thermosetting materials (also known as thermosets) are heated to a plastic state under pressure. Under these conditions of elevated temperature and pressure they are said to set, forming three-dimensional structures linked by covalent bonds. The thermosets therefore form a single large 3D network rather than a mass of molecular chains linked by secondary bonds, as is the case for the thermoplastics, as illustrated in Figure 1.4.25.

The thermosets are generally formed as part of a two part process in which linear chains are first formed followed by a second step in which these chains are connected (or cross-linked) to neighbours by primary bonds, forming a three-dimensional structure. Because the cross-link bonds formed between the chains are strong primary bonds, the chains cannot slide past each other and are not easily broken. This rigid three-dimensional structure leads to these materials exhibiting high strength but low ductility.

Thermoset materials cannot be reheated to a plastic state for reforming. On further heating the primary carbon bonds are broken, rather than the secondary bonds between the chains being weakened, and the material decomposes. Common thermosets are Melamine, Bakelite (Phenol formaldehyde) and Diallyl Phthalate (DAP).

Generally thermosets are rigid, unable to be remelted or remoulded, and possess higher strengths than thermoplastics.

Ceramics

Typically ceramics are a combination of one or more metallic elements with a non-metallic element. They form ionic/covalent bonds, giving them unique engineering properties. Ceramics are generally hard, brittle, chemically inert materials. They are also good electrical insulators and exhibit high temperature resistance, making them popular as refractories.

Common types used

Ceramics are employed where their physical properties make them most appropriate for service condition requirements. Environments and applications where thermal stability, wear-resistance and corrosion resistance are essential are often areas best suited to ceramics. Specific applications include but are not limited to:

- cutting tools

- refractory products

- electrical insulators

- biomedical implants

- pump components and seals.

Common ceramic materials include aluminium oxide (Al_2O_3) and silica (SiO_2). Their inherent brittleness, however, eliminates ceramics from many structural situations.

Forming and shaping

Ceramics display good compressive strength yet they have little tolerance for cracking, such that even microscopic defects can lead to failure well below their theoretical tensile strength. Processing techniques are therefore often directed to producing a compressive surface layer that must first be overcome before fracture will occur. A wide range of forming and shaping techniques are available for processing ceramics. The choice of process will be influenced by material choice, complexity of shape and final end use of the product. Some of the more common forming and shaping methods for ceramics include extrusion, slip casting, pressing, machining and injection moulding.

Composites

Composites represent a class of material whose properties derive from the combination of two or more materials that are bonded together such that each of the constituent materials contributes to an improvement in mechanical, physical, chemical or electrical properties.

One of the earliest man-made composite materials was straw reinforced bricks. At a much later time, cement, gravel and steel bars were combined to form reinforced concrete. Development of thin fibres and thermosetting polymers led to the creation of fibre-reinforced materials such as glass reinforced polymers (GRP). Much more recent examples are carbon-polymer and metal matrix composites.

Increasingly, composites are being employed to provide improved properties, increased efficiency, reduction of costs and provide additional functionality.

Timber

Timber (or wood) comes from trees and being an organic material is subject to the environment in which it grows, and thus its fundamental properties are subject to a great deal of variability. Timber is classified as a composite due to its cellular nature. Its structure can be best likened to a collection of thin-walled tubes made of cellulose. These cellulose 'tubes' are bound together with a weak glue called lignin giving wood its 'grain' (see Figure 1.4.26). It is the direction of the cellulose tubes within wood that is commonly referred to as the grain.

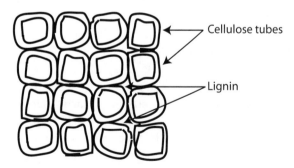

Figure 1.4.26 Cross-sectional cellular structure of wood

Timber can be described as an anisotropic material i.e. it behaves differently in different directions, or more accurately as an 'orthotropic material', having different properties in three mutually perpendicular directions. These are generally described in terms of one direction parallel to the grain or growth rings and two directions perpendicular to the grain, one radial and the other tangential to the growth rings. Wood is far stronger when loaded parallel to grain than perpendicular to grain. This difference can be as much as an order of magnitude.

Teak is one of the most valuable structural timbers in the world. It is durable, fire resistant and moderately hard. It resists attack from white ants and dry rot. It finds application in the furniture, shipbuilding and construction industries. Some specific uses include housing construction frames, flooring, pedestrian and vehicular bridges, fencing, wharves and landscape retaining walls.

Turpentine is a highly durable timber, allowing it to be used in range of applications and situations ranging from pilings in marine structures through to railway sleepers and decking.

River red gum is a moderately durable timber, making it suitable for a range of exterior applications including heavy commercial construction, general framing, floorboards and furniture.

Concrete

Concrete is classed as a composite due to its composition. It is a mixture of aggregate embedded in a cement binding matrix composed of sand, water and cement.

Concrete has a long history as a successful synthetic construction material. Its properties include durability, fire resistance and good compressive strength.

Concrete can have its physical properties modified and enhanced through the introduction of reinforcement materials ranging from steel rods to polymer fibres. Steel reinforcement in concrete may also be pre- or post-tensioned to improve the tensile properties of cast concrete. Modern application of concrete include dams, bridges, general construction, swimming pools, aircraft runways, ship hulls, etc.

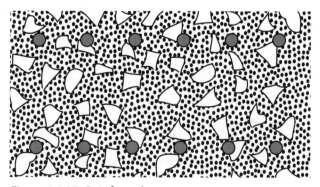

Figure 1.4.27 Reinforced concrete macrostructure

1.5 Communication

Freehand sketching in three-dimensional and third angle orthogonal projection

As a part of their everyday operations, engineers need to acquire the skills associated with graphical communication. The quick and easy nature of sketching as a design tool provides the engineer with a great deal of flexibility in the field. As a medium it requires little in the way of equipment and resources. Other than a pencil and paper, sketching may be done anywhere, anytime.

Sketching is a natural means of expressing ideas. Sketches, supplemented by written language, convey an idea very rapidly, completely and accurately. Engineers use sketches for a variety of reasons. The ability to freehand sketch has become an essential criterion of a successful engineer.

Sketching provides a quick way to jot down information and concepts. Three-dimensional sketches provide engineers with a sense of form, proportion and aesthetics while two dimensional sketches are able to isolate and detail more structural features. The ability to sketch well does, however, require some skill and training. At some later stage, these sketches may need to be translated into a more formal and accurate representation.

Orthogonal sketching

Orthogonal or orthographic drawing involves projecting two-dimensional views of objects onto vertical and horizontal planes. The placement of these objects into various 'quadrants' determines the arrangement of the projected views. First and third angle projections are commonly but for the purposes of the HSC, third angle projection is the only method explored.

To avoid confusion and misinterpretation between the two styles of drawing, an international convention requires the appearance of a standard symbol (see Figure 1.5.1) identifying the drawing to be either first or third angle projection.

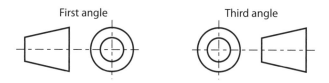

First angle   Third angle

Figure 1.5.1 International projection conventions

Figure 1.5.2 shows an example of a multiview orthographic drawing reproduced from a US patent (1913), showing two views of the same object. Third angle projection is used here to produce a front and left side view.

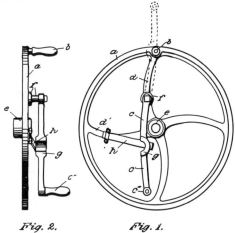

Fig. 2.   Fig. 1.

Figure 1.5.2 US patent showing a multi-view orthogonal drawing

Figure 1.5.3 shows two sketched orthogonal views of a bicycle. Note the projection between views positioning and aligning specific details.

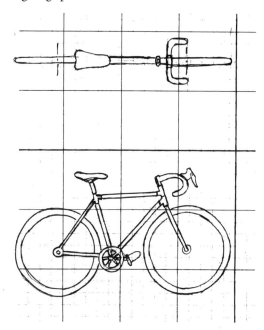

Figure 1.5.3 Orthographic sketch of a bicycle

Sketches (two-dimensional and three-dimensional) may be used to supply not only information about shape and proportion but may also display:

- partial cut-away views to reveal interior assemblies

- technical information relating to hidden detail as if the object were viewed through an X-ray.

3D sketching

The key to producing a sketch is not in the detail but the sequencing. When sketching in three dimensions it is important to establish the overall relationship of the height to the width and depth. The creation of an isometric 'box' or 'crate' provides the parameters within which the drawing will be constructed. From this point on, the outline of the overall shape is gradually built up maintaining proportional relationships between line length, angle and position. Once the outline is defined, details and features may be added. To add realism, shading and textures may be defined (see Figure 1.5.4).

Much of the theory of technical drawing and projection can be learned through the development of sketching techniques. The difference between sketching, instrument drawing and computer-aided design (CAD) is based around refinement of lines and not of theory. Engineers must be well versed in the theory of drawing before venturing into various technological techniques.

Figure 1.5.4 'Crating' to assist with 3D sketching

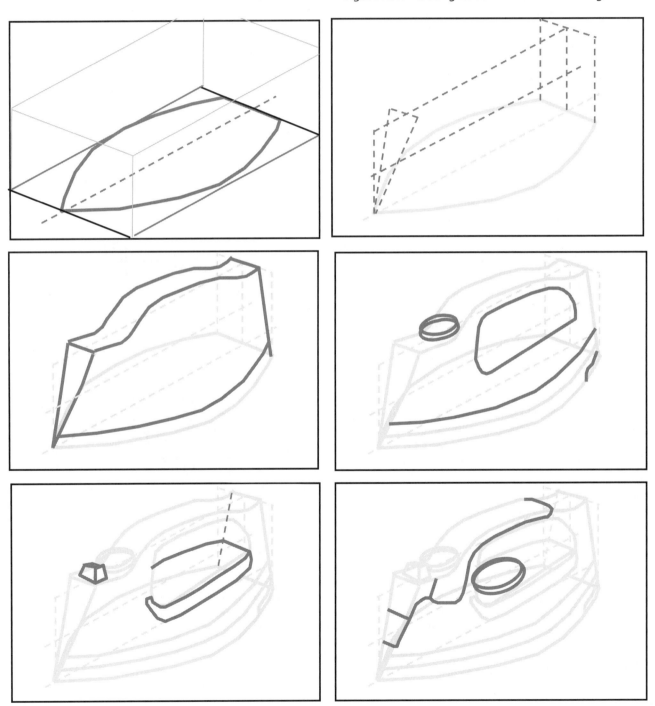

Research methods

Research using computer technologies and other resources

The biggest advantage of using computers and the internet as a source for research is that it provides researchers with a wealth of information from a variety of interdisciplinary perspectives. Researchers accessing published literature in libraries tend to limit searches to their own field of experience. This has a restricting effect on the type of information returned. Web searches trawl vast amounts of sources from a range of perspectives, even returning sources based in other cultures. The immediacy of the web and the ability to publish quickly and widely means information available in this fashion easily outpaces that produced by more traditional forms of publication. The internet also allows for quick and easy exchange of information between authors and researchers through the use of email.

Disadvantages associated with the use of the web for research include the validation of information and the vast amounts of data available to sift through. The use of computers and the web can be both a distraction and inefficient if used in an undisciplined fashion.

The two general categories of research methodology are qualitative and quantitative.

Qualitative research typically involves the use of language to record and describe the results. Such research is often associated with the investigation of cultural practices, attitudes, motivation, etc, and is most often employed within the humanities subjects such as history and ethnography. This form of research is often conducted in natural, holistic settings.

Quantitative research typically involves the numerical measurement of something, such as velocity, strength, altitude, pressure, force, etc, and is characteristic of research undertaken by the sciences and engineering. This form of research is often conducted within a laboratory setting where potentially confounding influences can be controlled.

Although the methodologies described above can be generally associated with either the humanities or the sciences and engineering, it is not unusual to find the use of some of the techniques of quantitative research being used by humanities researchers and vice versa.

Collaborative work practices

One of the hallmarks of modern engineering practice is the use of teams. Engineering projects are often large, complex and costly, necessitating the collaboration of a number of engineers to combine their skills to achieve an outcome in a cost effective and timely manner.

Much of the work undertaken by professional engineers also involves the coordination of others to accomplish a successful outcome. To be effective an engineer must therefore possess good interpersonal skills, including clear oral and written communication. Because of this, engineering courses today often emphasise the role of communication teamwork skills.

Engineering reports and their significance in engineering practice

Engineers use engineering reports as a communication tool. They may be written to address a variety of issues such as design evaluations, failure analysis, cyclic maintenance, environmental impact, etc. Reports may be commissioned on designs, parts, products or systems.

Well-researched, logically constructed and clearly written engineering reports form an important part of communication systems within the industry.

Within Engineering Studies, students will be required to write a number of reports. These reports will need to follow the format of an engineering report. Part of the documentation process is the acknowledgement in print of all sources used in compiling the report. This recognition is referred to as referencing or citation and allows the report writer to:

- demonstrate breadth of research undertaken

- inform readers of other sources of information related to the topic

- substantiate information upon which the report is based

- avoid charges of plagiarism.

Referencing occurs as citations within the text and as a list under a separate heading at the end of the document. Styles of referencing vary depending on the discipline but whatever style is adopted consistency is required. Widely used referencing styles include Harvard, APA and Physics Review.

1.6 Sample Preliminary questions and answers

Objective-response questions

1. Ionic bonds are formed between

   A metals and metals.
   B metals and non-metals.
   C non-metals and non-metals.
   D none of the above.

2. Scalar quantities consist of

   A direction only.
   B magnitude only.
   C magnitude and direction.
   D none of the above.

3. Identify the property not a characteristic of metals.

   A maleability
   B metallic lustre
   C insulation (heat and electricity)
   D usually solid at room temperatures

4. Identify which of the following shows polymer structures in order of weakest to strongest.

   A linear, cross-linked, network, branched
   B branched, linear, cross-linked, network
   C linear, branched, network, cross-linked
   D linear, branched, cross-linked, network

5. Identify which of the following is not an example of a laminar composite.

   A bimetallic strip
   B laminated glass
   C concrete
   D plywood

6. Thermoset polymers exhibit the following primary type of bonding.

   A covalent
   B ionic
   C saturated
   D van der Waals

7. Orthographic drawings

   A may contain 3D sketches.
   B must always be dimensioned.
   C can only be created using drawing instruments.
   D consist of multiple two-dimensional drawings.

8. Welding as a joining process is

   A permanent.
   B semi-permanent.
   C temporary.
   D all of the above.

9. The velocity ratio of a pulley system is

   A equal to the mechanical advantage.
   B the efficiency of the system.
   C the same as the number of pulleys.
   D found by counting the number of ropes supporting the lower block.

10. Identify the correct statement about second-class levers.

   A The load arm moves further than the effort arm.
   B The effort arm moves further than the load arm.
   C The system operates at a mechanical disadvantage.
   D The fulcrum is positioned between the effort and the load.

Short-answer questions

1. Draw a diagram classifying the following materials: aluminium, cast iron, glass, nylon, titanium, stainless steel, bakelite, brass, alumina.   (4 marks)

2. Explain why the properties of wrought iron are variable across any section.   (2 marks)

3. Describe with the aid of a diagram the molecular structure of thermosetting polymers.   (2 marks)

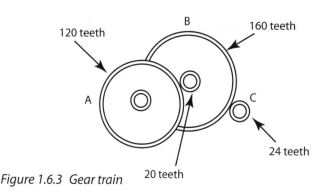

4. Calculate the height of a building given that the shadow it casts is 25 m long (see Figure 1.6.1). (2 marks)

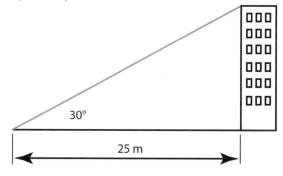

Figure 1.6.1 Building shadow

5. Explain the differences between brazing and welding. (2 marks)

Longer-answer questions

1. Explain why the movable pulley shown in Figure 1.6.2 has a velocity ratio of two, yet may only have a mechanical advantage of 1.6. (2 marks)

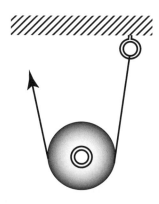

Figure 1.6.2 Movable pulley

2. Discuss the features of sketching opposed to more technical forms of drawing using instruments. (4 marks)

3. Outline advantages associated with collaborative engineering teams. (3 marks)

4. Explain why third-class levers operate at a mechanical disadvantage. (2 marks)

5. Calculate the final output speed for the gear train shown in Figure 1.6.3 if gear A rotates with an input speed of eight revolutions per minute. (3 marks)

Figure 1.6.3 Gear train

6. Calculate the velocity ratio of the gear system shown in Figure 1.6.4 if gear A is the driving gear. (2 marks)

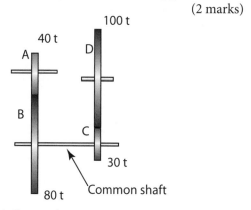

Figure 1.6.4 Gear train

Answers to objective-response questions

1. **B** Covalent bonding occurs between non-metals and between metals and non-metals.

2. **B** Vectors contain magniitiude and direction.

3. **C** Metals are conductors of heat and electricity.

4. **D**

5. **C** Concrete is a mixture.

6. **A** Thermosets are not ionically bonded, van der Waals forces are not a form of primary bonding and 'saturated' is not a form of bonding.

7. **D** Orthographic drawings do not have to be dimensioned and may be created using CAD software.

8. **A** Welding of all types is a permanent process.

9. **D**

10. **B** The load is always further from the fulcrum than the effort in second-class levers.

Answers to short-answer questions

1.

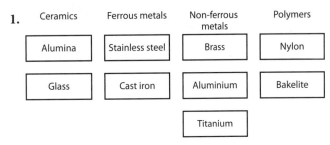

Ceramics	Ferrous metals	Non-ferrous metals	Polymers
Alumina	Stainless steel	Brass	Nylon
Glass	Cast iron	Aluminium	Bakelite
		Titanium	

Figure 1.6.5 Material classification

2. The inclusions of non-metallic slag, entrained in the iron during reduction of the ore, appear randomly throughout the iron matrix resulting in variable properties.

3. Thermosets appear as a three-dimensional network.

Figure 1.6.6 Thermoset structure

4. $\tan 30° = \dfrac{\text{height}}{25}$

   $25 \tan 30° = \text{height}$

   Height = 14.433 m

5. Welding in its various forms involves the fusion (melting) of parent materials together with or without a filler rod. Brazing involves the joining of metals together using a filler rod that melts above 500 °C.

Answers to longer-answer questions

1. The number of ropes supporting the load can be used to determine the mechanical advantage. In this case the effort rope must be considered as well and the velocity ratio is therefore two. The mechanical advantage of a pulley system, however, is affected by efficiency. For the mechanical advantage to be 1.6 the efficiency of the system must be 80% as determined by the formulae:

   Efficiency = MA ÷ VR

2. Sketching advantages:

   • quick to produce

   • little or no equipment required.

   Sketching disadvantages:

   • not as precise as instrument driven methods

   • does not necessarily conform to drawing standards and as such may be open to misinterpretation by others.

3. Collaborative teams rely on the expertise of more than one person. Team members may also be chosen from a variety of fields thus expanding expertise. Results may be produced in a more time efficient manner relative to the number of personnel involved in the team.

4. The positioning of the effort between the load and the fulcrum means the effort arm is shorter than the load arm, thus creating a mechanical disadvantage.

5. If the input gear is rotating is rotating at eight rpm or 960 teeth per minute (tpm) then the following calculations will apply.

For gear A	960 ÷ 20 or 48 rpm
For gear B	48 × 160 = 7680 tpm
For gear C	7680 ÷ 24 = 320 rpm

   Final output speed 320 rpm

6. Considering one revolution of gear A:

   gear B makes 40 ÷ 80 revolutions

   gear C also makes 40 ÷ 80 revolutions

   gear D makes 40 ÷ 80 x 30 ÷ 100 revolutions

   Therefore for one revolution of gear A, gear D makes 0.15 revolutions.

   given $VR = \dfrac{\text{speed of driving gear}}{\text{speed of driven gear}}$

   then   VR = 1 ÷ 0.15

   thus   VR = 6.67

1.7 Glossary

Amorphous
Like crystalline solids, amorphous materials are usually characterised by certain areas of short-range order. A long-range order, as in crystals, does not exist in amorphous substances. The terms *amorphous*, *non-crystalline* and *glassy* are interchangeable.

Austenite
Austenite is the face centred cubic (FCC) phase of iron containing some dissolved carbon.

Atomic bonding
Atomic bonding is an electrostatic attractive force within and between atoms that allows the formation of materials containing two or more atoms.

Brass
Brass is an alloy of copper and up to 43% zinc.

Bronze
Bronze is a term generally applied to an alloy of copper and up to 10% tin.

Cementite
Cementite is the name given to iron carbide with the general formula Fe_3C.

Ceramic
Ceramic is a multi-phase material containing phases composed of compounds of metals and non-metals. Ceramics are typically hard and good insulators.

Concrete
Concrete is a mixture of aggregate embedded in a cement binding matrix composed of sand, water and cement.

Composites
Composites represents a class of material whose properties derive from the combination of two or more materials that are bonded together such that each of the constituent materials contributes to an improvement in mechanical, physical, chemical or electrical properties.

Crystal
A crystal or crystalline solid is a material whose atoms or molecules are arranged in a predictable or ordered pattern based around all three-dimensional axes.

Density
Density is a measure of the quantity of mass per unit volume.

Ductility
Ductility is the ability of a material to undergo plastic deformation by extrusion or the application of tensile forces.

Ferrous
Ferrous metals are those based on the metallic element iron (Fe). The two most common of these are steel and cast iron, distinguished primarily by the percentage of carbon present.

Fulcrum
A fulcrum is a point of support and turning about which lever arms pivot.

Hardness
Hardness refers to the resistance of a material to scratching or abrasion. It may also refer to resistance to indentation, penetration or cutting.

Lever
A lever is a type of simple machine consisting of a rigid beam pivoting around a fulcrum that is used to transmit force.

Mass
The mass of an object is a measure of the amount of matter that an object contains. The unit of mass within the SI system is the kilogram (kg).

Metal
Metals are a solid materials, typically hard, opaque, ductile, malleable and shiny. They feature good electrical and thermal conductivity.

Non-ferrous	A material containing no, or minimal, iron
Pearlite	A phase of carbon steel and cast iron consisting of ferrite and cementite formed into distinct layers (or lamellae) on slow cooling from austenite
Polymer	A giant molecule based on carbon
Pulley	A pulley consists of a wheel and an axle arranged by itself or in conjunction with others to operate as a simple machine.
Scalar	Any measure that has a magnitude only
Screw	A screw is a form of simple machine used to translate rotary motion into linear motion.
Steel	An alloy of iron and up to 2% carbon, often with additions of other alloying elements such as manganese, silicon, chromium, nickel and molybdenum
Stiffness	Stiffness is the resistance of an elastic body to deflection by an applied force.
Timber	Timber (or wood) is an organic material consisting of thin-walled tubes made of cellulose. These cellulose 'tubes' are bound together with a weak glue called lignin.
Thermoplastic	A polymer that can be softened by heating
Thermoset	A polymer that can be set by heating but cannot be softened by reheating
Toughness	Toughness is the ability of a material to resist the propagation of cracks. It is often identified as the area under a stress-strain graph.
Vector	Any measure that has a magnitude and direction

ENGINEERED PRODUCTS

CONTENTS

STUDENT OUTCOMES

A student:

- identifies the scope of engineering and recognises current innovations.

- describes the types of materials, components and processes and explains their implications for engineering development.

- uses mathematical, scientific and graphical methods to solve problems of engineering practice.

- develops written, oral and presentation skills and applies these to engineering reports.

- applies graphics as a communication tool.

- describes developments in technology and their impact on engineering products.

- describes the influence of technological change on engineering and its effect on people.

- identifies the social, environmental and cultural implications of technological change in engineering.

- demonstrates the ability to work both individually and in teams.

© 2011 NSW Education Standards Authority

KEY TERMS AND CONCEPTS

Aluminium	Magnet
Alternating current (AC)	Martensite
Annealing	Normalising
Austenite	Non-ferrous
Brass	Pearlite
Bronze	Polymer
Case hardening	Potential difference
Cast iron	Quenching
Cementite	Slip
Cold working	Steel
Couple	Tempering
Current	Three force rule
Direct current (DC)	Toughness
Dislocations	Transformer
Ductility	Vector
Ferrite	Voltage
Ferrous	Work gardening
Heat treatment	

2.1 Skills of the professional engineer

Engineers as problem solvers, designers, communicators and project managers

Engineering involves people working as individuals and as part of a team, pooling their knowledge of mathematics, science and technology to generate creative and practical solutions to problems. On 22 February 2000, iconic astronaut Neil Armstrong delivered a speech to the National Press Club entitled 'The engineered century'. In this speeech he recounted many of the achievements of engineers over the past 100 years but also summed up the role of engineers and their place in society when he stated 'Engineers are dedicated to solving problems and creating new, useful, and efficient things. So should not the world admire and respect them?'.

The skills engineers possess and tasks they complete include:

- designing, making and operating the many systems, services and products that make up our everyday lives

- researching and producing new products

- testing things to make sure they are functional and safe

- developing new ways to make the world cleaner, safer and healthier

- project oversight or management.

Types of engineers and engineering

In the field of engineered products electrical and mechanical engineers play a significant role.

Mechanical engineering

Mechanical engineers turn energy into power and motion. Mechanisms (machines, tools and equipment) are designed, produced, tested and improved by mechanical engineering teams. Mechanical engineers also work in the areas of transport, energy and construction and on projects including:

- trains, cars, forklifts and trucks

- power generation

- cranes and lifts

- individual machines and their component parts.

Mechanical engineering applies knowledge of materials, energy and structures.

Electrical engineering

Electrical engineering is concerned with the way electrical energy is generated and used. Electrical engineering teams are involved in planning, making and using products, equipment and systems. Electrical engineering covers areas such as:

- power generation, including solar, wind, coal, hydro and nuclear, systems development, maintenance and distribution

- electrical manufacturing, electronics and computer systems

- telecommunications.

This discipline also provides the power, systems and products that make our lives safer (traffic lights, smoke detectors, earth leakage detection devices and so on).

Other types of engineering

There are many areas in engineering that do not fall into the above groups. Some are difficult to place into one category because they use the knowledge and skill from many branches of engineering and combine them for a specific purpose. People who work in these areas develop skills that are important and especially applicable for a precise field.

Each of the areas in these categories use a combination of knowledge and skills from the mechanical and electrical engineering fields. Examples of specific types of engineering fields other than those in the major categories described above include:

- chemical

- environmental

- marine and aeronautical

- materials or metallurgical.

2.2 Historical and societal influences

Engineering and the 20th century

In February 2000 the US National Academy of Engineering released its nominations for the top twenty engineering achievements of the 20th century. The criterion for selection on this engineering list was either invention and/or primary impact within the century. As might be expected, items such as electrification (1), the automobile (2), the aeroplane (3), radio and television (6), computers (8), and refrigeration (10), appear on the list. An item also appears on the list that initially seems incongruous in the company of such major technological development: household appliances (15). Selected for consideration below are the common clothes iron, domestic stove, refrigerator and lawn mower.

Historical development of various engineered products—household appliances

Until the advent of domestic electric power most household duties were performed by manual exertion, usually by the female members of a household. Appliances to assist in these tasks were generally rudimentary in design, being built for functionality and longevity rather than aesthetics.

The iron

One of the most common appliances within the home is the iron, used for the removal of creases in textile materials such as clothing. Such is the almost universal availability of this appliance that it played a pivotal role in the early history of the power generation industry and the availability of electricity in the home.

The practice of ironing appears to have developed independently in many civilisations, beginning with evidence of the manipulation and stretching of cloth to smooth it as represented on Grecian pottery of 540 BCE.

Evidence of the first recognisable ironing appliance, however, dates back to the Han dynasty of China, approximately 206 to 220 BCE. Irons of this period consisted of a small cast iron pan into which hot coals and sand were placed. These irons were still in use into the 18th century (see Figure 2.2.1).

Figure 2.2.1   Replica of Han Dynasty iron

In Europe, implements for ironing date from approximately the 10th century CE, when Vikings used glass in the shape of an upturned mushroom known as a 'smoothing stone'.

Heat does not appear to have been used for ironing in Europe until the 16th century, originating in Holland and spreading to the rest of the continent. Up until this time, most ironing processes relied on various weights passed over dampened cloth.

By the 17th century irons of a more contemporary design, consisting of a boat-shaped metal base of either a solid or hollow style, were in common use in Europe. A popular design of the time was the 'box' iron, consisting of a hollow container often cast in brass. The box iron was heated internally by inserting a heat source. The model shown in Figure 2.2.2 shows a hinged top developed for this purpose.

Figure 2.2.2   Box iron constructed in brass

The simplest form of box iron used slugs of iron, which had been heated in a fire. Using tongs, the iron slug could be replaced when cool by another waiting on the fire. This had the advantage of reducing the risk of soiling clothes with soot.

A similar iron of box construction was the 'charcoal' iron, shown in Figure 2.2.3. These irons were also heated from the inside by filling with hot charcoal. An advantage of these irons was that heat could be maintained for an extended period by fanning the charcoals inside. For this purpose, a small bellows was often supplied to pump air through a hole near the base. A small chimney was also often present to allow smoke to escape

Figure 2.2.3 Charcoal iron, image by Vincent de Groot, http-_www.videgro.net (own work) CC-BY-2.5 (www. creativecommons.org_licenses_by_2.5), via Wikimedia Commons

For those who could not afford the expensive brass variety, a cheaper solid iron made from wrought iron was available. These irons were commonly known as 'flat' or 'Sad' irons (meaning compact or heavy) (see Figure 2.2.4).

Figure 2.2.4 Flat or Sad iron

Although the technology to melt and cast iron had been available in China since the Han Dynasty, it was not generally available in Europe until the 16th century, a difference of over 1800 years. Even then, the production of cast iron in Europe tended to be restricted to the production of cannons until the early 18th century and the beginning of the Industrial Revolution. Most iron objects for everyday use in Europe, up until the 18th century, were largely constructed from 'wrought' iron. The production of wrought iron involves a process in which iron ore is reduced in a furnace at a temperature of approximately 1200 °C in the presence of carbon to form a solid 'bloom'. This bloom consists of a mixture of solid iron, slag and unburnt charcoal. The bloom is then hammered or 'wrought' to the desired shape.

In 1707, the Englishman Abraham Darby proposed to make thin-walled cooking pots from cast iron. Up to that time large cooking pots were generally cast into sand moulds using brass, a more expensive material. Darby established a furnace specifically for that purpose at Coalbrookdale, using a revolutionary fuel for the time, coke, instead of charcoal, which had been commonly used to that date and was becoming increasingly scarce. The greater strength and lower impurities of coke compared to coal, and lower cost compared to charcoal, helped to revitalise the British iron industry.

With the 18th century introduction to Europe of the technology to melt high quality iron, cast iron became available for everyday items. Irons were cast as solid objects that could be heated by placing them on the hot surface of a cast iron stove.

Weight was considered an advantage in the ironing process as the heat of the iron cooled relatively quickly.

A hugely successful modification of the Sad iron was patented by Mary Potts of the USA in 1871 and became known as the Mrs Potts's Sad iron (see Figure 2.2.5). This modification involved, in part, the separation of the handle from the base. A detachable wooden handle was created that allowed the cast iron base to be heated on a stove and which could be then picked up with the cold handle for use when ready. In addition, the base was reduced in weight by casting it hollow. Heat dissipation was reduced by subsequently filling the cavity with an insulating material such as plaster of Paris, clay or asbestos. This insulation also reduced the amount of radiant heat to which the operator's hand was exposed.

Multiple bases could now be used, transferring from one iron as it cooled to another waiting hot on the stove, using a single cool handle. The Mrs Potts's iron was often sold in sets consisting of several cast iron bases, a wooden handle and a stand known as a 'trivet' (meaning three feet). An advertisement for a Mrs Potts's ironing set is shown in Figure 2.2.6.

Toward the beginning of the 20th century little had changed with regard to irons, although chromium or nickel electroplating was often added to the surface to reduce corrosion and improve movement over the working surface by reducing friction. Gas-heated irons that could be connected by a hose to the mains gas supply were available in the 1880s but were cumbersome (see Figure 2.2.7).

Figure 2.2.5 Mrs Potts's Sad iron

Figure 2.2.6 Advertisement for Mrs Potts's Sad irons, image by the Alice Marshall Women's History Collection, Ephemera and Artifacts, Accession No. AKM 91/1.1. Archives and Special Collections at the Penn State Harrisburg Library, Pennsylvania State

FLETCHER, RUSSELL & CO.'S (LIMITED)

New and Simple Form of Internally Heated

SMOOTHING IRON.

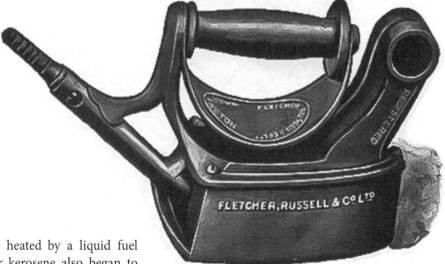

Figure 2.2.7 Gas-heated iron

About this time, spirit irons heated by a liquid fuel such as methylated spirits or kerosene also began to appear along with construction from pressed steel (see Figure 2.2.8). Fuel was often supplied to the combustion chamber from a small canister attached to the heel and the flow of fuel regulated by a dial on the top of the iron. Holes were positioned along the side of the cowl to allow the intake of air to maintain combustion.

methylated spirits added to a small tray and ignited (with a match) to heat the iron's base.

When the fuel was exhausted, the iron was ready for work. Although portable, the obvious disadvantage of the spirit iron was the safety aspects associated with the use of a flammable liquid fuel. The accompanying instructions read 'A pressing need for all on holiday, in bachelor rooms, on board ship and at empire outposts.'

Figure 2.2.8 'Spirit' iron, image by Sobebunny (own work) CC-BY-SA-3.0 (www.creativecommons.org/ licenses/by-sa/3.0), via Wikimedia Commons

Figure 2.2.9 Inverted 'Boudoir' travelling iron, image by Roger Graeme

In the 1920s smaller travelling irons were also available. The British made 'Boudoir' (Figure 2.2.9) used

The electric iron

The first patent for an electric iron was in 1883 to the Americans Dyer and Seely, who used an element consisting of thin carbon sticks to heat the sole plate. This iron was not commercially successful, not least of all due to the limited availability of electric power.

Even at the beginning of the 20th century electricity was still a relatively expensive commodity in comparison to other sources of energy such as gas, which was still well entrenched in the supply of energy for lighting, not to mention heating and cooking.

The availablity of electricity was confined to the provision of lighting and was therefore generated only during the evening. In 1903, however, an electrical power plant superintendent, Earl Richardson, while considering ways in which a greater demand for electricity might be encouraged developed an iron that could be heated by electricity. This 'electric iron' used an iron wire as the resistor wound around a brass core. As the wire was heated, the brass absorbed the heat and conducted it to the base of the iron. Richardson constructed a number of these irons and provided them to local households for a trial after convincing his company to generate power during the day, every Tuesday, during the trial period.

The irons proved very popular but suffered a major problem of overheating in the centre. After redesigning the heating elements based on suggestions from his wife, an iron was produced that contained heating elements more evenly distributed and which converged at the tip. This iron was subsequently marketed as the 'Hotpoint iron'. Introduced in 1905, the Hotpoint iron was immediately successful and created demand for power generation during the day. As distribution networks grew and electrical power became more available, a rapid increase occurred in the number of electrical appliances entering the market, encouraged and supported by the companies generating electricity.

By 1909, the iron resistor wire was replaced by the more reliable nickel–chromium alloy resistor. Until recently the cord connection for irons contained an insulating layer of asbestos beneath a cloth cover. Because iron cords incorporated an insulating layer of asbestos, frayed cords on old irons should be disposed of carefully.

Competition was still present however from alternate energy sources, particularly while the electricity supply was uncertain or expensive. 'Spirit irons' provided some initial competition in this respect.

Temperature control of the electric iron was the responsibility of the operator and was achieved by turning the power on or off as required, until the adjustable thermostat was introduced in 1927.

The last major improvement in the iron was introduced with the development of the 'steam iron' in the 1940s. The steam iron increased the efficiency of ironing by providing greater control over heating and allowing the simultaneous application of moisture and heat. Steam is also able to penetrate deeper into cloth, greatly assisting in the smoothing of the material. A number of other notable modifications were introduced in the following years, although the basic principle of operation remains largely unchanged. The timeline below shows some developments.

1930s: automatic thermostat introduced.

1931: a cast aluminium sole plate introduced.

late 1930s: an all cast aluminium iron introduced.

post WWII: stainless steel iron.

1965: Teflon™ coated sole plate.

The introduction of polymers to the design of irons first appeared in the handles, using thermosetting materials such as Bakelite (phenol–formaldehyde). These materials had a number of advantages in that they were:

- cheap

- strong

- durable

- heat resistant

- water resistant

- dimensionally stable.

Colours, however, were generally limited to black or brown.

Injection moulding techniques were later used to make the cowling from plastic and finally to incorporate the handle and cowling into an integral component. These developments allowed weight reductions while introducing colour. With these changes design became an important feature and irons are often purchased today as much for their style and fashion as for their functionality.

The sole plate of most irons today is usually die cast aluminium alloy although stainless steel or ceramic sole plates are available. Cowls are typically injection moulded plastic although chrome plated pressed steel components are still found, particularly in designs aiming for a 'retro' look.

The most common domestic steam iron is the 'drip type'. The drip type steam iron does not heat the water reservoir in the iron but rather allows a controlled flow of water to drop onto the inner surface of the heated sole plate where it is instantly converted to steam. Figure 2.2.10 shows two views of a steam iron with the cowl removed. The electrical connections can be seen at the rear. In Figure 2.2.10 (upper), the top of the steam chamber is seen. When ironing without the aid of steam the hole in the steam chamber top plate is blocked by a tapered rod connected to a selector dial on the body of the iron. When the selector dial is turned to steam a small spring raises the rod sufficiently to allow drops of water to enter the steam chamber and make contact with the inside surface of the heated sole plate where they are instantly turned to steam. The inside surface of the sole plate can be seen in Figure 2.2.10 (lower), following removal of the pressed steel steam chamber top plate. The steam exits the chamber through vents in the sole plate. If and when an extra shot of steam is required a pump action button on the handle can be used to remove a small quantity of water from the water tank and deliver it directly to the sole plate via a thin rubber tube.

Figure 2.2.10 Sole plate steam chamber and element

Heating of the sole plate is by electrical connections to an element buried within the sole plate.

An important feature of materials used for the sole plate, particularly of the early irons, was their ability to conduct heat (or their thermal conductivity). A comparative table of thermal conductivities is presented below in Figure 2.2.11.

Material	Thermal conductivity W/(m.K)
Silver	429
Copper	410
Aluminium	170
Magnesium	156
Brass	109
Cast iron	55
Carbon steel	54
Titanium	22
Stainless steel	16
Glass	4
Wood	0.13

Figure 2.2.11 Thermal conductivities

It is clear from Figure 2.2.11 why the early clothes irons made of brass were so popular with those who could afford them. Their high conductivity allowed the efficient transfer of heat from the internal heat source through to the clothes.

Cast iron was much cheaper but provided a less efficient means of transferring heat. The advantage cast iron could provide was cheapness and weight, which was useful in the smoothing process.

Today, because electric heating of the sole plate is available, weight is no longer a significant advantage when ironing. Indeed, many consumers may consider lighter weights preferable when selecting an iron.

Most modern irons use an aluminium alloy as a sole plate material. From Figure 2.2.12, the advantage of aluminium as a sole plate material is obvious.

In addition to high thermal conductivity aluminium offers low weight, corrosion resistance and suitability for die casting which allows precision manufacture capable of achieving thin walls and a fine surface finish.

The popularity of stainless steel in some modern irons is in large part due to its resistance to corrosion. Reduced corrosion has the dual benefits of avoiding the potential for the contamination of clothes by the products of corrosion and maintaining a smooth surface, eliminating drag between the sole plate and cloth.

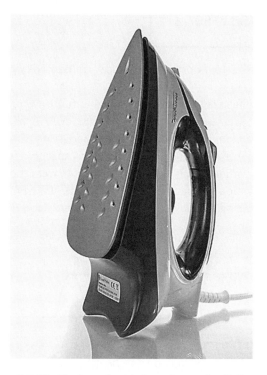

Figure 2.2.12 Modern electric iron, image by Colin (own work) CC-BY-SA-3.0 (www.creativecommons.org/ licenses/by-sa/3.0)], via Wikimedia Commons

Further reading

Constable, G and Somerville, B, *A century of innovation: Twenty engineering achievements that transformed our lives*, Joseph Henry Press, Washington DC, 2003

'The history of irons' (2004), retrieved 3 July 2013 from Garmento website, www.garmento.org/process&skills/ history_of_irons.pdf

The stove

While the cast iron cooking stove had been available in China since the Han dynasty, cooking in Europe remained the province of open fires within a special recess in the wall known as a hearth.

The hearth was an alcove type construction of brick or stone in which wood or coal was burnt as fuel. Smoke and excess heat was transported up a chimney. A beam of wood or iron, known as a backing bar, attached to the back wall of the hearth allowed cooking pots to be suspended over the fire. With increasing sophistication, these bars were replaced by a small swing crane, located to one side of the hearth, that allowed the cook pot to be moved in and out of position without the necessity of lifting it off its support (see Figure 2.2.13). Iron skewers and waffle irons were also used along with iron skillet pans supported over the fire on an iron tripod or trivet.

Figure 2.2.13 Open hearth stove, image by Johann Jaritz (own work) CC-BY-SA-3.0-2.5-2.0-1.0 (www. creativecommons.org/licenses/by-sa/3.0), via Wikimedia Commons

A major problem with this system, however, was the large amount of heat that was lost up the chimney. By the 19th century more compact appliances that enclosed the burning fuel were available, such that the stove often consisted of a large cast iron box with openings on the top for pots and pans and a baking oven. Gradually cleaner burning gas replaced wood and coal as the primary source of fuel. Even with the cleaner burning gas as fuel, cooking remained an imprecise activity until automatic oven temperature control was introduced in 1923.

Stoves were still however constructed of iron. The cleaning and polishing of stoves was a labour intensive process using products such as black-lead polish. In an attempt to reduce this chore and to introduce some colour to their products, manufacturers in the 1920s began offering stoves with enamelled side panels. By the 1930s most kitchen appliances had enamelled surfaces to facilitate cleaning.

With the introduction of electricity to the home at the beginning of the 20th century electric stoves began to appear. Iron also began to be replaced by thinner, lighter steel cabinets.

Electric cooktop

Traditional electric cooktops have relied on electricity being supplied to a resistance element often made of an alloy of nickel and chromium known as nichrome. This element in turn heats a cooking 'hob' in the shape of a plate or coil, made of cast iron. Heat transfers from the hob directly to the base of any cooking utensil by conduction.

Electromagnetic induction

Electromagnetic induction cooktops rely on the creation of a magnetic field, which induces a current in the base of a ferrous metal pot placed on the cooktop surface (Figure 2.2.14). The cooktop itself remains cool.

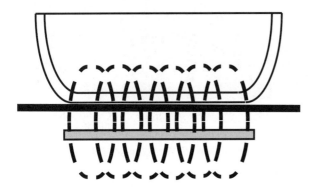

Figure 2.2.14 Induction cooktop

For this system to work efficiently electric power is converted to higher voltage and frequency by control systems within the cooktop. Electric power enters the cooktop as standard 240V 50Hz and is passed to power modules that control the cooking hobs. Figure 2.2.15 shows the typical sinusoidal AC wave form of the electric supply into the cooktop. Induction systems are safer, faster and more energy-efficient than a traditionally powered electric cooking surface.

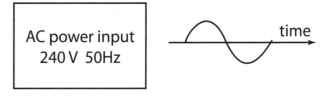

Figure 2.2.15 Electric power supply into a cooktop

Within each power module is a transformer, where the voltage is boosted to approximately 400V. Figure 2.2.16 illustrates the voltage boost provided by the transformer within a power module.

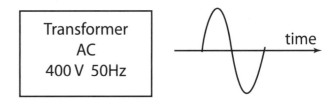

Figure 2.2.16 Boosted power supply into a cooktop

The voltage is then passed through a full wave rectifier circuit where the negative or reverse cycle is changed in direction, creating a continuous series of DC waves. Filters in the rectifier circuit contain capacitors, which act to smooth out the variation in current flow by their action of charging during the rise of current and discharging during decreasing current (see Figure 2.2.17).

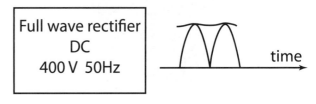

Figure 2.2.17 Rectification of the AC power to DC

An amplifier (containing an inverter circuit) changes the voltage and current back to AC, at which time the frequency is increased to 25–50 kHz as illustrated in Figure 2.2.18. This is accomplished with a switching circuit that is used to change the direction (or polarity) of the current, producing an alternating square wave while frequency is controlled by the switching speed.

High frequency AC is then supplied to the induction coils below the cooktop. A magnetic field extends from the coil and will induce high frequency eddy currents in any magnetic cooking pot of sufficient size sitting on the cooktop directly above the induction coil.

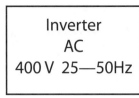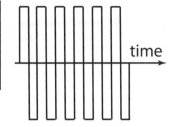

Figure 2.2.18 Inversion of the DC power supply into high frequency AC

A control module connected to the power modules allows frequency and voltage to be adjusted for different levels of heating.

Because induction heating relies on inducing a current within the cooking utensil it is only useful with magnetic materials. Cookware made of aluminium, copper or austenitic (non-magnetic) stainless steel are not compatible with an induction cooktop.

The refrigerator

Up until the late 1800s the ability to prolong the life of foodstuffs such as meat depended largely on drying or chemical curing with salt, herbs and spices, or smoke. Even the canning of food, begun in the early part of the 19th century, was of limited success until the discoveries of Louis Pasteur in the 1860s provided a scientific basis for the heating stage of the canning process. Despite this, Australia had built up a sizable trade in canned meat to Britain by the 1860s. Reliable transcontinental and intercontinental trade of meat, however, was to depend on refrigeration.

Natural ice

The use of ice from lakes and glaciers as a means of extending the useful life of food had of course been known for millennia. The Chinese had been building icehouses, kept cool by the evaporation of water, to store winter ice through the summer months since the 8th century BCE. Such means of food preservation were of limited use, however, in warmer climates such as those experienced in Australia.

Ice cut from lakes in the USA was imported to Australia in the 1850s for sale in the gold fields. Here the presence of many wealthy miners and the desire for a cold drink on a hot day could garner prices of four-pence a pound. Despite the high loss due to melting en-route, such prices made for a healthy profit. The famous American author Henry David Thoreau, in his well-known work *Walden*,

describes the harvesting of ice from Walden Pond in the winter of 1846–47 and observes 'Thus it appears that the sweltering inhabitants of Charleston and New Orleans, of Madras and Bombay and Calcutta, drink at my well'.

Outside of such specialty applications, ice was generally unavailable in Australia. In the absence of refrigeration, produce, particularly meat and milk products, could have only a very limited life. Storage was concerned not only with the effects of heat, but also of insects such as flies, and it was not unusual for meat to be sold in some degree of despoilation.

The meat safe

The meat safe was a common solution to the problem of flies and consisted of a cabinet with a wooden or metal frame enclosed by mesh that was hung in a cool location such as a veranda. The 'Coolgardie' safe was a development of the meat safe using the addition of a galvanized tray to the top and the hanging of hessian over the sides of the cabinet. With one end of the hessian in the water tray, capillary action would draw water down the sides. As air passed through the wet hessian, evaporation of water would occur, removing heat from the air and allowing cool air to flow over the contents of the safe. The origin and inventor of this product is uncertain, but is often credited to AP McCormick and to have been first used in the goldfield town of Coolgardie, hence the name Coolgardie safe.

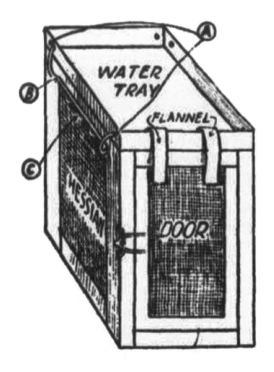

Figure 2.2.19 Coolgardie safe

Artificial ice

A Scottish immigrant to Australia, James Harrison, first accomplished the artificial manufacture of ice, for commercial sale, in 1851. Harrison was a printer by trade and noticed the chilling effect of sulphuric ether. He subsequently built a mechanical refrigeration unit to make ice, using ether as the refrigerant. With the aid of refrigeration, Harrison saw that an international trade of meat was possible. In 1873 he attempted to ship a consignment of frozen meat to England but, without refrigeration on board ship, the cargo was lost. Seeing the potential for international trade, a number of inventors around the world quickly developed freezer units and by the late 1880s ships with refrigerator units were beginning to routinely transport frozen meat. With the development of commercial cool rooms, perishable items could be stored for longer periods, reducing waste. Many of these commercial cool rooms were also often available to locals for the storage of foodstuffs.

Ice works also began to appear in cities and later in large country towns, supplying ice to commercial establishments and for private domestic use. By the turn of the century an ice chest was present in most kitchens.

Ice continued to be supplied to ice chests in Australia, particularly on industrial sites into the 1970s, well after most homes contained their own refrigerator.

Mechanical refrigeration

Refrigeration relies on a high latent heat of vaporisation (ΔHv), sometimes also called enthalpy of evaporation (see Figure 2.2.20). The units are expressed as either kilojoules per kilogram (kJ/kg) or kilojoules per mole (kJ/mol).

These units refer to the amount of heat absorbed from the environment in order for a given quantity of a liquid to change into a gas at the boiling point of the liquid. The higher the latent heat of vaporisation, the more heat is removed per kilogram. If the temperature of the surrounding environment is reduced to a point below that of the boiling point of the liquid, cooling ceases.

In practice the situation is a little more complicated, since some evaporation will occur from the surface of a liquid at temperatures well below the boiling point. If it did not, the Coolgardie fridge would not work and cooling of the body by the evaporation of sweat would not occur.

Name	Formula	BP	ΔHv	
		°C	kj/kg	kg/mol
Ammonia R717	NH_3	−33	1369	23.27
Freon 12 R12	CCl_2F_2	−29.8	139.3	16.84
Freon 22 R22	$CHClF_2$	−40.8	233	20.14
Carbon Dioxide	CO_2	−78	574	25.26
Ether		34.5	377	
Water	H_2O	100	2257	40.63
Sulphur dioxide	SO_2	−10	389.4	24.94

Figure 2.2.20 Latent heats of vaporisation

For the purposes of refrigeration, a low boiling point is also desirable. Many substances used as refrigerants have a boiling point below zero at normal atmospheric pressure. Other refrigerants have a relatively high boiling point at normal atmospheric pressure. The boiling point can be reduced substantially, however, by reducing pressure. Conversely, by placing a substance that is gaseous at normal temperature and pressure under elevated pressure, it can be liquefied.

Mechanical refrigeration relies on the circulation of a refrigerant in a closed system and can be achieved by using one of two basic principles:

- absorption
- gas compression.

Absorption

The absorption method of refrigeration uses heat to initially vaporise a liquid refrigerant, such as ammonia. An early domestic refrigeration unit using this technique was the 'Crosley ice-ball'. The appeal of this apparatus was that it could be retro fitted to ice chests that were already present in most homes.

Crosley ice-ball

The Crosley ice-ball was a refrigerating device widely available in the 1920s for domestic use. It operated on the absorption principle. It consisted of two galvanised steel spheres, connected asymmetrically by a pipe as shown in Figure 2.2.21. A handle was attached to the pipe connection to allow the lifting of the 'ice-ball'. The Crosley ice-ball weighed approximately 16 kg and was a removable/portable device that could be used almost anywhere.

Figure 2.2.21 Crosley ice-ball, image modified from Jeremy Mikesell (own work) CC-BY-SA-2.5 (www.creativecommons.org/licenses/by-sa/2.5) or GFDL

The higher of the two spheres, known as the 'hot' ball, was partially filled with a mixture of water and ammonia, similar to household ammonia.

Preparation of the ice-ball, known as 'charging', was accomplished by gently heating the hot ball while the other sphere, the cold ball, sat immersed in a bucket of water. During heating ammonia evaporated from the water in the hot ball and travelled through the connecting pipe to the cold ball where it condensed. When this process was completed, the cold ball was placed in a cabinet containing the foodstuffs to be cooled. The hot ball was positioned on the outside of the cabinet. Because ammonia has a boiling point of minus 33 °C the ammonia evaporated in the cold ball and returned to the hot ball where it was absorbed by the water. The latent heat of evaporation taken from the immediate region of the cold ball resulted in the formation of ice on the outer surface of the sphere, cooling the contents of the cabinet. In this manner, food could be kept cold for over 24 hours before needing to recharge the ice-ball. Because the Crosley ice-ball was a sealed unit and ammonia was not lost, the device had a potentially long life and low operating cost.

The Australian refrigerator, 'The Silent Knight'

The Crosley ice-ball was also available in Australia and formed the basis for a manufacturing company that was to lead to the development of an Australian refrigerator. Edward Hallstrom established E. Hallstrom Pty Ltd to manufacture beds and furniture, including chests to accommodate the imported Crosley ice-ball. Work grew to include the repair of ice balls and the invention of a special valve, welded into a connecting pipe to refill gas. In 1927, Hallstroms Pty Ltd manufactured its own ice-balls and chests (see Figure 2.2.22).

Figure 2.2.22 Upright cabinet with ice ball c 1924, image by the Hallstrom family

Later Hallstrom tried putting the heating flame under the outside cylinder to create a permanent frozen core inside the chest. External water cooling tanks were added later (see Figure 2.2.23).

Figure 2.2.23 Hallstrom model A, c1932, image by the Hallstrom family

Advertisements of the period such as that shown in Figure 2.2.24 promoted the ability of the cabinet to keep meat and dairy products cold without the need for electricity, which was still in relatively short supply, particularly in country areas.

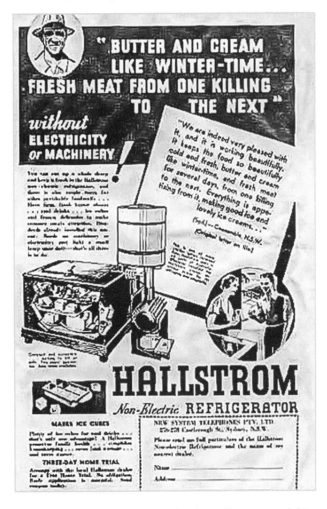

Figure 2.2.24 Advertisement for the Hallstrom model A, image by the Hallstrom family

Edward then turned the cabinet on its end and placed the cooling tank on top. Kerosene burners were added and the resulting refrigerator became known as the 'Super-Freezer' (see Figure 2.2.25).

In 1944, the Hallstrom refrigerator was renamed the 'Silent Knight'. This refrigerator and others based on the absorption method were extremely popular in Australia into the 1950s. Edward Hallstrom was later noted as the founder of Sydney's Taronga Park Zoo, serving as director of the park from 1941 to 1967. He was knighted in 1952 for services to philanthropy. Hallstroms Pty Ltd ceased the manufacture of refrigerators in 1970.

Figure 2.2.25 Advertisement for the Hallstrom Super-Freezer, c1936, image by the Hallstrom family

Gas compression

The gas compression cycle, also known as the vapour compression cycle, relies on the vaporisation of a liquid refrigerant and consists of four stages consisting of the:

- compressor

- condenser

- expansion valve

- evaporator.

In the compressor, vapour is compressed using an electric compressor, resulting in a temperature increase. The hot vapour enters the condenser stage where the refrigerant condenses to liquid as heat is removed either by radiation to the surrounding air or by conduction (if surrounded by a coolant such as water). This section of the cycle is found on the outside rear of most domestic refrigerators. The liquid refrigerant is next passed through an expansion valve where it undergoes rapid expansion and vaporisation as it enters the evaporator. To maintain this expansion, heat energy is taken from the surroundings, resulting in a cooling of the immediate environment. It is the evaporator section of the cycle that is located within the refrigerator.

Refrigerators based on the gas compression cycle began to appear for domestic use in the 1920s (see Figure 2.2.26).

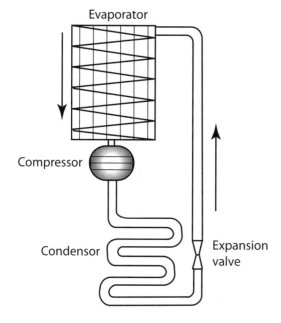

Figure 2.2.26 Gas compression regenerative refrigeration cycle

Early refrigerators used a variety of toxic gases such as ammonia (NH_3), ethyl chloride (C_2H_5Cl), or sulphur dioxide (SO_2), until the halogenated hydrocarbon 'Freon' was introduced in the 1920s as a non-toxic alternative. The production of Freon 12 was discontinued in 1996 after it was found that it affected the Earth's ozone layer.

Further reading

'Applications' (2012), Air Liquide, www.gaz-industriels. airliquide.com/en/applications-2.html

'How Refrigeration Changed the World' (2013), Asymetric War, www.asymmetricwar.com/ howrefrigeration-changed-the-world/

Elert, G, 'Refrigerators' (2013), The Physics Hypertextbook, www.physics.info/refrigerators/

Effects of various engineered products on people's lives and living standards—household appliances

With the increasing production of iron during the Industrial Revolution many household appliances such as cooking pots, irons and cast iron stoves became available. However, domestic duties remained largely unchanged from those of the preceding centuries. Those duties were performed almost exclusively by the female members of a household, and occupied a substantial part of their day. For wealthy families however, these duties were performed by servants. Cheap labour meant that many middle-class families could afford to employ servants. Under these conditions, interest in labour-saving devices was low. By the mid 19th century the supply of cheap labour began to decrease as more lower-income families chose to find employment in the burgeoning factories and as staff in the growing number of department stores.

With the decrease in the availability of servants, the desire for household appliances that reduced the need for servants became an economic driving force for innovation. As electrical power became increasingly available, the presence of such labour-saving devices in the household also became an expression of modernity, a view encouraged by electrical power suppliers who actively promoted the purchase of electrical appliances in order to utilise the power being generated since the supply of power for lighting no longer covered generation costs. Large domestic electric appliances such as gas compression cycle refrigerators and electric stoves were particularly targeted for promotion due to their higher electricity requirements.

As the number of household electrical appliances grew, the corresponding increase in demand for electricity resulted in reduced unit costs of electricity to the consumer and an ever-increasing improvement in the electrical power infrastructure. By the end of WWI electricity was widely distributed and a growing number of electrical appliances were available. With the increasing availability of electrical household appliances, significant social changes, particularly with respect to domestic work, were to take place. Indeed, it has been suggested that the introduction of electrical household appliances had a much more profound impact on the household than the electric light, for which supply of electricity had originally been envisioned.

A significant reduction in the physical drudgery that had accompanied many activities followed the introduction of domestic electrical appliances. However, the lack of automatic control on appliances such as the stove and washing machine meant that roughly the same amount of time was often required to perform tasks. Until the introduction of automatic control systems, regulation of these appliances was imposed by switching the power on and off at the appropriate time.

Despite this shortcoming, advertising of the day could highlight the ease with which chores could be performed compared to the older methods. Following WWI a growing unease was also raised about the cleanliness of the home. It should be remembered that Louis Pasteur's germ theory was only proposed in 1861 and that the flu pandemic of 1918 known as the 'Spanish flu' had killed over 20 million people and was fresh in the mind.

Many advertisements of the time, therefore, highlighted the need for diligence in eliminating germs and safeguarding the family. It has been suggested that because of this campaign the frequency and intensity of many household activities, particularly those involved in cleaning, increased. This change in the level of domestic activity was such that despite the increasing availability and sophistication of household appliances, surveys performed in the late 1920s and after WWII found similar time was spent on housework.

Today, many households have both partners working and have limited time for domestic cleaning activities. To overcome this situation, a number of small businesses have emerged offering their services in domestic cleaning. While issues of inequality had remained between domestic workers and the householder, the rise of the small business model has changed this dynamic somewhat. Under such a model domestic services may no longer be a lowly-paid position within the households of the wealthy, but rather a profitable business for the self-employed, as shown in Figure 2.2.27.

Figure 2.2.27 Domestic cleaning services advert, image by James' Home Services

Environmental implications of the engineered product—household appliances

The development of household appliances very closely followed the patterns of development associated with the Industrial Revolution in that there was a shift from devices powered by human energy to machinery developed to be driven by electric motors.

As a consequence of the Industrial Revolution and the shift in energy requirements, greenhouse gas production continued to rise. Many scientists believe this was a direct consequence of the burning of fossil fuels for power generation, land clearing and changing agricultural practices.

Today, cheap, readily available and reliable supplies of electricity continue to meet the needs of many industrialised nations to produce and use engineered products. In Australia alone, coal-fired power stations produce the bulk of the electricity consumed. The International Energy Association (IEA) quotes electricity production by coal in Australia at 78% (2012).

Combustion of coal and oil produces both significant amounts of nitrogen oxides, sulphur dioxide, carbon dioxide and mercury compounds. Nitrogen oxides and sulphur dioxide contribute to the formation of acid rain. This in turn has led to the acidification of soils and waterways as well as the corrosion of buildings and civil structures. Sulphur dioxide is also associated with respiratory disease and the aggravation of existing cardio-vascular problems. While carbon dioxide is a good transmitter of light, its resistance to the free passage of infrared radiation passing from the Earth contributes to global warming and all of its associated issues.

The burning of coal and fuel oil also releases particulate matter into the atmosphere. Mixing with sulphurous impurities and water vapour, this mixture creates a chemical fog, or smog, that covers many industrialised cities. Toxic ash is an after-product of the burning of coal and is most often simply disposed of in landfill.

Natural gas is the cleanest of all the fossil fuels to burn, producing lesser amounts of carbon dioxide and carbon monoxide than oil and coal. Water vapour is a harmless by-product of combustion, but small amounts of sulphur dioxide and oxides of nitrogen and particulate matter are generated.

Notable changes have also occurred in the field of engineered products outside the home. One such case in point is the lawn mower, within the field of engineered landscaping products.

Historical development of various engineered products—lawn mowers

The wide scale manipulation of the landscape for aesthetic purposes, requiring specialised equipment, is a relatively recent concern. One of the leading proponents of such manipulation was the Englishman Lancelot 'Capability' Brown (1715–1783). While grand gardens had been created for centuries, often on geometric designs, Brown worked on a scale previously unheard of to create a 'natural' look. Typical of his style was the creation of large areas of undulating grassland combined with artificial lakes created by the damming of rivers. Perhaps the pinnacle of Brown's work was the landscaping of 2000 acres of parkland for Blenheim Palace.

Lawn mowers

By the end of the 18th century, and largely due to the popularity of landscaped grounds, the upkeep of large country estates was a highly labour intensive practice. On the estates at Blenheim Palace over 200 labourers were employed, 50 of these being used on the pleasure gardens and fine lawns alone. Maintenance of the expanses of lawn was performed by skilled labourers known as scythesmen or 'mowers', who used scythes to crop the grass as they moved in lines over the estate.

The scythe consisted of a curved serrated blade of 65 to 70 cm length attached to one end of a pole to which were attached two handles (Figure 2.2.28). Maintaining the blade the required distance above the ground, a sweeping action was made across the grass, resulting in a relatively uniform lawn. Every ten days in the height of the season, the mowers would start early in the morning when the dew was on the grass. Women and children employed on the estate would collect the clippings later in the day. Larger areas of parkland were often maintained through the grazing of fallow deer and sheep.

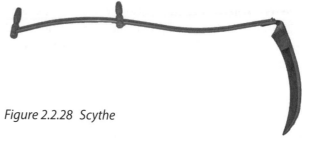

Figure 2.2.28 Scythe

In 1830, Edwin Beard Budding, an engineer from Gloucestershire, England, was granted a patent for a new invention—the cylinder lawn mower. Budding developed the idea after visiting a local cloth mill where a cutting cylinder (or bladed reel) was used to smooth cloth after weaving. Budding applied this concept to the cutting of grass through the mounting of rotating blades held in a wheeled frame. The blades were riveted to arms or 'spiders' attached to the axle. Grass was cut in a scissor-like action as it was trapped between a rotation blade and a stationary blade in the mower base.

Budding made potential customers aware of his new product by placing an advertisement in 'The Gardener's Magazine' (Volume VIII) in 1832. The illustration reproduced in Figure 2.2.29 showed a rather elegant be-hatted gentleman effortlessly pushing his mower. The advertisement assured would-be customers the device did the work of eight men and went on to say 'Gentlemen may find, in using the machine themselves, an amusing, useful and healthy exercise'.

When comparing this new development to currently available scythe technology the author added, 'Grass growing in the shade, and too weak to stand against a scythe to be cut, may be cut by this machine as closely as required; and the eye will not be offended by those circular scars, inequalities, and bare places so commonly made by the best mowers with the scythe, and which continue visible for several days'.

Figure 2.2.29 Budding's advertisement of 1832

'The Gardener's Magazine' also provided a detailed technical description of both the construction and operation of Budding's machine. The following is an image (Figure 2.2.30) and excerpt from the text:

'Budding's Machine for cropping or shearing the vegetable Surface of Lawns, Grass-plots,&c. — The machine being pushed forward, the hollow cylinder or cast-iron roller (a) is put in motion, and also the smaller cylinder or gage roller (b), the purpose of which is, to regulate the height of the rectangular steel plate (c), The operation of shearing is performed by from four to eight spiral cutters (d) which revolve in a horizontal axis.'

When the mower was pushed from behind, cast iron gear wheels transmitted power from the rear roller to the cutting cylinder (the ratio was 16:1). Sharpened knives mounted on the front cutting reel shaved the lawn.

'In the specification of the patent, it was unnecessary to notice that all the grass cut off may be collected in a box; but this we consider a valuable addition, as saving sweeping, and as completing the operation of mowing as it proceeds; so that the operator may leave off at any moment, and at the same time leave what he has done perfectly neat and finished.'

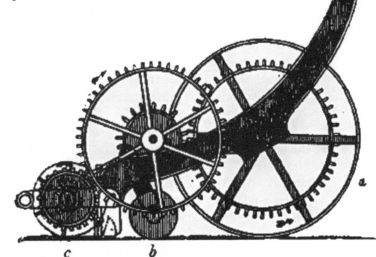

Figure 2.2.30 Elevation of Budding's machine for cropping or shearing the vegetable surface of lawns

At the same time as Budding's invention, Ransome's iron-founders undertook a wide range of general work including building iron bridges in Suffolk and production of chairs, fastenings and other railway equipment. One of Ransome's principal products was ploughshares. Ransome patented the chilling process that enabled shears to sharpen themselves as they worked the soil.

Ransome purchased the patent from Edwin Budding and commenced producing lawn mowers in 1836.

The size of the Budding mower meant that larger estates would still require a significant number of workmen. The solution to the economic mowing of large estates was provided by Alexander Shanks of Arbroath in Scotland who developed a reel mower with a 675 mm wide cut in 1841 and a mower with a 1050 mm wide cut the following year. Mowers of this size, however, could not be pulled or pushed by a workman and required a pony or horse to supply the motive power. These machines provided very large savings in labour costs on large estates and public parks. Operation was reduced to two labourers, one in front to lead the pony or horse and one behind guiding the mower.

In the mid 1850s Green and Son of Leeds & London introduced a mower called the Silens Messor (silent cutter). Using a chain drive connected to the rear roller these machines were lighter and quieter than the early gear-driven Ransome machines.

Around 1867, Alexander Shanks introduced its range of Caledonia mowers and Ransome's introduced the Automaton. Both were available with either gear or chain drive with grass collection boxes an optional extra. The Automaton was a popular model with over 1000 machines being sold in the first season.

The Budding style of machines were largely abandoned by manufacturers by 1864. In 1869, Follows & Bate introduced a major innovation through the world's first side-wheel lawn mower: the 'Climax' (see Figure 2.2.31).

Before the Climax was developed all lawn mowers had been driven using a combination of gears or chains that linked a rear land roller with the cutting cylinder or reel. The Climax cutting cylinder was driven directly by gearing cast onto the inside of two wheels mounted on the outside of the main chassis or side frame. When pushing the mower forwards the outer gearing engaged with smaller gear wheels on the ends of the cutting cylinder, causing it to turn at high speed. The first models even had thin rubber tyres fitted to the outside of the wheels to provide improved traction. The revolutionary design of the side-wheel lawn mower provided many advantages including:

- reduced production costs

- simplified production and operation due to fewer moving parts

- lighter weight through the elimination of the cumbersome rear roller and heavy side frames found on traditional mowers.

FOLLOWS & BATE'S
PATENT LAWN MOWERS,
The "CLIMAX" and the "ANGLO-AMERICAN."

Between 5000 and 6000 of these celebrated Machines were sold last year, and 10,000 are being prepared for the present season.

"In all things, but proverbially so in Mechanics, the supreme excellence is simplicity."—JAMES WATT.

These words are very applicable to the simple Wheel and Pinion driving power of the Climax Lawn Mower.

THE "CLIMAX" PATENT BACK DELIVERY LAWN MOWER

Is now sufficiently well known for its simplicity and easy working to require but a very short description. The two novel features in its construction, and in which it differs from all other machines of the kind, are (firstly) the entire absence of the heavy iron roller behind the knife, and the substitution of the grass collecting box in its place, so that, every impediment being removed from the front, the machine can be worked close up to walls and trees, or underneath shrubs, without removing the collecting box—the grass being cut as it grows, and disposed of with equal rapidity whether wet or dry; (secondly) in the revolving cutter being propelled by a simple wheel and pinion—which gear direct instead of being connected by intermediate wheels or chains—the most uninitiated will at once understand this simple arrangement, and readily admit its non-liability to get out of order. When used without the Box (see Illustration) either size will cut Grass 6 inches long if required. Every Machine is made of the best materials, and no pains are spared in finishing every one, even the cheapest, in the best possible manner.

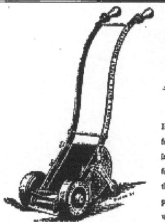
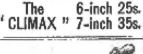

The "CLIMAX" 6-inch 25s. 7-inch 35s.

THE ADVANTAGES OF THE "CLIMAX" LAWN MOWERS
May be thus enumerated:—

They are CHEAP, SIMPLE, WELL MADE, NOT LIABLE TO GET OUT OF ORDER, and can be EASILY worked by LADIES or CHILDREN.

They Cut LONG GRASS as well as SHORT, and WET Grass as well as DRY, and do not CLOG.

As they have no ROLLER in FRONT, the Knives Cut the Grass as it GROWS, and do not miss the BENTS.

They Cut CLOSE up to Walls and Trees, or UNDERNEATH Shrubs, and are invaluable for SLOPES and STEEP EMBANKMENTS.

By their regular use CROQUET GROUNDS can be kept in the PERFECTION of order.

They do not RIB the Grass, but leave the Lawn with a beautifully even and velvety appearance, very different to Scythe Mowing.

Having a BACK-DELIVERY they are EQUALLY adapted for Collecting the Grass in the usual manner, or for scattering the Cuttings on the Ground, thus COMBINING the ENGLISH and AMERICAN Systems in ONE Machine.

The "CLIMAX" 8-inch 45s. 10-inch 55s.

Figure 2.2.31 Climax advertisement from 'The Gardeners' Chronicle and Agricultural Gazette', 28 December 1872

A later modification introduced larger diameter side wheels allowing higher gearing between the side-wheel and cutting cylinder. Mowers of this type were known as 'high wheel' models and were produced by a number of manufacturers. This system delivered more power and speed to the cutting blades thus enabling wider cutting cylinders with blades and the ability to cut longer grass.

Regular maintenance was required to keep the knives sharp and a number of alternatives were developed to maintain blades in good condition. These included:

• reversing the cutting cylinder to maintain even wear

• using a wooden handle inserted in one of the side gears to manually rotate the cutting cylinder in reverse

• placing 'flowers of emery' (grinding material) on the edge of the knives to allow the cylinder to be ground-in

• removing the cutting cylinder and placing it on a machine bed for grinding using specially designed tools.

The first American patent for a reel mower was not issued until 1870 but by 1885 the USA was challenging the British domination of the industry and was exporting mowers around the world.

From 1890 some American manufacturers fitted ball bearing races, giving greater accuracy of cut. Around this time American mowers tended to be a little cheaper and in many cases the castings were of a better quality iron than their English counterparts. This resulted in less metal being used, resulting in lighter machines while retaining strength.

In 1893 the first steam lawn mower (developed by James Sumner of Leyland, Lancashire) was introduced (see Figure 2.2.32). The mower weighed approximately two tons and produced a 40 inch wide cut (100 cm). The boiler was fired by paraffin under pressure and was able to reach working pressure in ten minutes. The water tank, slung under the handle arms, generated additional weight on the rear roller, which helped when turning. The first trials of steam mowing were held at Lords Cricket Ground in London.

These mowers were little more than a horse mower with a steam engine mounted on top and a simple arrangement of gears to transmit power to the rear roller.

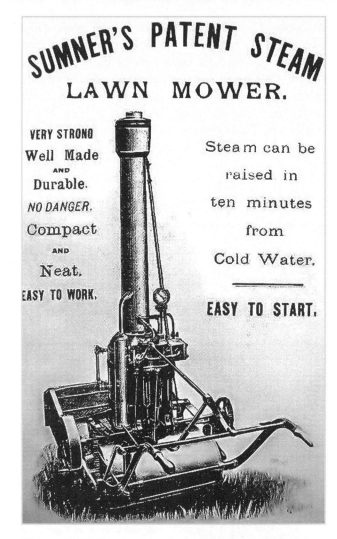

Figure 2.2.32 Sumner's patent steam engine, image from 'Shire' album 'Old Garden Tools' by Kay N Sanecki

In theory the steam mower offered a number of advantages, including:

• it could be operated by one person

• it did not need to be sheltered and fed like a horse or pony

• it was suitable for large areas such as sports grounds.

Steam mowers were generally oil-fired, oil being preferred to coal because it fired the boiler faster. They were used only on larger lawns due to their size and weight. The fact that oil-fired boilers generated pressures around 1.38 MPa represented something of a safety hazard. Unfortunately they were also expensive and difficult to operate.

In 1896, American WJ Stephenson-Peach produced a prototype internal combustion engined lawn mower. However, Ransome's of Ipswich, England were the first company to patent and commercially produce petrol engine powered lawn mowers in 1902.

Up until WWI the bulk of lawn mower sales remained with the hand-pushed and animal-powered machines. Motor mowers were generally classed as a luxury, with prices outside the range of most people. Many were still in use up until the 1940s.

It is still possible to see mowers of this type (pulled by oxen) operating in places such as India. The highly mechanical nature of these early mowers also meant that the operator had to be trained. Most of the early operators doubled as chauffeurs, adding to the cost.

In 1914 Europe was at war. Lawn mower development, production and consumption slowed and by 1915 most mower companies were involved with production of munitions for the war effort. At this time in America, Worthington patented a new mower consisting of three side-wheel mowers connected via a frame and pulled by a horse. These 'gang' mower units could be combined to produce an increased cutting width.

Cast aluminium sides allowed a significant reduction in weight. Cast iron frames continued to be used however, although this material also changed. Flake grey iron castings that could be brittle were replaced by malleable iron which exhibited improved mechanical properties, particularly with respect to ductility.

Mass production techniques also began to impact on mower manufacture at this time, with the use of standardised parts allowing interchangeability between company models.

In the early 1920s, the Dennis motor mower (Figure 2.2.33) was introduced and met the demand for a high-quality machine to mow sports grounds and ovals. Even though the original machine (based on aluminium castings) was dropped from production within the year, it reappeared in 1923 with a frame made from sheet steel. It was built for heavy-duty work and soon gained a market with councils and government departments. The Dennis incorporated separate drives for the roller and cutting cylinder and two large levers on the handle bars used to engage either or both drives. This feature allowed the mower to be driven without cutting the grass, thus converting it into a makeshift roller.

By the end of the 1920s most companies had switched to using steel for mower construction due to its greater availability and improved strength characteristics.

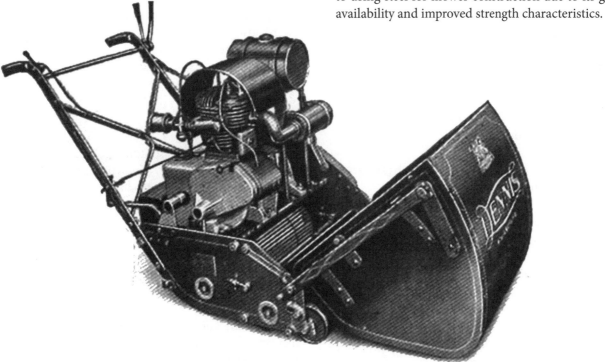

After the war a raft of new companies showed an interest in lawn mower development and production. At this time push mowers began to appear using the latest available material, aluminium.

Figure 2.2.33 Dennis mower

The rotary mower, developed in 1933 by Power Specialities of Slough, Berkshire, was a radical change in concept from Budding's original patent. The theory was developed around a turning grass-cutting disc driven by a motor. The turning disc was covered by a deck or hood that allowed a vacuum to form when the disc was driven at speed. This vacuum lifted clippings away from the ground and sent them to a catcher attached behind. The two-stroke engine employed was an advantage as it maintained lubrication at different angles. The smaller 25 cm and 32 cm models were electrically-powered while 37 cm and 45 cm models were powered by a petrol engine.

Effects of engineered products on people's lives and living standards—lawn mowers

By the end of the 18th century the lawn had become a popular part of any garden for wealthy land owners around the world.

The introduction of mechanical cutting of grass with a lawn mower simultaneously resulted in a reduction of skilled labour while improving the consistency of the finished lawn. In turn, the introduction of mowers with larger cutting widths further reduced the time and labour required to mow large estates and public parkland.

With advances in sport in the 1880s a new demand for lawn began to grow, such that more companies were becoming involved in the manufacture of grass-cutting machinery.

By the 1930s a new market opened for the lawn mower with the middle classes becoming first-time buyers of homes with small garden lawns.

Environmental implications of the engineered product—lawn mowers

Two-stroke engines are the predominant power source for small motors used in landscaping machinery (brushcutters, lawn mowers, chainsaws, etc). Two-stroke engines by design are:

* inexpensive

* manoeuvrable

* extremely reliable

* lightweight yet powerful.

Unfortunately, two-stroke engines are also inherently dirty with regard to exhaust due to incomplete combustion of fuel. Despite this they continue to outsell four-stroke engines which are:

* costly

* complex in operation

* consuming in time to repair.

In an internal combustion engine, fuel is ignited in a cylindrical chamber. The explosion pushes down a piston, which turns a shaft thus providing power to drive a variety of machines. In two-stroke engines the incoming fuel charge is used to expel exhaust gases from the previous combustion. Through this process about 30% of the new fuel mix escapes unburned, releasing polluting hydrocarbons and oxides of nitrogen (NOx), two primary precursors of ozone, into the atmosphere.

Over time two-stroke engines have been modified to reduce emissions, ensuring engines run with a lower proportion of fuel in the fuel-air mix.

In an effort to reduce fuel emissions further, engineers have developed a variety of alternatives outlined below.

* Stratified charge designs inject pure air between the exhaust gases and the fresh charge of incoming fuel. This engine emits air (instead of ejecting a third of the fuel) through the exhaust. This technique improves fuel consumption by 34% and allows the engine to run quieter.

* Models employing a catalytic converter (used in conjunction with a stratified charge design) emit cleaner exhaust gases. Catalytic converters reduce emissions to water and carbon dioxide. Unfortunately they are expensive, add weight to the product, and produce high-temperature exhaust exceeding 540 °C.

* Better control of the air-fuel transfer from the crankcase to the combustion chamber also reduces the loss of unburned fuel.

Engineers are constantly looking for improvements in fuel efficiency, performance and emission reduction. Work is currently being conducted on reducing emission of vapours from the fuel tanks of small petrol-powered motors.

2.3 Engineering mechanics

Forces

Nature and type of forces

A number of forces treated as a group are known as a force system. Force systems fall into the four general types of:

- parallel

- co-linear

- concurrent

- co-planar.

Parallel force systems are composed of forces with parallel lines of action: they do not have a common line of action. They also potentially have a different direction or sense (see Figure 2.3.1).

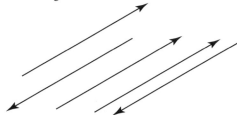

Figure 2.3.1 Parallel forces

Co-linear force systems contain forces with a common line of action but again may have a different sense (see Figure 2.3.2).

Figure 2.3.2 Co-linear forces

Concurrent force systems incorporate forces whose lines of action all intersect at a common point but may lie on different planes (see Figure 2.3.3).

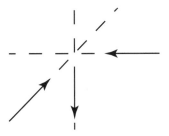

Figure 2.3.3 Concurrent forces

Co-planar force systems (Figure 2.3.4) constitute forces all contained within the same plane.

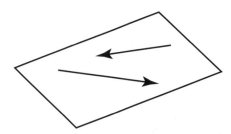

Figure 2.3.4 Co-planar forces

Addition of vectors

When a quantity has a magnitude, direction and sense it is considered to be vector quantity or simply a vector. Direction is often specified in terms of angle relative to the horizontal (or x-axis). Force is considered to be a vector quantity, since an adequate description of a force requires information about its magnitude, direction of action and sense.

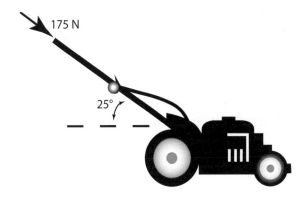

Figure 2.3.5 Vector forces

The vector in Figure 2.3.5 displays the following features:

- magnitude 175 N

- direction 25° to the horizontal

- sense downwards to the right.

Resultants and equilibrants

Vectors may be added together mathematically or graphically such that the result of their combined influence can be determined. The vector that describes the result of such an addition of vectors is known as the resultant. Similarly, an equilibrant is identical to the resultant in magnitude and direction but is opposite in sense. Equilibrants are balancing forces used to maintain equilibrium within a system.

Resultants may be used when we wish to replace multiple forces with a single force and equilibrants may then be used to replace multiple forces with a single balancing force. Figure 2.3.6 shows an example where two forces may be replaced with a single force.

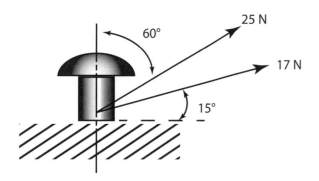

Figure 2.3.6 Multiple forces

Space and free body diagrams

A free body diagram assists engineeeers to represent vectors and the bodies they act upon in a more visual fashion. These diagrams are not drawn to scale but may assist with calculations.

Drawn graphically as a vector or force diagram, the resultant force may be read directly from the vector diagram both in terms of direction and magnitude.

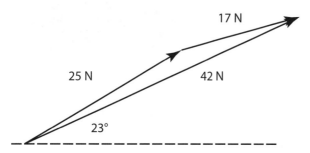

Figure 2.3.7 Force polygon

The resultant read from the force polygon in Figure 2.3.7 shows the force to be 42 N inclined at an angle of 23° to the horizontal.

The sense is decided by whether the solution requires a resultant as above (the combination of two forces) or an equilibrant (the balancing of forces). In the case of the equilibrant the sense would be in the opposite direction.

The same approach may be used to break down a force into its constituent vertical and horizontal components (Figure 2.3.8).

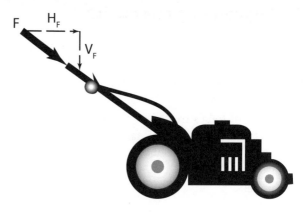

Figure 2.3.8 Multiple forces

Equilibrium of concurrent forces

Vectors may be added together either mathematically or graphically. In the case shown in Figure 2.3.9, a 47 kg mower is being hoisted by two cables. The system may be represented on a space diagram on which all the forces are shown in their relative positions. The space diagram would appear as shown in Figure 2.3.10.

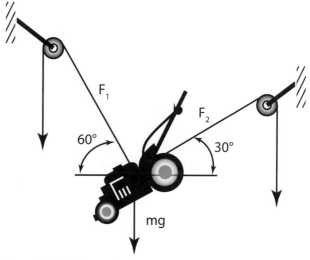

Figure 2.3.9 Mower hoist

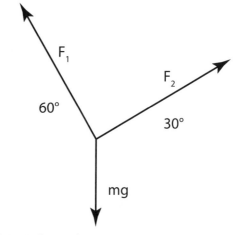

Figure 2.3.10 Space diagram

By rearranging the space diagram into a force diagram or force polygon the system will close if it is in equilibrium (Figure 2.3.11). Through the creation of a scale and drawing the known vertical force 470 N, the unknown forces F1 and F2 may now be read directly from the newly created force polygon. It is important to understand the results produced using this technique will be approximate only. Minor variations will occur in translating the scale when measuring from the diagram.

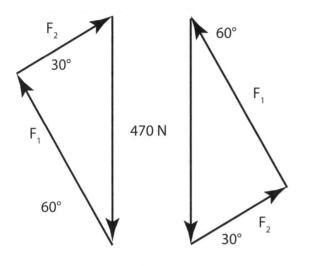

Figure 2.3.11 Force diagram

Using an appropriate scale and measuring from the diagram produces the following results:

$F_2 = 230$ N $F_1 = 400$ N

Notice also the polygon may be formed in a variety of ways to obtain the same result.

The polygon formed in Figure 2.3.11 is a right-angled triangle and therefore the unknown forces may be precisely calculated using trigonometry. When using graphical methods to solve problems, results will be approximate only due to errors in construction and measurement.

The solution to the problem is as follows:

$F_2 \div 470 = \sin 30°$ $F_1 \div 470 = \sin 60°$

$F_2 = 470 \sin 30°$ $F_1 = 470 \sin 60°$

$F_2 = 235$ N $F_1 = 407.03$ N

Principle of transmissibility of forces

The external effect of a force on a rigid body is the same for all points of application of the force along its line of action. In simple terms the effect of a force on a rigid body is the same whether the force is a push or a pull along the same line of action (see Figure 2.3.12).

Figure 2.3.12 Transmissibility of force

Three force rule for equilibrium

When three forces act on a body and the body is in a state of equilibrium, then the three forces must be concurrent (i.e. they will all intersect at a common point).

If more than three forces are involved, the only way to use the three force rule and establish a point of concurrency is to combine sufficient forces together by vector addition until only three remain.

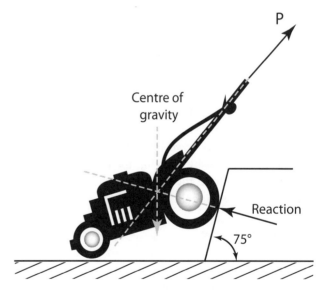

Figure 2.3.13 Force equilibrium

In Figure 2.3.13 a number of concurrent forces are shown to be acting on the mower as it is pulled up the step. The line of the reactive force at the wall is determined by the location of the intersection of the two known vectors (P and mg).

The space diagram for a 35 kg mower as shown in Figure 2.3.14 would appear as:

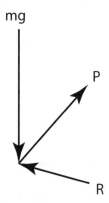

Figure 2.3.14 Space diagram

Rearranged and drawn to scale to produce a closed force polygon or force diagram the force system now appears as show in Figure 2.3.15. By drawing the forces at their correct angles and applying a scale to the known force (350 N), a force triangle may be created that closes and is therefore in equilibrium.

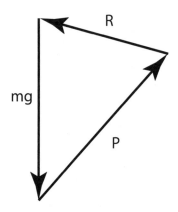

Figure 2.3.15 Force triangle

The magnitude of the two remaining unknown forces may be determined by applying the original scale. By applying this method the reaction at the wall is 260 N and the force P pulling the mower up the step is 375 N.

Moments of a force

If a force is applied to a body fixed in space, this force tends to create a rotating effect on the body. An example of moments created by a force includes the use of a spanner to loosen or tighten a nut. Moments are determined using the formula:

Moment = force × perpendicular distance

The perpendicular distance is calculated from the turning point or fulcrum at 90° to the force causing moment. Moments are vector quantities and are measured in newton metres (Nm).

Note: a force applied to or through the fulcrum will have no turning effect on the body.

When attempting to create equilibrium in a system the mathematical formula stating the sum of the clockwise moments equals the sum of the anticlockwise moments or:

$$\Sigma M^{\circlearrowleft} = \Sigma M^{\circlearrowright}$$

This formula is simply the third law of equilibrium put into practice.

The example shown in Figure 2.3.16 demonstrates how the balancing of turning moments may be used to calculate tension in a cable.

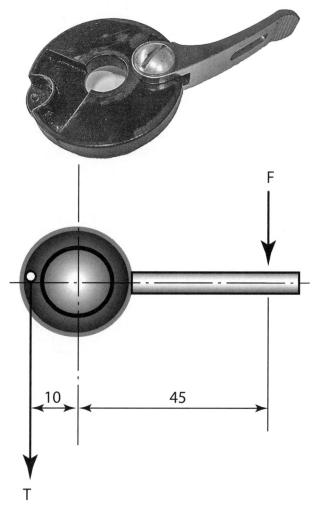

Figure 2.3.16 Lawn mower throttle moment

If a force of 7 N is applied to the throttle arm similar to the one shown in Figure 2.3.16 then a moment is created about the fulcrum and the following equation can be used to balance the system:

$$\Sigma\, M^{\circlearrowleft} = \Sigma\, M^{\circlearrowright}$$

$$F \times d_1 = T \times d_2$$

$$7 \times 45 = T \times 10$$

$$T = 315 \div 10$$

$$T = 31.5\ \text{N}$$

Therefore, for the system to be in equilibrium the tension in the cable must be 31.5 N. The tension in the cable provides the balancing force to the initial load placed on the lever, making it the equilibrant for this system.

Force-couple systems

A system of forces that exerts a resultant moment, but no resultant force, is called a force-couple. The simplest example of a force-couple consists of two equal and opposite forces acting some distance apart.

The effect of a force-couple may be characterised by a single vector moment M.

To calculate the moment of a couple, the distance between the forces (moment arm) is generally used and produces the formula:

Moment of couple, M = F × arm of the couple

The application of this formula is shown in Figure 2.3.17.

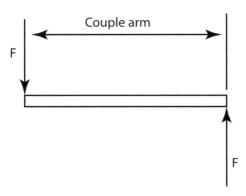

Figure 2.3.17 Moment of couple

Note that a force-couple:

- has a zero resultant force

- can only be balanced by another couple

- maintains the same resultant moment about all points.

Examples of couples include turning on/off a tap, winding a clock and the forces exerted by the tip of a screwdriver on the head of a screw. The SI units for a moment or a couple are newton metres (Nm).

In engineering, the moment of a force or couple is known as torque. A spanner tightening a nut is said to exert a torque on the nut and similarly a belt turning a pulley exerts a torque on the pulley.

Figure 2.3.18 shows a clockwise couple of 0.9 Nm is required to turn the tap on. Determine the value of the force required at A and B to effect this couple.

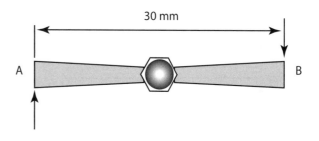

Figure 2.3.18 Tap couple

$$M = F \times d$$

$$0.9 = F \times 0.03$$

$$F = 0.9 \div 0.03$$

$$F = 30\ \text{N}$$

Replacing forces with a force-couple

The effect of the force F on the bracket assembly (Figure 2.3.19) creates not only a vertical downwards force but also a rotational force-couple balanced by another rotational force-couple produced by the wall anchor bolts.

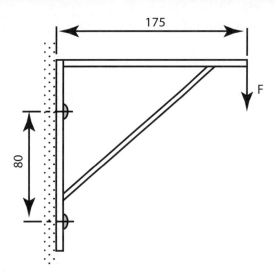

Figure 2.3.19 Bracket

To consider the effect a single force has on this system, two balancing forces of equal magnitude and opposite sense are placed at the other extreme of the element in question. This system may then be represented as a force-couple and force system (Figure 2.3.20).

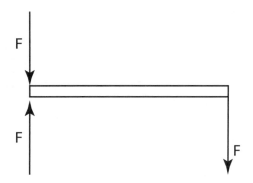

Figure 2.3.20 Force-couple

The resolution of these forces then translates into a force and couple system (Figure 2.3.21).

Figure 2.3.21 Force and force-couple system

Worked example 1

Calculate the force exerted on each anchor bolt by 140 N force pressing down on the end of the bracket as shown in Figure 2.3.22.

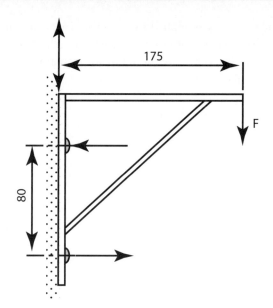

Figure 2.3.22 Bracket problem

The force-couple (FC) induced by the load must be balanced by an equivalent couple at the wall such that:

$$FC \circlearrowleft = FC \circlearrowright$$

$$140 \times 175 = 80 \times F_{bolt}$$

$$F_{bolt} = 140 \times 175 \div 80$$

$$= 306.25 \text{ N}$$

Note that due to the nature of the force-couple, the top force on the bolt would be trying to pull the bolt from the wall while the lower of the two forces would be forcing the bracket against the wall.

Equilibrium of concurrent co-planar forces

Worked example 2

Determine graphically the resultant force acting on the object shown in Figure 2.3.23.

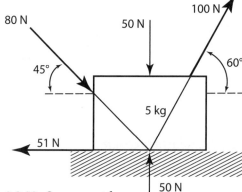

Figure 2.3.23 Concurrent forces

Solution

To solve the problem the forces are organised, as arrows, in a tip-to-tail arrangement as shown in Figure 2.3.24. The order in which the arrows are arranged within the diagram is not particularly important but clarity may favour one arrangement over others.

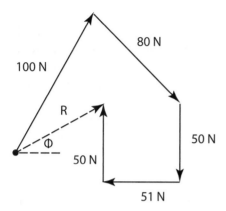

Figure 2.3.24 Force polygon

The magnitude and angle of the resultant force can now be measured directly from the diagram using a rule and protractor, if the diagram has been constructed to scale.

A force of 63 N acting at an angle of 28° is indicated.

Because of inaccuracies in drawing and measurement, the answer obtained by the graphical method described will not be exact, but rather a good approximation. A more accurate although time consuming method of determining the resultant vector would be to solve analytically by resolving each vector into its x and y components.

$$+\uparrow \Sigma y = 100 \sin60 - 80 \sin45 + 50 - 50$$

$$= 100 \times 0.866 - 80 \times 0.707$$

$$= 86.6 - 56.57$$

$$= 30.03 \text{ N} \uparrow$$

$$+\rightarrow \Sigma x = 100 \cos60 - 51 + 80 \cos45$$

$$= 100 \times 0.5 - 51 + 80 \times 0.707$$

$$= 50 - 51 + 56.56$$

$$= 55.56 \text{ N} \rightarrow$$

Therefore the resultant could be represented as:

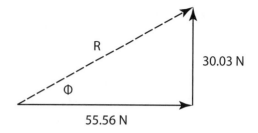

Figure 2.3.25 Analytical solution

$$\tan\phi = 30.03 \div 55.56$$

$$= 0.54$$

$$\phi = \tan^{-1} 0.54$$

$$= 28.37°$$

By Pythagoras:

$$R = \sqrt{(30.03)^2 + (55.56)^2}$$

$$= \sqrt{3988.7}$$

$$= 63.16 \text{ N}$$

2.4 Engineering materials

Modification of materials

Work hardening

Once the elastic limit has been passed and plastic deformation takes place, Hooke's law no longer applies and stress is no longer directly proportional to strain.

Work hardening is a result of plastic or permanent deformation of the crystal structure. Under micro-examination separate grains can be seen to be elongated and distorted in the direction the metal has been deformed.

Figure 2.4.1 Slip planes

The process of deformation, on an atomic scale, involves the movement of planes of atoms moving relative to each other in a process known as slip. As slip progresses, defects within the crystal lattice known as dislocations (representing regions in which the regular lattice order has been locally disrupted) increase. An increase in the number of dislocations will begin to interfere with the ease with which slip can take place and the material is said to be undergoing work hardening.

During work hardening or strain hardening an increase in stress is required to continue deformation. This effect is considered to be the result of increasing resistance to slip within the grains of a polycrystalline material.

The movement of crystallographic planes is believed to be assisted by the movement of the aforementioned dislocations. A number of different types of dislocations have been identified that help explain the different forms of plastic deformation encountered.

In Figure 2.4.2 an illustration of a dislocation is presented. As can be seen the lattice is distorted and a stress field is associated with the dislocation. These dislocations can move through the metal lattice and will do so freely until they meet an obstacle. As dislocations pile up at grain boundaries, a back-pressure is created that restricts the motion of dislocations in the lattice, making further deformation more difficult.

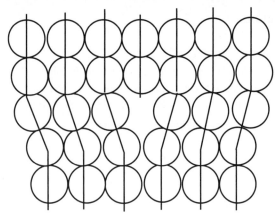

Figure 2.4.2 Dislocation in lattice arrangement

A higher stress is therefore required to continue plastic deformation, which we identify as work hardening. The movement of a dislocation through lattice is represented in Figure 2.4.3.

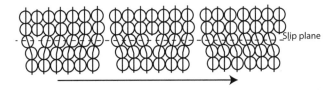

Figure 2.4.3 Dislocation movement through metal lattice

Through work hardening an increase in hardness and strength can be achieved although ductility is reduced. Past a certain point, the energy required to continue deformation may be prohibitive or the likelihood of tearing becomes significant. If further shaping is required then the metal must undergo a heat treatment to recover sufficient ductility to reduce the degree of work hardening and regain ductility.

The surface of a polished and etched sample of austenitic stainless steel is shown in Figure 2.4.4 in which lines of slip can be seen within different grains.

Figure 2.4.4 SEM surface image of plastically deformed austenitic stainless steel revealing slip lines

Heat treatment

The process of controlling the manner in which materials are heated and cooled to produce a variety of mechanical properties is known as heat treatment.

Heat treatment of metals is routinely undertaken to modify mechanical properties. The intention of the heat treatments performed varies considerably depending on the mechanical properties required and several different heat treatments may be undertaken before the final properties are achieved. Typical heat treatments include:

- stress relief

- normalising

- full annealing

- process annealing

- quench and temper.

Steel is an excellent example of the application of heat treatment to modify mechanical properties. Steel is principally an alloy of iron and less than 2 wt% carbon, and depending upon the carbon content and the level of secondary alloying elements, the response to heat treatment can vary significantly.

When heated above a critical temperature (~723 °C) the structure changes from body centred cubic (BCC) to face centred cubic (FCC). At this time a greater level of carbon can be contained in the crystal structure. It is said that more carbon is contained in solid solution. On cooling below 723 °C, the structure will change back to BCC and excess carbon will be ejected from solution, forming iron carbide. As a result, the microstructure at room temperature will typically consist of iron carbide (Fe_3C), also known as cementite, and almost pure iron known as ferrite.

Heat treatments such as annealing and normalising typically produce softer materials.

Stress relieving

Stress relieving is applied to both ferrous and non-ferrous alloys in order to remove internal stresses most often generated by prior manufacturing processes such as cold rolling. Without stress relieving further processing may lead to distortion, cracking or component failure. This operation causes little structural change to the material because it is performed at relatively low temperatures. Stress relieving may be used to remove the internal stresses of work hardening without softening the material.

Annealing

Annealing is a softening process that is commonly used after casting, forging and rolling operations to reduce internal stresses, increase ductility and allow for further processing. Both ferrous and non-ferrous alloys may be annealed. After heating to the appropriate temperature the material is furnace cooled.

Normalising

The purpose of normalising is to counter the effects of prior manufacturing processes, (e.g. rolling, casting, forging etc.), by refining the existing grain structure to improve machining and forming characteristics. It may be applied to steels to soften, harden or stress relieve. The normalising process consists of heating suitable steels, typically in the temperature range 830–950 °C, and subsequently cooling in still air.

Quench hardening

If cooling is sufficiently rapid that excess carbon cannot be ejected from the iron crystal lattice as it transforms to BCC, a distorted BCC structure is created, known as a body centred tetragonal lattice, and a microstructure known as martensite is produced.

Steels to be hardened are heated to an appropriate temperature, typically 800–900 °C, held at that temperature and then rapidly quenched in oil or water.

Martensite is not in a state of equilibrium and receives its very high strength and hardness (and lower ductility) from its distorted, stressed lattice structure.

Tempering

Tempering is a heat treatment operation applied to ferrous products after hardening. A low temperature tempering heat treatment is routinely performed following quenching to regain some ductility, reduce quenching stresses and increase toughness at the expense of a small reduction in hardness.

Steel produced in this way is described as being quenched and tempered and the resulting structure is known as 'tempered martensite'. This material is often specified with a tempering range.

As may be appreciated, responsiveness to the quenching and tempering heat treatment process depends on the initial carbon content of the steel.

Case hardening

Modification of the surface chemistry of steel to increase the carbon content is often undertaken to improve wear resistance on items such as gears and shafts. Using a process known as carburisation, the item is heated to an elevated temperature while in the presence of a high carbon atmosphere. Carbon diffuses into the steel surface resulting in a high carbon steel shell surrounding the original low carbon steel core. The depth of carburisation is determined by the time and temperature of the treatment.

On quenching and tempering, a high carbon martensitic surface is formed providing high hardness and wear resistance, while maintaining a low carbon core with greater ductility. In essence a composite material has been produced.

The sectioned and polished gear, typical of a range of engineered products and shown in Figure 2.4.5, has undergone a carburising treatment. This figure shows the hardened perimeter of the gear. The hardened 'skin' traces the pattern of the teeth and indicates the presence of additional carbon absorbed into the structure.

Figure 2.4.6 Macro examination of carburised gear tooth

Under a microscope the carburised 'skin' displays a martensitic structure. The structure is described as needle-like and is know technically as acicular (see Figure 2.4.6).

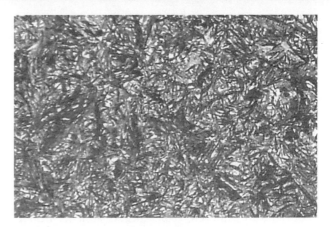

Figure 2.4.6 Martensitic structure

Induction and flame hardening

Induction and flame hardening techniques rely on the existing carbon content of the steel to achieve the hardness levels required. Both the surface and the depth of heat treatment is controllable.

Induction hardening involves placing the component to be hardened within a shaped coil that has a high-frequency alternating current passed through it. Rapid heating of the component surface situated within the electromagnetic field occurs.

Flame hardening involves the direct application of an oxy–gas flame onto the surface to be hardened. Quenching operations follow heating for both induction and flame hardening techniques.

Alloying materials

Alloys are metals produced by mixing two or more metals. They are developed in order to gain improved properties not available from the pure metal. While metal alloys occur in nature, the industrial manufacture of an alloy allows the precise control of the alloy composition with consequential confidence in the material properties. Alloys may be ferrous or non-ferrous. The most common examples are listed below.

Ferrous alloys

Stainless steel	iron, chromium, nickel
Steel	iron, carbon (plus other elements)
Cast iron	iron, carbon, manganese, silicon

Non-ferrous alloys

Brass	copper, zinc
Bronze	copper, tin

The alloying of a metal typically occurs in one of two ways depending on the size of atomic radius of the alloying element(s) relative to that of the base metal.

In those instances where the atomic radius of the alloying (solute) element differs by no more than 15% from that of the base (solvent) metal a substitution of one for the other can occur within the metal lattice. Such an alloy addition forms what is known as a substitutional solid solution. As the size difference between the substitutional atom and the lattice increases, an increasing strain is created in the lattice.

This lattice strain acts as an impediment to dislocation movement, leading to an increase in strength, although above a difference of 15% substitutional solubility is limited. Therefore the larger the mismatch in atomic radii, the greater is the strengthening effect of the alloy addition.

The arrangement of substitutional elements within the lattice can vary from disordered, meaning that there is no particular position or pattern within the lattice in which they may be found, to a clustered arrangement in which local groupings arise, to a highly ordered structure as illustrated in Figure 2.4.7.

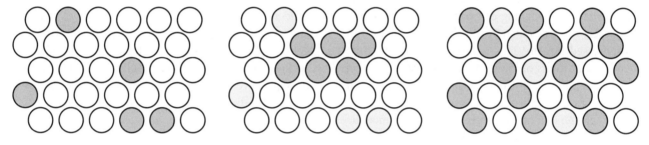

Figure 2.4.7 Illustration of a metal lattice containing substitutional alloying elements (grey)

An interstitial alloying element by contrast finds a position in the metal lattice in the spaces or interstices between the lattice positions of the base metal (see Figure 2.4.8). Such an alloy addition is possible if the difference in atomic radii is greater than approximately 60%, although other factors also affect the ability and extent to which interstitial additions will occur. Such an alloy addition forms what is known as an interstitial solid solution. As the size of the element taking up an interstitial site increases relative to the size of the vacancy within the lattice, an increase in lattice strain occurs. Hydrogen, when present, would be an interstitial addition in most alloy systems. Hydrogen, nitrogen, oxygen, carbon and boron are present as interstitial additions in iron, with most of the other elements being present as substitutional alloy additions.

Note: Lead (Pb) does not have any solubility (interstitial or substitutional) in the iron lattice due to the exceptional difference in their atomic radii.

By introducing strain into the lattice, both substitutional and interstitial alloying hinders the movement of dislocations and as a result increases the yield and tensile strength of the metal (see Figure 2.4.9). This phenomenon is known as solution hardening.

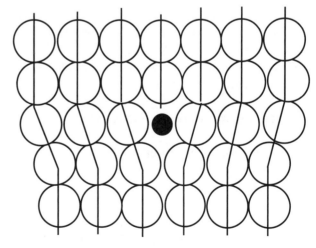

Figure 2.4.9 Illustration of a metal lattice with a dislocation, hindered in movement by the presence of substitutional and interstitial alloying elements

Figure 2.4.8 Illustration of a metal lattice containing interstitial alloying elements (dark)

Increasing the percentage of the alloying element leads to an increase in strength by increasing the number of regions of lattice strain, up to the point at which the solid solubility of the alloy is exceeded. At this point the excess atoms often form in groups or clusters at the grain boundaries by diffusion leading, under conditions of slow cooling, to the formation (precipitation) of a second phase consisting of a fine intermetallic compound.

Substitutional and interstitial solutes can also interact, leading to the formation of this second phase precipitation. The result is that some of the solute atoms are removed from the lattice and a decrease in solid solution hardening occurs, though a process known as precipitation hardening can occur. If rapid cooling takes place, the precipitation of this second phase can be suppressed but the alloy is unstable and with time or under conditions of low temperature heat treatment (called an aging heat treatment) the second phase will precipitate as a fine dispersion throughout the matrix. If these clusters of atoms forming the intermetallic compounds remain coherent with the lattice, i.e. they maintain the same crystallographic orientation, they also act to impede dislocation movement and strengthening by precipitation hardening is said to occur.

The alloy duralumin (Al-4wt% Cu) represents a common precipitation-hardening alloy. The time and temperature of the aging treatment needs to be closely controlled however, since if these precipitates grow too large they lose cohesion with the lattice, leading to a reduction in lattice strain and consequential loss of strength. At this point the alloy is said to have been over-aged.

Dispersion strengthening is similar to precipitation hardening in that a second phase is dispersed throughout the matrix, which restrains dislocation movement (slip). In dispersion hardening, however, the second phase dispersion is usually an oxide and powder metallurgy processes often produce the alloy.

Engineering applications of materials

Ferrous material applications

Stainless steel

Ferrous alloys with elevated contents of such elements as nickel and chromium create the group of metals commonly known as stainless steels. Stainless steel gets its name from its apparent resistance to discoloration by corrosion. In engineered products its application is most beneficial where corrosion resistance is required in

mosisture-laden or hot environments or where hygiene is important. Examples include kitchen appliances, iron sole plates, refrigerators, stoves etc. The sole plate of most irons today is usually die cast aluminium alloy although stainless steel or ceramic sole plates are available.

Steel

Among the most commonly referred to classes of steel is a group of plain carbon steels known as 'mild steel', which typically have a carbon content of 0.15wt% to 0.30wt% carbon. The category of plain carbon refers to the fact that there are no other special alloy additions.

Mild steels are typically used in the as-rolled condition and exhibit a tensile strength of up to 500 MPa with good weldability, suiting them to structural applications such as beams, channels and angles. Despite the growth in popularity of aluminium, polymers and composites, steel is still the most specified material for car bodies.

Steels are also found in ball bearing races where support of rotating shafts and the reduction of friction are paramount (see Figure 2.4.10). Many household appliances and motor systems employ ball bearing races to improve overall energy efficiency.

The ball bearing is a variation of the roller bearing. It is easier and therefore cheaper to produce balls of high accuracy than rollers of high accuracy. Ball bearings reduce friction during rotation and locate and support shafts against both axial and lateral loads. They may also continue to operate under slightly misaligned loads.

Figure 2.4.10 Steel ball bearing race

Cast iron

The strength and hardness of cast iron is provided by the metallic matrix in which the graphite is distributed. The properties of the metallic matrix vary with the carbon content and may exhibit the following.

- A matrix consisting entirely of ferrite, maximising machinability but having reduced wear resistance and strength.

- An entirely pearlitic matrix (typical of high strength grey irons).

- A matrix of both ferrite and pearlite will provide intermediate hardness and strength.

- Alloy additions and/or heat treatment can be used to produce grey iron with very fine pearlite or with an acicular matrix structure.

The majority of the carbon in grey cast iron is present as graphite, which has little strength or hardness. However, the presence of the graphite in cast irons provides several valuable characteristics, including:

- self-lubricating

- high vibration damping

- good thermal conductivity

- the ability to produce sound castings economically in complex shapes

- good machinability even at wear resisting hardness levels and without burring

- dimensional stability under differential heating.

Cylinders and liners are generally made from grey cast iron because it is easily cast and has self-lubricating properties due to the graphite flakes.

Non-ferrous material applications

Aluminium and its alloys

Aluminium is obtained by the electrolysis of bauxite and is therefore an intensive user of electricity. Recycling programs for scrap aluminium, however, significantly reduce the energy requirements of reprocessing.

Pure aluminium has a low density at 2.7×10^3 kg/m^3 making is useful for weight reduction applications where strength is not important. When strength is required, alloying with elements such as Si, Mg, Cu and Zn can significantly improve mechanical properties. The good strength–to–weight ratio has resulted in the extensive use of aluminium alloys in the aerospace industry.

Aluminium is non-magnetic and exhibits high thermal and electrical conductivity while its high reactivity results in the formation of a tight adherent oxide surface film leading to excellent corrosion resistance. The properties of aluminium and its alloys has led to their widespread use in engineering applications.

Properties exhibited by aluminium include:

- non-toxicity

- high recyclability

- good corrosion resistance

- low density (reduced weight)

- good strength-to-weight ratio

- ability to be wrought and cast

- good thermal and electrical conductivity.

Today, aluminium castings are often used as an alternative to iron castings to save weight. The higher thermal conductivity of aluminium compared to cast iron is also advantageous when heat dissipation is required.

Cylinder heads are a typical example of such substitution and are commonly produced by low-pressure die-casting. The aluminium alloy AA413.0 (12%Si, 1.3%Fe, balance Al) is used extensively in the production of die-cast outboard motor and mower parts such as pistons, connecting rods and housings. The silicon in the melt assists with fluidity when casting, enabling thin sections to be successfully cast.

Copper and its alloys

Pure copper has high thermal conductivity combined with good corrosion resistance and ductility. These are properties important in its extensive early use in household equipment such as cooking pots and irons. Today, the high electrical conductivity of copper has led to its major use in electrical wiring. Pure copper has a density of $8.93 \times 10^3 \, kg/m^3$.

The major alloying materials for copper are Zn, Sn, Al, Pb, Ni and Fe.

Brass is an alloy of copper and up to 43% zinc. Brasses with a zinc content of up to 35% consist of a single phase alpha (α) structure. Alloying brass with zinc results in an increase in strength and ductility and a decrease in electrical conductivity. Cartridge brass (70%Cu/30%Zn) is a common alloy within this group. The addition of zinc over approximately 35% results in the introduction of a second phase known as beta (β), leading to a duplex alpha-beta (α + β) structure and a further increase in strength although ductility decreases. A commonly used example of this group is 60/40 brass. Brass is used in a wide range of applications where the following features may be useful: decorative appearance, low coefficient of friction, corrosion resistance and conductivity (both thermal and electrical). It is often used where it is important that sparks not be struck, as in gas fittings and fixtures.

Bronze is a term generally applied to an alloy of copper and up to 10% tin. More specifically these alloys are referred to as tin bronze, as alloys of copper and up to 10% aluminium are known as aluminium bronzes and alloys of copper and up to 5% silicon are known as silicon bronzes. Bronze finds extensive use as a casting material for bearings, pumps and valves due to its excellent castability, strength and corrosion resistance.

Aluminum bronzes such as the one shown in Figure 2.4.11 have exceptional corrosion resistance, high strength, toughness and wear resistance. They also exhibit good castability and welding characteristics.

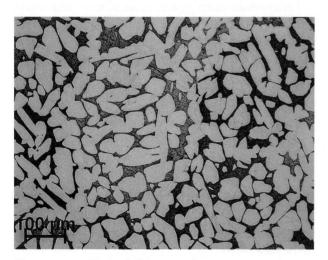

Figure 2.4.11 Typical aluminium bronze structure

Recyclability of materials

Implications for recycling

Design engineering

Research shows the overwhelming percentage (80% to 90%) of committed costs (including manufacturing, distribution and servicing) is locked-in at the design stage. Clearly the role of the design engineer is of paramount importance when considering the financial aspect of every stage of product development.

Constantly in search of a competitive edge, engineers play a crucial part when designing products that are differentiated from others in the market. Many of today's consumers require knowledge that engineered products limit damage to the environment either during the manufacturing, use or disposal phases of their lives.

In terms of recycling, the greatest opportunities for increased materials recovery rates involve plastics, rubber, glass and electronic components. Plastics have traditionally been the largest proportion of non-recycled materials in vehicles. The amount of waste per vehicle continues to decline as manufacturers reuse a variety of production wastes and recycle material from scrapped vehicles, therefore using less landfill disposal and requiring smaller amounts of virgin materials.

As an example, refrigerators provide opportunities for reuse, repair and recycling. In 2009, the 14 model Electrolux Refrigeration Collection won the award for Excellence in Sustainable Design in the Australian International Design Awards. All of the models were designed to be highly energy efficient and consume only 51% of the energy used by comparable models ten years ago, through the use of low wattage defrost systems and high efficiency compressors. Iso butane, a non-synthetic refrigerant with a shorter life in the atmosphere, is also used in all of these models. The judges were also impressed by Electrolux's commitment to product stewardship with a 'take-back' service for previously owned fridges, product package recycling and a product life expectancy of 20 years or more.

Legislation

Historically, disposal of discarded packaging, cars, refrigerators and other engineered products has long been the responsibility of governments. Traditionally these unwanted items have been buried in landfill or incinerated with little consideration given to reuse or recycling. Not only is this process wasteful of many materials that may be recycled but it also has serious impacts on the environment.

Suitable landfill sites close to the source of waste materials are increasingly difficult to find and consume land that would otherwise be public space. Even when appropriate sites are found, the burying of community and/or industrial waste generates its own set of problems including:

- risk of subsidence

- generation of odours and flammable and toxic gases

- attraction of scavenging bird and vermin populations

- release of pollutants into the atmosphere in the event of a fire

- pollution of surface and groundwater through run-off and leaching.

'Take-back' legislation or extended product responsibility (EPR) requires manufacturers to either manage their own waste or engage a third party to be responsible for managing waste products and packaging over the entire product life cycle. The product life cycle starts with materials acquisition and finishes with product end-of-life and waste disposal. This period is often referred to as 'cradle to grave'. Legislation now requires a product specific approach, however, one immediate result is the reduction or elimination of landfill and incineration as the means of dealing with product end-of-life waste.

Directive 2002/96/EC of the European Parliament and of the Council on Waste Electrical and Electronic Equipment (WEEE) noted the pace at which consumer electrical and electronic products were growing without sufficient concern for waste management and recycling. The council 'insisted on the need for promoting waste recovery with a view to reducing the quantity of waste for disposal and saving natural resources, in particular by reuse, recycling, composting and recovering energy from waste and recognised that the choice of options in any particular case must have regard to environmental and economic effects'.

'Take-back' schemes for WEEE items now exist throughout the EU and non-member countries. These programs place the responsibility of end-of-life waste management on manufacturers. The legislation has the intention of reducing the quantity of toxic waste, increasing recyclability of products and reducing pollution at its source.

'Take-back' policy has implications for manufacturers, engineers and designers across the entire product life cycle. The legislation essentially aims to reduce environmental impacts through a three-stage process of:

- increasing recycling rates

- reducing or eliminating pollution at every stage

- reducing the volume and toxicity of waste disposal.

Typically, EPR strategies used by designers and manufacturers include:

- producing more durable products

- identifying materials to aid recycling

- choosing materials that recycle more easily

- reducing the amount of materials used in products

- eliminating toxic materials in the product design stage

- developing and managing recovery, reuse and recycling systems

- designing modular or component-based construction, assisting repair or maintenance

- improving ease of recycling through design for disassembly approaches.

Because manufacturers in Europe are financially responsible for the management of their products entire life cycle, these costs must be included within the retail price. To remain competitive in the market, companies and therefore designers have to make this process as efficient as possible.

Consequently there is an incentive for innovation as designers and manufacturers strive to reduce toxic waste materials while incorporating recyclable and recycled materials into their products. It should be noted waste management programs can add to production costs if not carefully integrated into designs that incorporate recyclable materials or reusable components that may lower future product costs and in some cases even generate an income.

In Australia, mandatory take-back requirements affecting engineered products are limited only to those products containing ozone damaging components such as refrigerants and even then it is only the offending material that requires gathering.

The Environmental Protection and Heritage Council (EPHC, formerly ANZECC) is currently negotiating with the government and manufacturers for a national product stewardship or EPR program.

Curently these groups are focusing on developing programs surrounding mobile phones, televisions and computers but hope to expand to other engineered products over time.

Common problems associated with recycling involve product assemblies and even individual components that are often made up of more than one kind of material or the inclusion of some sort of fibre (as in composites). This adds to the difficulties of recycling. In a conscious effort to facilitate the recycling process, manufacturers have begun to design and make parts in a different way. Engineers are limiting the variety of materials used and redesigning assemblies to facilitate their removal and separation when recycling.

Dismantling and recycling complex products such as cars, refrigerators, washing machines and other engineered products containing a variety of metal types and polymers can be an expensive and time consuming process. Shredding of partially disassembled products results in particulate matter of mixed quality yet, to be successful, the recycling of light metals such as aluminium and magnesium require high purity material due to their susceptibility to contamination.

Metal sorting technologies have increased in both speed and efficiency. Magnetic and eddy current separators can easily separate iron and ferrous alloys but with the advent of X-ray technologies it is now possible to separate a variety of alloys and also distinguish composite materials and organic polymers.

Recycling specific materials

Steel

There are essentially two methods for making steel using recycled scrap. The basic oxygen furnace (BOF) process, using a minimum of 25% recycled steel, and the electric arc furnace (EAF) process, can use up to 100% recycled steel. As with other recycling programs, steel recycling primarily reduces the solid waste stream, saves valuable energy, reduces emissions and saves natural resources. Every tonne of steel recycled, saves over 1100 kg of iron ore, 635 kg of coal, and 50 kg of limestone.

Aluminium

One of the reasons aluminium is not regularly specified is often due to its high associated production costs. Recycled aluminium is considerably cheaper to produce than virgin aluminium, using only 700 kWh or 5% of the electricity required to produce one tonne of virgin aluminium. With no difference in engineering properties between virgin and recycled aluminium, recycling programs will continue to grow in popularity. Current estimates show we recycle up to 60% of aluminium.

Brass

Brass is readily recycled without loss of properties. A basic melt of scrap of similar composition to that required may be adjusted by the addition of small amounts of new copper or zinc to meet specifications before casting.

Polymers

Not all polymers are recyclable. Common polymers recycled include:

- polystyrene

- polypropylene

- polyvinyl chloride

- polyethylene (both high and low density).

A common problem with recycling plastics is that plastics are often made up of more than one kind of polymer or there may be some sort of fibre added to the plastic (a composite) to give added strength. This adds to the difficulties of recycling.

To aid in the identification, sorting and recovery of polymers a coding system has been developed based on the 'recycle triangle' that uses a series of numbers and letters as shown in Figure 2.4.12.

Figure 2.4.12 Recycle triangle code

Rubber

Crosslinked rubbers are usually moulded and shaped before they are crosslinked. Crosslinking occurs at high temperatures and gives the product its thermosetting properties. The vulcanising process delivers increased strength and resistance to changes in temperature. It also renders rubber impermeable to gases and resistant to heat, chemical action and abrasion.

Reclaiming is a process of de-polymerisation, wherein vulcanised waste rubber is ground, then treated with application of heat and chemicals before being intensely worked mechanically. Reclaimed rubber does not have properties comparable to virgin rubber but still has many uses.

Recovered rubber can cost half that of natural or synthetic rubber to produce and recovered rubber has some properties that are better than those of virgin rubber. This recycling process also conserves non-renewable petroleum products used to produce synthetic rubbers. Physical reuse of rubber can be simply achieved by reducing it to a granular form and then reprocessing. Granulate can be used for low-grade products such as rubber wheels for carts and barrows and can also be added to asphalt for road construction.

Costs and benefits of recycling materials

The economic, political, social, technological and environmental reasons for recycling materials today are strong. Recycling offers both environmental and economic benefits by:

- reducing volumes of material that end up in landfills

- saving energy by reducing the need for mining and smelting

- reducing production energy requirements and emissions

- relieving environmental impacts on the land and water

- conserving raw materials.

Companies require costs to be minimised through innovative packaging and generating designs that use fewer materials, produce less waste and contain more recycled and recyclable materials. These reduced costs may be directly passed on to the consumer.

Recycling is often defined as the series of activities, including collection, separation and processing, by which products or other materials are recovered from the waste stream for use as raw materials in the manufacture of new products. Recycled products may be reprocessed back into their original form e.g. used glass jars recycled back into new bottles or it may involve materials being reprocessed into a new product such as waste paper being recycled into cardboard. This reprocessing excludes the recovery of materials for energy and does not include reclaiming materials for use as fuel for producing heat or power by combustion.

Further reading

Alexander, C and Reno, J, (eds), *Economies of Recycling: Global Transformations of Materials, Values and Social Relations*, Zed Books, 2012

Allen, DT and Shonnard DR, *Sustainable Engineering: Concepts, Design and Case Studies*, Prentice Hall, 2001

Braungart, M and McDonough, W, *Cradle to Cradle: Remaking the Way We Make Things*, Northpoint Press, 2012

Braungart, M and McDonough, W, *The Upcycle: Beyond Sustainability—Designing for Abundance*, Northpoint Press, 2002

Graedel TEH and Allenby BR, *Industrial Ecology and Sustainable Engineering*, Prentice Hall, 2009

2.5 Engineering electricity/electronics

Basic principles

Potential difference and current

Potential difference is a measure of the work that must be done to move an electric charge from one point to another. Potential difference is measured in volts and is symbolised by the capital letter 'V'. The relationship can be represented by the equation below:

$$V = W / Q$$

where W is the work expressed in joules, required to move the charge Q.

The electric charge Q on an electron is measured to be 1.6×10^{-19} Coulombs. Electrical current is a measure of the flow of electrons past a point in a unit of time and can be represented by the equation below:

$$I = Q / t$$

where I is the electrical current measured in amperes and expressed in the units amps symbolised by the capital letter 'A'.

Fundamentals of AC and DC currents—simple circuits and components

Resistors

Resistors are components within an electrical circuit that retard or resist the free flow of electrons. Resistance is measured in ohms and is symbolised by the Greek letter omega (Ω). When drawing circuits, resistors are represented by a sawtooth line or rectangle (Figure 2.5.1).

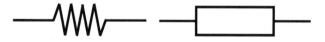

Figure 2.5.1 Resistor graphic

Resistance is related to voltage and current by Ohm's law, stated as:

$$V = I R$$

Voltage source

A battery is a source of steady continuous voltage and is represented within a circuit diagram as two uneven lines normal to the circuit as indicated in Figure 2.5.2. The battery is a source of direct current since Ohm's law relates voltage to current.

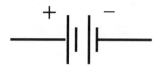

Figure 2.5.2 DC source graphic

A source of alternating voltage is represented within an electric circuit as indicated in Figure 2.5.3 and is also a source of alternating current (AC).

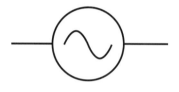

Figure 2.5.3 AC source graphic

Switches

Within a circuit a switch that completes or breaks the circuit is represented as shown in Figure 2.5.4.

Figure 2.5.4 Switch graphic

Direct current (DC)

Direct current systems provide a constant flow of electrons in a single direction from negative to positive.

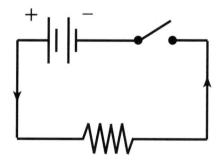

Figure 2.5.5 Electrical DC circuit

Note: The circuit diagram in Figure 2.5.5 shows current flow to be from the positive terminal to the negative terminal. This is often designated as the conventional current direction. This direction of flow was proposed in a theory developed by Benjamin Franklin (1706–1790) before the existence of electrons was known. The conventional current direction as described above (from positive to negative) is still used today even though electron flow around a circuit proceeds from negative to positive

Direct current can be produced from a generator or batteries where it can be stored chemically. Unfortunately transmission losses through a conductor mean that DC current cannot be sent efficiently over long distances. Within a DC circuit, voltage and current can be considered as unchanging with time so that Ohm's law represents the relationship:

$$V = I \times R \text{ or } R = V / I$$

Therefore for a constant resistance (R), voltage (V) and current (I) must maintain a constant ratio. If R = 1 ohm, V and I must maintain the same ratio: 1:1, 3:3, -2.8 : -2.8, and so on.

Similarly if R = 2.5 ohm, the ratio V : I must be constant, e.g. 5:2, 8:3.2, -0.12:-0.048, etc.

Alternating current (AC)

Alternating current gets it name from the way that the direction of electron flow changes or alternates. In this process the positive and negative charges at either end of the conductor switch positions results in reversals of electron direction.

As shown previously by Ohm's law, for a given resistance voltage and current maintain a constant ratio i.e. they vary in unison. Each reversal of current is termed a cycle. A schematic representation of an AC circuit is shown in Figure 2.5.6.

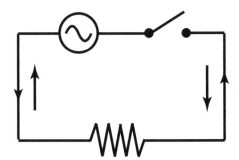

Figure 2.5.6 Electrical AC circuit

Alternating current is generated using rotating-coil generators in which a cycle is completed for every complete rotation of the generator shaft. At various times during a cycle the value of current or voltage can be determined by sin θ where θ represents the angle of rotation of the generator shaft.

The variation of current and voltage in an AC circuit can therefore be represented by a sine wave moving with respect to time as shown in Figure 2.5.7. In Australia alternating current electricity is supplied at 50 cycles a second or a frequency of 50 Hz. Therefore one complete cycle is completed every 0.02 seconds or 20 ms.

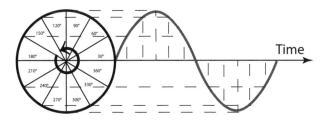

Figure 2.5.7 Variation in current and voltage with rotation of rotor in AC power generation

Nicola Tesla is generally credited with the establishment of alternating current as an efficient means of electrical transmission in 1888. While AC current cannot be stored in a battery for later use, it can be readily transformed to higher or lower voltages. Because of this, very high voltages can be transmitted from power stations and later stepped down by local transformers for domestic use. Similarly, small individual transformers can be used to operate portable low voltage appliances.

Magnetic induction

Michael Faraday (1791–1867) discovered in 1831 that a current could be made to flow through a second wire by a process called electromagnetic induction if the wire is exposed to a moving magnetic field.

Figure 2.5.8 shows the instant a current begins to flow in the primary coil. A galvanometer attached to the secondary coil deflects and returns to zero, registering the momentary flow of current in the secondary coil.

A similar deflection of the galvanometer is recorded at the instant of terminating the flow of current in the primary coil. As the magnetic field initially develops around the primary coil, towards an equilibrium state, it can be thought of as moving outward.

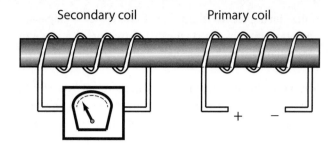

Secondary coil   Primary coil

Figure 2.5.8 Experiment performed by Faraday in which a current was induced into a secondary coil when current is switched on or off in the primary coil

The developing magnetic field is therefore moving relative to the secondary coil and an induced current is created in the secondary coil. The same phenomenon occurs when the current in the primary coil is switched off: an instantaneous flow of current is detected in the secondary coil as the lines of magnetic force decrease about the primary coil although in this case deflection of the galvanometer occurs in the opposite direction (see Figure 2.5.9).

Faraday also found that a current could be induced in a coil if a magnet was moved relative to the coil. A generator operating on the principle of electromagnetic induction converts mechanical energy to electrical energy.

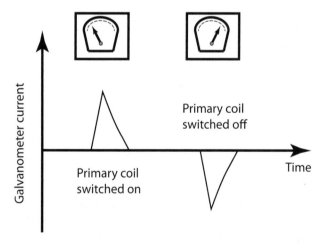

Figure 2.5.9 Change in current in secondary wire

Induction motors

The AC induction motor is the most common motor used in industry and mains-powered home appliances. Induction motors are also sometimes called 'squirrel cage' motors because of the appearance of early rotors.

AC induction motors offer users simple, rugged construction and easy maintenance. AC induction motors consist of two basic assemblies: stator and rotor. In this instance however the stator is an electromagnet and current is induced in the coil of the rotor as the AC current in the stator alternates. In induction motors, the magnetic field of the stator is constantly changing due to the reversal of current direction associated with the AC supply of the stator winding. An induced current is therefore produced in the rotor, resulting in associated magnetic field leading to rotation of the rotor. The motor's name comes from the alternating current induced into the rotor by the rotating magnetic flux produced in the stator.

The absence of brushes in induction motors leads to an extended motor life and reduced maintenance. Their simpler design makes induction motors easier and cheaper to construct.

Induction cooktops use the same principle of magnetic induction to heat food.

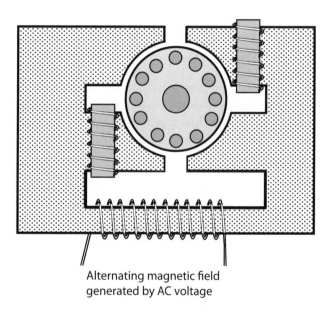

Alternating magnetic field generated by AC voltage

Figure 2.5.10 Diagram of an AC induction motor demonstrating a rotating magnetic field created by additional coils on the pole pieces

Field force in currents

Magnetic fields are produced by moving electric charges and are measured in teslas.

Electric fields may be produced by moving charges or stationary charges.

The magnitude of the force (F) felt by a charge (q) moving with velocity (v) through a magnetic field B is illustrated below.

$$F = qv \times B$$

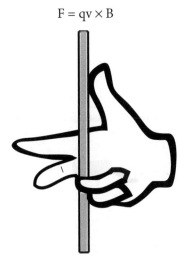

Figure 2.5.11 Right-hand rule

The direction of the force is perpendicular to both v and B. The right-hand rule illustrated in Figure 2.5.11 is used to determine the direction of F.

To find the direction of F use your right hand and:

- point the thumb into the direction of v

- extend the index finger into the direction of B

- the direction of the force will be perpendicular to the palm and may be reprsented by the crooked middle finger

- closed fingers curl into the direction of the force.

If the charge is negative, the direction of the force will be opposite.

Electrical safety

The hazards represented by electricity depend on the amount of current, its frequency, the duration of exposure and the path taken through the body.

Earth leakage circuit breakers (ELCBs) or ground fault circuit interrupter (GFCI) devices are electronic devices for protecting people from serious injury due to electric shock. These systems constantly monitor electricity flowing in a circuit.

If the electricity flowing into the circuit differs even slightly from that returning, the device will quickly shut off the current. The advantage of using these devices is that they can quickly detect amounts too small to activate fuses or circuit breakers. By limiting the duration of exposure to a fraction of a second they help protect consumers from the dangers of severe electric shocks and electrocution.

Related Australian electrical safety standards

Power cords and AC adaptors for use in Australia must be tested for compliance with state electrical safety authority regulations. The product must be marked with a valid Electrical Safety Certificate Number and an RCM (Regulatory Compliance Mark) issued by Standards Australia (SAA). A C-tick marking may also appear on an AC adaptor showing compliance with EMC (Electromagnetic Compatibility) standards. Shown in Figure 2.5.12 are the C-tick mark, and RCM mark. The Electrical Safety Certificate number is below each prefixed by the capital letter 'N'.

Figure 2.5.12 C-tick mark (left) and RCM mark (right)

A C-tick mark may also appear on products which are required to comply with Australian electromagnetic compatibility requirements and radio communications standards. It signifies that the product may be legally sold in Australia.

Electric motors and generators

There is a small but important difference between motors and engines. An engine is a device that converts chemical energy (in the form of gasoline, diesel or natural gas) to rotating mechanical energy. An electric motor is a device that converts electrical energy (from a power source) to rotating mechanical energy. In an electric motor a current is passed through a wire which is suspended in a magnetic field. This causes the wire to move. The direction of movement is determined by the direction of the field and the direction of the current. The speed of movement is determined by the strength of the field and the amplitude of the current. This principle is used in electric motors to produce rotation.

Many devices that operate on the principle of rotation such as fans, pumps, conveyors and power tools rely predominantly on electric motors. Electric motors play an important role in many of today's highly productive industries, contributing to our quality of life in general.

The principle of the electric generator is related to the operation of electric motors. The electric generator converts the mechanical energy of rotation into electrical energy using the principle of electromagnetic induction. In this situation a wire coil is rotated in a magnetic field. As it rotates it cuts the lines of magnetic flux associated with each pole of the magnet. Voltage and current are subsequently induced in the coil, reaching a maximum when the coil is directly in line with a pole and a minimum when at right angles to the poles. A conductive ring known as a 'commutator' passes current to an external circuit through brushes (Figure 2.5.13).

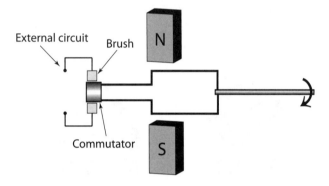

Figure 2.5.13 Basic DC electric generator

With every complete rotation of the armature, the coil will be aligned with the poles of the magnets twice, leading to two peaks of current for every complete rotation as illustrated in Figure 2.5.14.

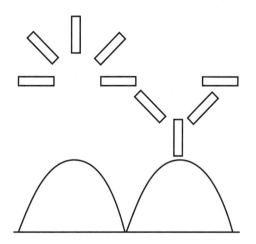

Figure 2.5.14 Variation of current from a basic DC electric generator

A similar situation exists for an AC generator although a separate commutator is present on the ends of the coil. For every complete rotation of the commutator one alternating cycle is produced, as illustrated in Figure 2.5.15.

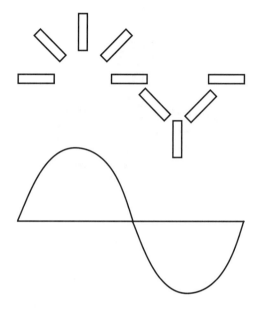

Figure 2.5.15 Variation of current from a basic AC electric generator

In an electric motor the reverse operation takes place. Current is passed through a commutator to a coil creating an electromagnet (also known as the armature). The electromagnet is placed between the poles of a permanent magnet. The poles of the electromagnet repel the like poles of the permanent magnet and the electromagnet spins, turning a drive shaft (Figure 2.5.16).

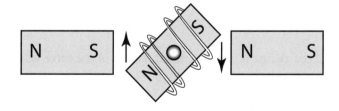

Figure 2.5.16 Basic electric motor

The rotating electromagnet is also known as the rotor while the fixed permanent magnet is known as the stator. A motor of the sort shown above would be considered a single phase motor in that for each rotation of the rotor a single cycle is produced. Because magnetic forces travel poorly through air, the stator has shaped metal attachments known as 'shoes' designed to fit as closely to the poles of the rotor as possible (see Figure 2.5.17). The end result is a stronger, more stable magnetic field.

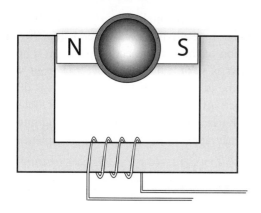

Figure 2.5.17 Electromagnet with 'shoes'

Adjustment of current in DC motors can be made by reversal of the wires at the battery terminal while AC current oscillates on its own.

Single phase motors

Many motor applications use single phase power, especially for smaller horsepower motors. Most of these applications are residential and light commercial, where three phase power is generally unavailable. In a three phase motor, the incoming power produces a rotating magnetic current on its own. This allows the three phase motor to be self starting. Single phase motors require additional power in order to produce a rotating magnetic field. Once started, the motor has a changing magnetic field at each pole, allowing the motor to continue running.

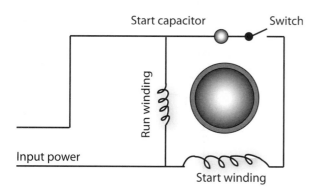

Figure 2.5.18 Single phase motor

The most common method of starting a single phase motor combines a capacitor and auxiliary winding or start circuit. Figure 2.5.18 shows an auxiliary starting winding, a capacitor, and a centrifugal switch. The auxiliary winding is actually a second winding in the motor. When current is applied to the motor, both the run winding and the start winding produce magnetic fields. Because the start winding has a lower resistance,

a stronger magnetic field is created which causes the motor to begin rotation.

Once the motor reaches about 80% of its rated speed, a centrifugal switch disconnects the start winding. From this point on the single phase motor can maintain enough rotating magnetic field to operate on its own.

Three phase motors

Three phase motors are identical to single phase motors with the exception that three pairs of magnets surround the rotor (at separations of 120°) instead of one pair. Three phase AC power is therefore comprised of three independent voltages. The sinusoidal curve for each voltage is displaced (out of phase) 120° from the others. When phase one (A) is at zero volts, phase two (B) is near its maximum voltage and flowing in the positive direction. The third phase (C) is near its maximum voltage as well, but flows in the negative direction (see Figure 2.5.19).

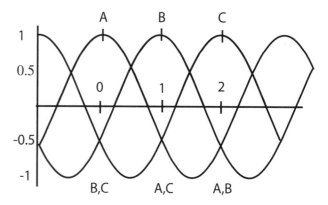

Figure 2.5.19 Three phase power

These three phases will change from positive to negative as the AC signal runs through each cycle. A rotating magnetic field is produced if each of the three phases is connected to an electrically independent winding in an AC motor stator.

AC power cycles 60 times per second between positive and negative. In a fraction of a second, the phases have shifted 60° causing the relationship of the north and south poles to change at the same rate. Because the motor has established an induced magnetic field, the opposite fields of the rotor and stator attract each other, causing the rotor to follow the stator's magnetic field change. As the rotor continues to follow the stator's magnetic field, the three phases will shift yet another 60°. It is this continuous change in polarity that causes the rotation of the motor.

2.6 Communication

Orthogonal and pictorial drawings

Orthographic drawing uses lines of sight that are always perpendicular to the viewing plane to produce a projected image, hence the name orthographic projection (see Figure 2.6.1).

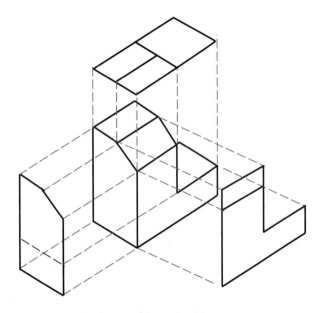

Figure 2.6.1 Orthographic projection

A variety of different forms of orthographic projection exist depending on the positioning of the object and the observer in relation to the plane or planes of projection. The different styles of orthographic projections are named around four quadrants or angles (see Figure 2.6.2).

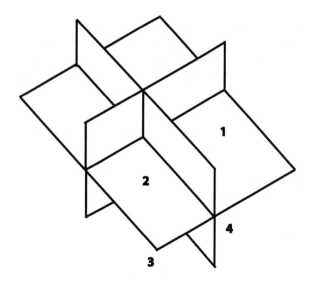

Figure 2.6.2 Quadrants or angles

The frontal and horizontal planes of projection are perpendicular to each other, however using the line of intersection of the two projection planes as a hinge, the top view is swung directly above the front view. Frequently the folding line between the views is drawn on the paper. Above the folding line a HP notation indicates a horizontal plane. Below the folding line the letters VP may appear, indicating a vertical plane (see Figure 2.6.3).

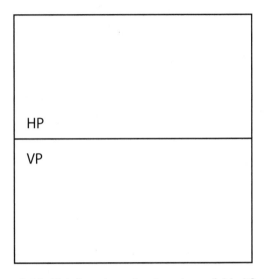

Figure 2.6.3 Third angle projection planes folded flat

First and third angle projections are both used extensively throughout the world. When the first quadrant is used, the lines of sight travel from the observer's eye to the object and then to the plane of projection. When third angle projection is used, the lines of sight travel from the observer's eye through the plane of projection to the object. Views obtained by the two systems are identical. Only their relative positions on paper are different.

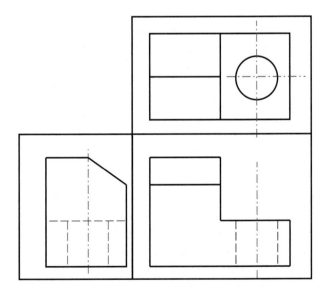

Figure 2.6.4 Third angle projection view placement

The three-view drawing shown in Figure 2.6.4 shows a number of line types. The Australian Drawing Standard AS1100 specifies a minimum thickness (in mm) for each line type when used on A2, A3 or A4 sheet sizes.

Line types and weights include:

- visible outlines   (0.35)

- hidden detail   (0.25)

- dimension/projection (0.18)

- centre line   (0.18)

Dimensioning

Linear dimensions are expressed in millimetres without the need to write the symbol 'mm' after every dimension. Most often a general statement such as 'all dimensions in millimetres' may appear in the drawing title block. Angular measurements should be shown in degrees.

Dimension lines should be drawn lightly and kept away from the drawing wherever possible. Arrow heads on the end of dimension lines should be drawn more firmly and be roughly 3 mm long and 1 mm wide.

Light projection lines determine the limits of dimensions. They should not touch the drawing and should extend past the dimension line by a couple of millimetres. Figure 2.6.5 shows the relationship between a drawing's projection and dimension lines.

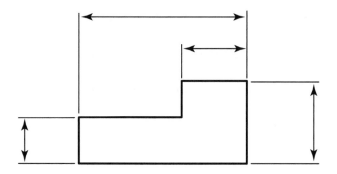

Figure 2.6.5 Dimension lines

Figures on dimension lines should be placed above the line and be readable from the bottom or right-hand side of the drawing (see Figure 2.6.6).

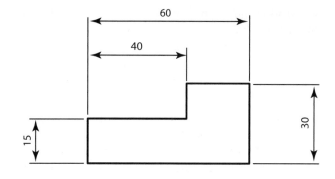

Figure 2.6.6 Dimensioning drawings

Circles are defined by their diameter using the symbol Ø. Depending on the size of the circle and its position in relationship to other drawing features, a variety of dimensioning techniques may be used as shown in Figure 2.6.7.

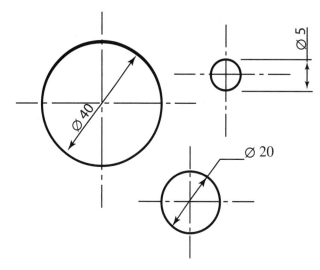

Figure 2.6.7 Circle dimensioning

Materials lists

Many drawings are often accompanied by a materials list. It regularly appears in table form. The purpose of the list is to identify specific quantities of materials and directly associate them with the identified part(s).

Computer graphics such as computer-aided drawing (CAD)

CAD stands for computer-aided design. CAD drawings exist as electronic data files that are created using specialist software. CAD software may be used to create either 2D or 3D drawings. These drawings may be technical or conceptual in nature. They may incorporate additional information through the inclusion of tables, dimensions, tolerances, assembly notes, materials lists or flowcharts. There are essentially two types of computer graphics:

- raster or bitmap graphics composed of pixels (or patterns of individual dots)

- vector graphics generated by mathematical relationships describing points, lines and shapes.

Paint programs use bitmap images whereas most drawing, animation and modeling packages use vector graphics.

Vector graphics are more flexible and contain more detail. They may be scaled, stretched or resized and most often produce a file of smaller size than their bitmap counterparts.

CAD drawing packages allow users to design in 3D to give designers and engineers the opportunity to view models as they would appear in real life. No longer are complex orthographic drawings created and converted into 3D figures. These 3D models can quickly be viewed as wire-frame or solid. They are able to be rotated and viewed from any direction, as well as resolved into oblique, isometric or perspective views. These 3D models such as the one shown in Figure 2.6.8 instantly provide recognition and realism for engineers, clients and consumers. Notice how the features in the CAD drawing (upper) are instantly recognisable in the final manufactured part (lower). Three-dimensioanl drawings created in CAD packages may be viewed in a variety of forms including wire frame, isometric, oblique, perspective, showing hidden lines, shaded, textured and toned. They may also be reworked at the click of a mouse button to be viewed as orthographic, exploded isometric, fully dimensioned, sectioned or animated assembly/disassembly and so on.

The ability to sketch directly in 3D has also enhanced the engineer's ability to perceive potential design flaws. This process, known as virtual design, is increasingly used in industry to generate computer models of real

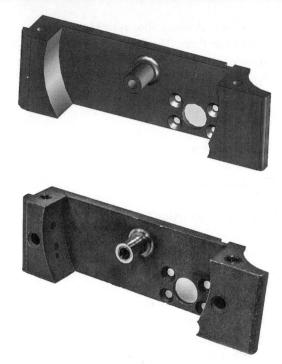

Figure 2.6.8 CAD model and CNC machined part

components or assemblies. Animation of moving and mating components can show areas of on-alignment or 'clashing'. Flow simulation software can analyse effects, such as turbulence and drag, without recourse to expensive models and wind tunnel tests. Stress analysis can also be performed on these virtual products to identify weaknesses and make modifications before the first physical component is produced.

Figure 2.6.9 is a computer-generated dimensioned orthographic projection of a spark plug. The drawing shows the standard layout of top, front and side view. Dimensions and application of drawing standards indicate all of the major features including:

- threaded sections shown with parallel lines

- AF (across the flats) dimensions

- radius (R) dimensions

- circle diameters (Ø)

- linear dimensions

- nested dimensions

- part identification.

Details of parts and additional information pertinent to the interpretation drawings is often provided in

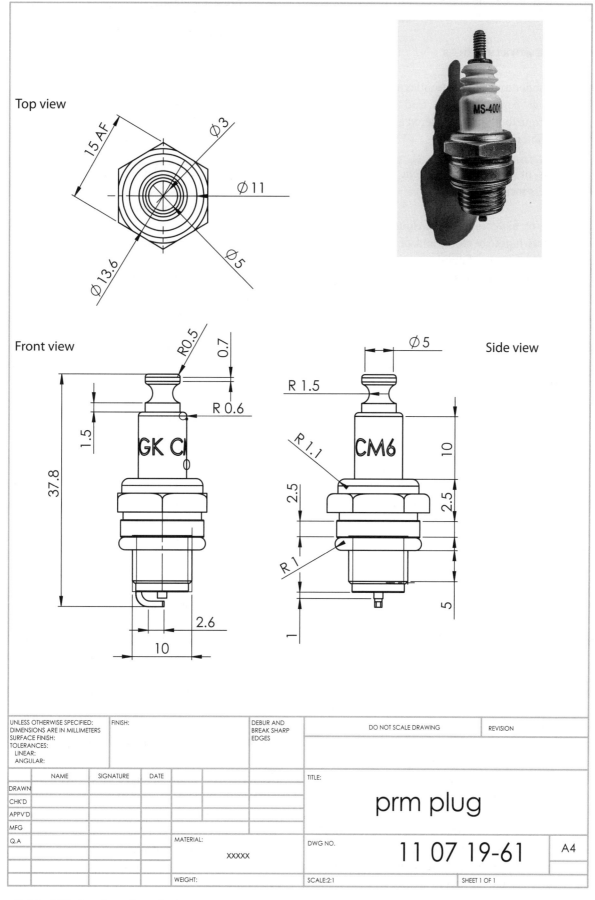

Top view

15 AF
Ø3
Ø11
Ø13.6
Ø5

MS-4001

Front view

R0.5
0.7
R 0.6
1.5
37.8
GK C
2.6
10

Side view

Ø5
R 1.5
CM6
R 1.1
2.5
10
2.5
R 1
1
5

UNLESS OTHERWISE SPECIFIED:
DIMENSIONS ARE IN MILLIMETERS
SURFACE FINISH:
TOLERANCES:
  LINEAR:
  ANGULAR:
	FINISH:				DEBUR AND
					BREAK SHARP
					EDGES
							DO NOT SCALE DRAWING	REVISION

	NAME	SIGNATURE	DATE			TITLE:		
DRAWN								
CHK'D						**prm plug**		
APPV'D								
MFG								
Q.A			MATERIAL: XXXXX			DWG NO. **11 07 19-61**		A4
			WEIGHT:			SCALE:2:1	SHEET 1 OF 1	

Figure 2.6.9 CAD drawing of spark plug

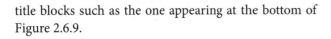

title blocks such as the one appearing at the bottom of Figure 2.6.9.

Collaborative work practices

CAD packages offer many opportunities and advantages for fast remote communication and collaboration, particularly if contributors are scattered around the site, city, state, nation or even globe.

This feature is of even greater benefit in remote or difficult to access locations.

Email, the use of file compression, cloud services etc. have allowed drawings to be stored and/or distributed for consultation at every stage of development. Consultation and approval takes place efficiently. Through the use of CAD software, adjustments can be made without the need for manual redrafting. Closer scrutiny is available through electronic zoom features and hard copies may be produced on paper for non-electronic viewing. Photo realistic rendering, virtual environments and digital animations may all be used to enhance the engineer's and/or the client's experience of the design process.

CAD programs also have the ability to export data in spreadsheet form. Selected objects, components or assemblies may be exported in a table form that communicates materials, volumes and quantities. A materials list may then be generated and costs established when materials are matched with financial data.

A similar process applies to the production phase. CAD software can also generate production flow charts, allowing manufacturers to predict production times and allocate hourly rate estimates.

Australian Drawing Standard AS 1100

A standard sets out specifications and procedures to make sure a material, product, method or service can do what it is meant to do and perform consistently the way it is meant to perform.

Australian Standard AS 1100 for technical drawing covers conventions required by architects, designers, engineers, surveyors and so on. It is published by Standards Australia and based upon standards established globally and determined by the International Standards Organisation (ISO). Essentially this standard establishes how to construct and interpret technical drawings in a consistent fashion.

The Australian Standard specifies:

- sectioning

- types and uses of lines

- methods of projection

- scales and their application

- materials, sizes and layout of drawing sheets

- dimensioning techniques, including tolerances

- use of abbreviations, lettering, numerals and symbols.

Third angle projection is the preferred drawing style of engineers. This method provides more detail than may be available in pictorial styles of drawing such as isometric. Orthogonal drawings consist of as many views as necessary to satisfactorily specify an object sufficient for manufacturing. Views may include top, front, left, right, base and a range of sectional views. Important information additional to the drawing may appear in the form of annotations and include such information as surface finish, joining technique, material, assembly and so on.

Figure 2.6.9 shows a dimensioned orthographic drawing in the style of third angle projection. It shows a top, front and side view of a standard spark plug. Details of the threaded barrel of the spark plug appear as two parallel lines. The end of the thread or 'run out' is terminated with a 45° line.

The top view is oriented so that both the front or side views show an across the flats (AF) view of the hexagonal body. Dimensions, as the document states, are all shown in millimetres and are read from the base of the drawing or right-hand side as mandated by convention. Radii are identified by a capital 'R' and diameters are recorded with the diameter symbol ($\emptyset$) .

Developing an engineering report

The following engineering report provided by Bureau Veritas is typical of the type of non destructive materials analysis undertaken by materials engineers (metallurgists). The part, a pinion, is a common part of many engineered products requiring transmission of rotational motion. Some client-specific details have been removed.

MATERIAL IDENTIFICATION REPORT

Report: xxxxx

Client: xxxxx

Attn: xxxxx

Order xxxxx

Date: xxxxx

Component : Pinion Material Identification

Move forward with confidence

Bureau Veritas Asset Integrity and Reliability
Services Pty Ltd
ABN 86 000 928 816
29 Rosegum Close, Warabrook
Newcastle NSW 2304 Australia
Tel: 61 2 4908 2500 Fax: 61 2 4908 2555
Email: airs@au.bureauveritas.com

The tests marked 'X' were carried out to determine the material grade, heat treatment, etc.

X	Chemical Analysis – AES/ EDS
	Mechanical Testing
	Microexamination
	Replication
X	Hardness Test
	Site Hardness Test

A pinion was received from xxxxxxxx for non-destructive material identification testing. Images of the pinion are provided in Figures 1 and 2. The following identification was present on one end.

62402   13   L = 196,83   TA

A visible heat tint was present on the ends of the pinion and top land of each tooth suggesting selective surface hardening.

Chemical analysis was performed using Atomic Emission Spectrometer (AES) on the end of the pinion and the results presented below in Table 1.

C	Mn	P	S	Si	Ni	Cr	Mo	Al	Cu
0.44	1.20	0.009	>0.12	0.16	0.13	1.31	0.25	0.024	0.21

These results indicate the pinion had been manufactured from a medium carbon free machining low alloy steel similar to 41CrMoS4 (Wk No 1.2331). This material approximates a resulphurised version of AS1444/4140. This material is suitable for induction hardening. A sulphur print was performed on the end of the pinion to confirm the high sulphur result and is shown in Figure 3.

Hardness tests were performed on the end of the pinion, tooth top land and tooth flanks using an Equotip portable hardness tester using an LD+15 impact device with the results presented below.

Flank hardness 267-296 HV (HL_{D+15})

Top land and End hardness 296-322 HV (HL_{D+15})

The results suggest that despite evidence of a heat tint on the end of the pinion and top land of the teeth, that the surface had not been effectively induction hardened.

Comments

A free machining grade would not normally be recommended for gear components and a change in specification to AS1444/4140 is suggested.

Figure 1   General view of the pinion as received

Figure 2   View of heat tint indications along top tooth land and end of pinion

Figure 3   View of sulphur print performed on end of pinion confirming high sulphur content

2.7 Sample Preliminary questions and answers

Objective-response questions

1. Brass may be best described as

A   an alloy of copper and zinc.
B   lamellar composite material.
C   mixture consisting of copper and tin.
D   a compound of copper and zinc.

2. Force systems consisting only of forces that intersect at a common point are known as

A   co-planar.
B   co-linear.
C   concurrent.
D   codependent.

3. Resultants and equilibrants are

A   identical.
B   the same except for sense.
C   the same except for magnitude.
D   the same except for direction.

4. Work hardening most often results in

A   an increase in strength with a decrease in ductility and hardness.
B   an increase in hardness with a decrease in ductility and strength.
C   an increase in ductility and hardness with a decrease in strength.
D   an increase in hardness and strength with a decrease in ductility.

5. Alloys produced from metals of similar atomic size form structures known as

A   interstitial.
B   substantial.
C   intermetallic.
D   substitutional.

6. Grey cast iron's strength comes from

A   the casting process.
B   the homogeneity of its structure.
C   high concentrations of martensite.
D   its metallic matrix in which graphite is distributed.

7. The direction of the force exerted on a moving charge by a magnetic field may be determined by

A   the rule of force.
B   the left-hand rule.
C   the right-hand rule.
D   the three force rule.

8. Magnetic fields are produced by

A   stationary charges.
B   stationary or moving charges.
C   moving electric charges measured in teslas.
D   moving electric charges measured in faradays.

9. The absence of what leads to greater longevity of induction motors.

A. a stator
B   brushes
C   windings
D   moving parts

10. Induction cooktops rely on

A   the creation of a magnetic field.
B   induced current in the pan base.
C   direct contact between the cooktop and pan.
D   heat transferred from the cooktop to the pan.

Short-answer questions

1. From where does martensite get its very high strength and hardness?   (2 marks)

2. Explain why DC current is unsuitable for transmission over longer distances.   (1 mark)

3. Explain why the properties of wrought iron are variable across any section.   (2 marks)

4. Explain the 'three force rule' used for solving some force systems.   (2 marks)

5. Explain the principle of 'force transmissibility'.   (2 marks)

6. What are the advantages of vector graphics over those saved in a bitmap format?   (2 marks)

Longer-answer questions

1. Explain the process and purpose of case hardening.
(2 marks)

2. Describe the process of work hardening at a structural level, i.e. movement of individual grains.
(3 marks)

3. Explain (at a molecular level) how cross linking affects the properties of rubber.
(2 marks)

4. Discuss the 'green' or environmentally friendly credentials of steel.
(4 marks)

5. Discuss what will happen if two saucepans, one made of copper and the other made of mild steel, are placed on the hobs of a new induction cooktop to heat some soup. Both hobs are turned to the same heat setting.
(2 marks)

Answers to objective-response questions

1. **A** Brass is an alloy of copper and up to 43% zinc.

2. **C** Concurrent force systems incorporate forces whose lines of action all intersect at a common point but may lie on different planes.

3. **B** An equilibrant is identical to the resultant in magnitude and direction but is opposite in sense.

4. **D** Work hardening is a result of plastic or permanent deformation of the crystal structure that increases hardness and strength but reduces ductility.

5. **D** Substitutional alloys form when the atomic radius of the alloying (solute) element differs by no more than 15% from that of the base (solvent) metal. Intermetallics are compounds and interstitial alloys occur when atomic radii differences are large.

6. **D** Grey cast iron does not have a homogeneous structure nor does it contain martensite. The casting process does not add any strength but its largely metallic matrix does improve strength.

7. **C** The three force rule refers to vectors. The left-hand rule deals with charged particles entering a magnetic field. The right-hand rule is used to determine the direction of the force felt by a charge moving with velocity through a magnetic.

8. **C** Moving electric charges create magnetic fields that are measured in teslas.

9. **B** The absence of brushes that would normally wear out lead to low maintenance and an extended lifetime for induction motors.

10. **A** Electromagnetic induction cooktops rely on the creation of a magnetic field, which induces a current in the base of a ferrous metal pot placed on the cooktop surface. The cooktop itself remains cool. Just placing a pot in contact with a cooktop surface does not prodcue any heat.

Answers to short-answer questions

1. Steels to be hardened are heated to an appropriate temperature, typically 800–900 °C, held at that temperature and then rapidly quenched in oil or water producing a distorted, stressed lattice structure.

2. Transmission losses through a conductor mean that DC current cannot be sent efficiently over long distances.

3. The process of plastic deformation used to create wrought iron deforms both the slag inclusions and the iron matrix throughout the material, resulting in variable properties.

4. When three forces act on a body and the body is in a state of equilibrium then the three forces must be concurrent (i.e. they will all intersect at a common point). The three force rule thus allows these forces to be resolved using a force vector diagram to determine unknowns.

   If more than three forces are involved the only way to use the three force rule and establish a point of concurrency is to combine sufficient forces together by vector addition until only three remain.

5. The external effect of a force on a rigid body is the same for all points of application of the force along its line of action. In simple terms, the effect of a force on a rigid body is the same whether the force is a push or a pull along the same line of action.

6. Vector graphics are more flexible and contain more detail. They may be scaled, stretched or resized and most often produce a file of smaller size than their bitmap counterparts.

Answers to longer-answer questions

1. Case hardening involves the modification of the surface chemistry of steel to increase the carbon content. Popular processes include flame or induction hardening, carbuurising, nitriding and cyaniding.

   Using a process known as carburisation the item is heated to an elevated temperature while in the presence of a high carbon atmosphere. Carbon diffuses into the steel surface resulting in a high carbon steel shell surrounding the original low carbon steel core. The depth of carburisation is determined by the time and temperature of the treatment. On quenching and tempering, a high carbon martensitic surface is formed providing high hardness and wear resistance, while maintaining a low carbon core with greater ductility. In essence a composite material has been produced.

2. Work hardening is a result of plastic or permanent deformation of the crystal structure. Under micro-examination separate grains can be seen to be elongated and distorted in the direction the metal has been deformed.

   The process of deformation involves the movement of planes of atoms moving relative to each other in a process known as slip. As slip progresses, defects within the crystal lattice, known as dislocations, increase. An increase in the number of dislocations will begin to interfere with the ease with which slip can take place and the material is said to be undergoing work hardening.

3. Cross-linking or vulcanisation occurs at high temperatures in rubber when additives modify the polymer by forming crosslinks or bridges between individual polymer chains. This cross-linking gives the rubber its thermosetting properties. This process imparts increased strength and resistance to changes in temperature. It also renders rubber impermeable to gases and resistant to heat, chemical action and abrasion.

4. The production of virgin steel can be quite damaging to the environment. After the initial damage to the environment from the mining and ore transportation processes, coke production is one of the major sources of pollution from steelmaking. Emissions such as coke oven gas, naphthalene, ammonium compounds, crude light oil, sulphur, coke dust and excess heat are released from coke ovens, while serious water contamination occurs when water is used to cool the hot coke. Slag, sulphur dioxide and hydrogen sulphide gases are also a direct by-product of steelmaking.

   The use of recycled steel, however, to make 'new' steel is considerably more environmentally friendly.

   Two methods for making steel using recycled scrap are the basic oxygen furnace (BOF) process (using a minimum of 25% recycled steel) and the electric arc furnace (EAF) process, which can use up to 100% recycled steel. As with other recycling programs, steel recycling primarily reduces the solid waste stream, saves valuable energy, reduces emissions and saves natural resources. Every tonne of steel recycled saves over 1100 kg of iron ore, 635 kg of coal and 50 kg of limestone.

5. Induction cooktops rely on inducing a current in the cooking utensil to heat its contents so the cooking utensil must be made from a magnetic material. Therefore, only the mild steel saucepan will be heated and in turn heat the soup. Copper saucepans, although made from a high conductivity material, are non-magnetic and therefore will not be heated by this method.

2.8 Glossary

Aluminium
A metal and element, aluminium (Al) is lightweight, corrosion resistant, ductile, malleable, machinable and has excellent castability.

Alternating current (AC)
Alternating current gets it name from the way that the direction of electron flow changes or alternates. In this process the positive and negative charges at either end of the conductor switch positions which results in reversals of electron direction.

Annealing
The purpose of annealing may be to remove stresses, soften, obtain a desired structure or improve machinability and cold working properties. It involves heating steel to and holding at a suitable temperature, followed by relatively slow cooling.

Austenite
A face centred cubic (FCC) phase in the iron-carbon equilibrium diagram, designated by the symbol gamma (γ), Austenite is a non-magnetic solid solution of carbon in iron.

Brass
Brass is an alloy of copper and up to 43% zinc.

Bronze
Bronze is a term generally applied to an alloy of copper and up to 10% tin, known as tin bronze. Alloys of copper and up to 10% aluminium are known as aluminium bronzes, while alloys of copper and up to 5% silicon are known as silicon bronzes.

Case hardening
Case hardening is a process of surface hardening involving a change in the composition of the outer layer of a ferrous alloy. Typical hardening processes are carburising, cyaniding, carbonitriding and nitriding.

Cast iron
Cast iron is an alloy of iron and carbon in which the carbon is in excess of the amount that can be retained in solid solution in austenite at the eutectic temperature. Carbon is usually present in the range of approximately 2% to 4.5%. In addition, silicon, manganese, sulphur and phosphorus are contained in varying amounts.

Cementite
A hard brittle iron carbide compound with the formula Fe_3C, found in carbon steel

Cold working
Involves changing the shape or size of metal by plastic deformation; carried out below the recrystallisation point, usually at room temperature; hardness and tensile strength are increased while ductility and impact values are lowered

Couple
A force-couple is a system of forces that exerts a resultant moment but no resultant force.

Current
Current refers to the rate of flow of electrically charged particles measured in amperes.

Direct current (DC)
Direct current provides a constant flow of electrons in a single direction from negative to positive.

Dislocations
Discontinuities in the crystal lattice of a metal; the movement of dislocations under stress may be used to explain slip, creep, etc.

Ductility
The ease with which a material deforms plastically while undergoing tensile forces

Ferrite
Body centred cubic (BCC) phase in the iron–carbon phase diagram; may exist in either a low temperature alpha (α) or a high temperature delta (δ) form

Ferrous
Ferrous metals are those in which the primary constituent is iron (Fe).

Heat treatment	Heat treatment applies to any one of several processes involving heating metals to controlled temperatures for specific periods of time, and afterwards cooling them at controlled rates. Heat treatments may be applied to soften work-hardened material but more generally they are used to strengthen alloys.
Magnet	A magnet is a piece of iron or other material exhibiting the properties of magnetism, i.e. it generates a force or magnetic field that attracts other ferromagnetic materials such as iron and attracts or repels other magnets.
Martensite	A hard phase produced when steel is cooled from the hardening temperature at a speed greater than its critical cooling rate, martensite is an acicular (needle-like) phase when seen under microscopic examination.
Normalising	A heat treatment process for ferrous alloys involving heating the material above the upper critical temperature then cooling in still air, the objective being to enhance toughness by refining grain size
Non-ferrous	Contains no, or minimal, iron
Pearlite	A phase of carbon steel and cast iron consisting of ferrite and cementite formed into distinct layers (or lamellae) on slow cooling from austenite
Polymer	A giant molecule based on carbon
Potential difference	The work or energy per unit charge needed to move an electron from one point to another; measured in volts
Quenching	Quenching involves the use of a variety of rates of cooling to cause a steel to harden. Quenching media include water, brine and oil.
Slip	Slip involves the movement of planes of atoms moving relative to each other.
Steel	An alloy of iron and up to 2% carbon often with other additions of other alloying elements such as manganese, silicon, chromium, nickel and molybdenum
Tempering	Reheating of a quenched steel to a sub-critical temperature in order to improve ductility and toughness
Three force rule	When three forces act on a body and the body is in a state of equilibrium, then the three forces must be concurrent, i.e. they will all intersect at a common point.
Toughness	The ability of a material to withstand shock loading (opposite to brittleness)
Transformer	Transformers reduce or increase the voltage of an alternating current.
Vector	When a quantity has a magnitude, direction and sense it is considered to be a vector quantity or simply a vector, e.g. displacement, velocity, acceleration.
Voltage	The amount of energy required to move a small electric charge along a path
Work hardening	Work hardening is a result of plastic or permanent deformation of the crystal structure.

BRAKING SYSTEMS

CONTENTS

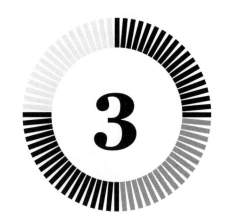

STUDENT OUTCOMES

A student:

- identifies the scope of engineering and recognises current innovations.

- describes the types of materials, components and processes and explains their implications for engineering development.

- uses mathematical, scientific and graphical methods to solve problems of engineering practice.

- develops written, oral and presentation skills and applies these to engineering reports.

- applies graphics as a communication tool.

- describes developments in technology and their impact on engineering products.

- describes the influence of technological change on engineering and its effect on people.

- identifies the social, environmental and cultural implications of technological change in engineering.

- demonstrates the ability to work both individually and in teams.

- applies skills in analysis, synthesis and experimentation related to engineering.

© 2011 NSW Education Standards Authority

KEY TERMS AND CONCEPTS

Amorphous	Hydraulics
Anisotropy	Kinetic energy
Asbestos	Matrix
Austenite	Normal
Band brake	Plasticity
Castability	Power
Cast iron	Pearlite
Ceramic	Shear
Coefficient of friction	Sintering
Composites	Strain
Compression	Steel
Corrosion	Tension
Ductility	Torsion
Elastic limit	Toughness
Energy	True stress
Engineering stress	Ultimate tensile stress
Friction	Weldability
Hooke's law	Young's modulus

3.1 Historical and societal influences

Historical developments of braking systems including band, drum, disc, ABS, regenerative brake systems and automotive hand brake

Braking systems are amongst the most important systems in vehicles of all types. They are responsible for bringing a vehicle to rest from any speed or (once stopped) holding it in a stationary position.

A moving vehicle possesses kinetic energy. To stop a vehicle at speed (because energy cannot be created or destroyed) a way must be found to channel this energy, safely dissipate it and bring the vehicle to a halt.

A brake converts kinetic energy into thermal (heat) energy, and then dissipates this energy into the atmosphere. Brakes must do this time after time without failure, from varying speeds, under a range of loads, in all weather conditions and on all road surfaces.

The essential components of friction braking systems are a rotating part, such as a wheel, axle, disc or brake drum, and a stationary component that is forced against the rotating part to cause it to slow or stop. The stationary part is lined with a material selected for the amount of friction it can generate while still providing wear resistance and heat dissipation thus ensuring a long service life.

Additional requirements of braking systems include:

- low noise
- light weight
- ease of maintenance
- resistance to corrosion
- stable and consistent friction
- acceptable cost versus performance.

Historical developments of braking systems

The history of brakes is synonymous with the invention of the wheel. Since the invention of the wheel, one of the most difficult problems engineers encountered was the problem of bringing a moving vehicle safely to a halt.

The first brake might have been some sort of chock or anchor, or perhaps a stake attached to the chassis that could be stuck into the ground.

One of the more primitive methods employed to slow a cart was to drag a log on the end of a rope. This approach used the additional load generated by the dragging log to slow the vehicle.

Another early method of slowing carts was to drag a wedge just in front of the moving wheel. Braking was achieved when the wedge jammed against the wheel, causing the wheel to skid. One of the problems associated with this type of brake system was the difficulty in slowing both sides of the vehicle evenly. Unfortunately the cart tended to turn to one side and in some situations would overturn.

Spoon brakes

An effective braking method was not introduced until 1838 when Kirkpatrick Macmillan, a Scottish blacksmith, invented the spoon brake. This device employed a lever that pressed a block of wood against the tyre (an iron band).

Coaches and early motor vehicles adopted the spoon brake, although some used a variation in which the block contacted one of the transmission pulleys. These systems were again little more than a wooden friction block being applied to the rim of the wheel (Figure 3.1.1). Known as 'lever and shoe' type brakes they were designed to be operated by hand or foot and could even serve as a parking brake.

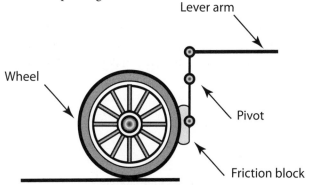

Figure 3.1.1 External spoon brake

Lever or shoe type brakes were often activated by a long lever. While a wooden friction block was adequate when pressed against the iron rims of early cart wheels the introduction of rubber tyre rims were more problematic when it came to braking. The application of the friction block quickly ground down solid rubber tyres.

Despite this, the wooden brake shoe continued to be widely used on carriages and many early autos.

A variety of different friction block materials were experimented with in an effort to increase the overall performance of the system. Unfortunately brakes remained relatively inefficient due in part to their exposure to the elements and relatively small contact area. In wet conditions these crude brakes would lose their effectiveness.

When bicycles first appeared, the only way to slow them down was to wedge your shoe against the turning wheel. Henry Ford's 1896 quadricycle also had no brakes. Ford rigged a lever that loosened a drive belt allowing the vehicle to coast to a stop. To bring the vehicle to a complete stop, Ford would often rub his feet against the front wheels. As a warning, a friend rode a bicycle in front of the vehicle to alert people with horses. The first cars to incorporate a braking system were small mine trucks running on rails. The miners engaged a lever which pressed a wooden block against the moving wheel, duplicating the braking system commonly used on carts.

Band brakes

One of the first successful automobile brakes was the external contracting type or band brake. This brake consisted of a flexible metal band or cable with a friction material lining wrapped around a drum attached to the car's back axle. The increased drag area of this design, as well as the turning of the hub which helped to tighten the strap, made this a much improved development.

The brakes were engaged by pulling a lever that pulled the band tightly about the drum. Band brakes were better than the early block type brakes but still suffered from:

- overheating

- erratic operation

- brakes unwrapping on hills and giving way

- the need for externally applied chocks on hills

- lack of development of durable friction materials

- having no protection from dirt caused bands and drums to quickly wear (brake maintenance every 320 to 480 kilometres was considered normal).

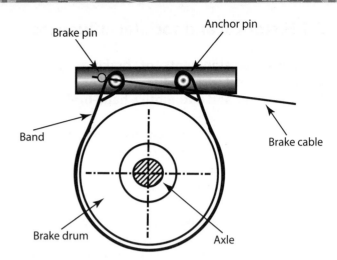

Figure 3.1.2 Lever-operated band brake using a band to tighten on a drum mounted behind the wheel

By 1904, practically all carmakers were building cars with an external band brake on each rear wheel such as the one shown in Figure 3.1.2.

Roads and tyres of the time were not good, and early cars had to share the road with horses. It was considered undesirable to fit brakes to the front wheels as testing had shown vehicles under heavy braking locked their front wheels, thus affecting steering.

In an effort to maintain steering control early automobiles were fitted with brakes only on the rear axle.

A spot-type disc brake was invented as early as 1898 by the American EA Sperry. Designed for an electric car, the system operated on the front wheels. Early disc brakes were not as effective at stopping as the contemporary drum brakes of that time and were soon forgotten.

In 1902 a British patent was awarded for a non-electric spot disc braking system similar in principle to systems in use today. However, a major disincentive was the noise generated from metal-to-metal contact between copper linings and the disc. The problem was solved in 1907 when Herbert Frood used lining pads made with asbestos.

Asbestos brake linings were quickly adopted by car manufacturers who found the new lining outlasted other friction materials by a wide margin, with brakes now lasting up to 15 000 kilometres between servicing.

In time, many of the problems associated with the external brake were overcome by the development of internal braking systems.

Drum brakes

Development of the drum brake, or more correctly the internal expanding shoe drum type brake, was a major step forward in automotive braking. In drum brakes, two semicircular brake shoes covered with a friction material are located inside a circular drum. When the brakes are applied, these brake shoes are forced outwards against the drum.

The drum brake had several advantages over the earlier external contracting band brake, including:

- better resistance to overheating

- improved response to driver demands

- greater freedom to design several different methods of applying the shoe to the drum (leading to servomotor action drum brakes, and drum brakes with more than two shoes)

- brake drums made of lightweight metals such as aluminium and fitted with a liner of cast iron, giving the added advantage of weight reduction.

Originally, drums were pressed from steel but they were susceptible to flexing and amplified squeals. Cast iron drums soon replaced steel, capitalising on the greater vibration damping characteristics of cast iron. In 1919 Hispano-Suiza introduced finned aluminium drums with iron liners in order to reduce weight while maintaining heat dissipation.

Another important development occurred in the 1920s when drum brakes were employed on all four wheels instead of only the back axle.

Up until the early 1920s the activation of the braking system, regardless of design, relied on mechanical linkages. Originally cables with long levers were used, followed by more intricate types of cable routing and connections. Hand levers gave way to the pedal, however, mechanical arrangements involving cams, cables and levers remained.

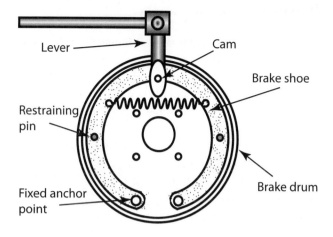

Figure 3.1.3 Lever and cam operated drum brake

The brake system shown in Figure 3.1.3 incorporates a rotating cam, which causes the shoes to expand and the linings to bear on the surrounding drum. This system has both one leading shoe and one trailing shoe. A typical brake shoe assembly is shown in Figure 3.1.4.

Brake systems have also been developed with two leading shoes activated by an individual hydraulic cylinder and piston for each shoe.

Figure 3.1.4 Drum brake—brake shoe assembly

While the mechanical systems were simple and mostly reliable, they did suffer from some disadvantages including:

- corrosion of the actuating components (particularly bad with sheathed cable systems)

- problems resulting from wear and misadjustment, producing uneven braking and often causing turning of the vehicle (yawing)

- slow response times of larger systems due to the mass of the moving components, rubbing surfaces and friction in the system.

Hydraulics

Hydraulic systems eventually eliminated cables and levers which required constant adjustment as cables stretched, rods and pins wore and brake shoes or pads wore down. Cables also suffered from mechanical failure often at the most critical of times (under heavy braking).

In 1918, Malcolm Lougheed (who later changed the spelling of his name to Lockheed) applied the principles of hydraulics to braking. Through the use of cylinders and tubing, fluid transmitted pressure against brake shoes, pushing the shoes against the drums.

In 1921, the first passenger car (the Model A Duesenberg) was equipped with four-wheel hydraulic brakes. Self-adjusting brakes appeared in the 1925 Cole.

Car makers did not adopt hydraulic braking systems either quickly or universally. By 1931 (ten years after the Model A Duesenberg), hydraulic systems were used by only a few companies. All other manufacturers persisted with cable-operated mechanical brakes. It was not until 1939 that the last major manufacturer (Ford) switched to hydraulic brakes.

Most of the disadvantages of the cable-operated mechanical systems were overcome with the introduction of hydraulic brakes. Hydraulic systems provided:

- an overall reduction in weight

- a greater freedom of design considering hydraulic lines did not need to be mounted on rigid mountings in the same fashion as cable systems and were more flexible

- distribution of equal force to each brake surface

- improved response times, and a better transfer of energy between the driver's foot and the brake.

Hydraulic systems also allowed the development of lightweight and effective power assistance devices.

Disc brakes

Disc brake systems were used during World War II on aircraft. This system was later adapted for use in automotive applications, first on racing cars in 1952, then in production cars in 1956. Disc brakes did not become standard on European cars until the 1950s, and were not adopted by American manufacturers in mass produced non-performance cars until around 1965.

Disc brakes (Figure 3.1.5) have greater stopping power than drum brakes and consist of a metal disc or rotor that is connected to the wheel via the wheel nuts.

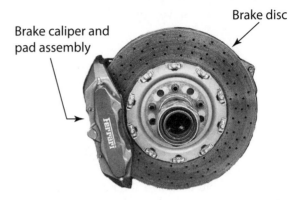

Brake disc

Brake caliper and pad assembly

Figure 3.1.5 Disc brake assembly

A device called a caliper holds two friction pads, one on either side of the rotor. Operated hydraulically the friction pads are driven by two opposing pistons. When hydraulic pressure is created, the pads are forced against the rotating metal disc (rotor), exerting a normal force on each contact surface. These two normal forces cancel one another axially but generate tangential frictional resistance which opposes the disc's, and therefore the wheel's motion. A typical disc pad assembly is shown in Figure 3.1.6.

Disc brakes are considered superior to drum brakes because they:

- do not trap water

- are simpler in design

- dissipate heat more quickly

- provide better braking performance

- handle higher braking temperatures

- allow greater air ventilation (cooling)

- are significantly better in their resistance to brake fade due to heat dissipation.

Figure 3.1.6 Disc pad assembly, image by Treemonster86

Both drum and disc brakes contain several features to dissipate the large amount of heat produced by friction. To aid heat dissipation rates many rotors are vented and/ or have cooling fins sandwiched between the faces of the rotor (Figure 3.1.7).

Overheating of the brake drums and shoes causes the brakes to fade and lose their effectiveness when held in engagement for a considerable length of time.

If the coefficient of friction between pad and rotor materials is raised, then so is the frictional resisting force, hence the sourcing of materials with high coefficients of friction for braking surfaces.

As a design consideration, automotive engineers design disc brakes with two contacting surfaces (pads) to be forced against the rotor, thus effectively doubling the resisting force (Figure 3.1.7).

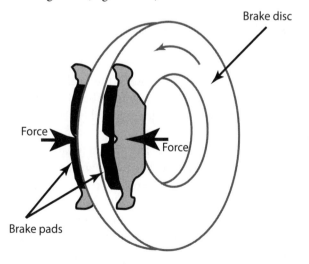

Figure 3.1.7 Normal forces applied to either side of brake disc

In motorcycles, gyroscopic effects due to weight become an issue (the heavier the wheel and brake unit, the more gyroscopic resistance to changes in direction). Thus a motorcycle's steering requires higher effort with heavier drum brakes than with lighter discs.

Advances in tyres, suspension, hydraulic systems and brake boosters have also made it possible to decelerate faster without locking up.

Through the use of hydraulics, the introduction of greater braking pressures (kPa exerted by the shoe or pad against the drum or rotor) has allowed more force to be available. This development alone allows the swept area (square millimetres of contact between shoe or pad and rotor or disc) to be reduced, resulting in less material in use and lighter designs.

Anti-lock braking systems

Anti-lock braking systems (ABS) have been around for some time. Patent applications were made for mechanical versions in the 1920s.

The first anti-lock braking system was developed by the Frenchman Gabriel Voisin in 1929 for use in aircraft. The first implementation of ABS in cars was in 1936 when Bosch and Mercedes Benz introduced the first (albeit slow responding) electronic ABS on Mercedes Benz cars. The first of the modern ABS devices was developed by Chrysler and Bendix in 1971.

ABS are designed to reduce braking distances on vehicles by preventing wheels 'locking up'. This maintains tyre grip and traction between the tyres and the road surface by preventing skidding. They operate using a microprocessor to monitor and control the application of the brakes. When braking, the processor monitors rpm and braking pressure on each of the vehicle's wheels. Using this information, measured amounts of pressure are sent to each wheel in the form of hydraulic pulses (at speeds of up to 40 times per second) to the calipers. These pulses achieve the desired braking pressure without allowing the wheels to lock up. This process greatly increases control during hard deceleration (a locked wheel cannot be steered) and reduces stopping distances. It also serves to reduce damage to tyres.

Inherent problems of 'irregularities' at the friction surfaces such as disc thickness variations, drums 'out of round' and 'hot spots' reduced the efficiency of ABS until the advent of electronic control systems.

Today these systems are commonplace on most passenger vehicles and not only prevent wheel locking but also make adjustment to front-to-rear brake bias.

Regenerative brakes

In traditionally powered vehicles under braking, all of the energy expended is wasted as heat in the brakes. Regenerative braking however recaptures some of the vehicle's momentum as electrical energy.

At this time this feature is found only in electric vehicles and hybrid-electric cars where systems take advantage of the fact that opposing magnetic fields created within the electric motor itself will slow the vehicle. Regenerative braking occurs whenever a driver eases back on the accelerator or applies the brakes steadily. Regenerative braking handles up to 80% of all vehicle braking situations.

When a driver releases the accelerator pedal, the electric motor changes into a generator, recapturing the energy from the moving car and transforming it back into electricity. The extra electricity is then used to recharge and extend the driving range of the batteries. Advantages of this system include:

- reduced emissions

- improved fuel economy

- extended life of the battery pack

- less wear on brake drums, rotors and pads

- the system can be added to existing powertrains

- reduced need for using the vehicle's hydraulic brakes.

While the concept appears simple and uncomplicated this is far from the truth. Some of the problems associated with these systems currently include:

- noise generated by the system

- the need for different driving techniques

- limited to electric or hybrid-electric vehicles

- leakage problems with seals and valves

- removing air from hydraulic fluid can be difficult

- additional components including pulse suppressors, filters and an electric circulator pump for cooling the main pump/motor

- applications only on driven wheels, therefore the need to be coupled with ABS.

Kinetic energy recovery systems (KERS) are another form of of braking where energy may be stored either in a flywheel, battery or super capacitor.

Hand brakes

All vehicles have a hand brake or parking brake used to lock the wheels when the vehicle is parked. Parking brakes use levers and cables, rather than hydraulics, to activate and are most often connected to the rear brakes only. In a total hydraulic failure, the parking brake could be used as an emergency brake to stop the vehicle.

Air brakes

Air brakes have advantages over hydraulic brakes in that they provide a 'cushion' to the brake system due to the compressibility of air.

Compared with hydraulic systems, air brakes are significantly more expensive at the time of installation and in their maintenance but have still been widely adopted by heavy transport industries.

Brake-by-wire systems

Car makers are experimenting with replacing mechanical, pedal-pressure-powered brakes with systems that work electronically through the introduction of brake-by-wire systems.

These electronic braking systems use sensors to determine how hard and quickly the brake pedal is pushed. They electronically customise braking force to each wheel according to its stopping ability at that time.

Issues arise in that it is the 'feel' in a standard power-assisted brake system which drivers are accustomed to, i.e. as the pedal effort increases, pedal travel also increases. In an effort to preserve this feel in electronic systems 'something' is required to provide feedback to the driver. Engineers are currently developing a pedal feel emulator that can be 'tuned' to produce responsive feedback at the pedal.

As a fail-safe, this system can also be used to operate a standard hydraulic brake system if the by-wire system fails. Unfortunately, in this case pedal effort would be very high, making this an emergency backup system only. Brake-by-wire systems are being developed to offer a variety of other functions and may include the following.

- Electronic brake prefill. In emergency situations, if a driver's foot is lifted off the accelerator suddenly this system brings the brake pads into contact with the discs in anticipation of the driver's next braking action.

- Brake disc wiping. Intended to counter the problem of moisture build-up in wet conditions this system momentarily touches the brake pads against the discs at regular intervals.

- 'Hill-hold-control stops unintentional roll-back on hill starts.

- 'Soft stop' reduces braking pressure just before the vehicle comes to rest thus smoothing out the stopping process.

Further reading

Birch, TW, *Automotive braking systems* (3rd ed.), Delmar, Albany NY, 1998

Dirksen, S, 'Brakes' (n.d) from 'History of the Brake', retrieved 3 July 2013 from Bryant website, www.web.bryant.edu/~ehu/h364proj/sprg_97/dirksen/brakes.html

Johnson, A, *Hitting the brakes: Engineering design and the production of knowledge*, Duke University Press, Durham, 2009

Patrascu, D, 'Braking systems history', 2009, retrieved 3 July 2013 from Auto Evolution website, www.autoevolution.com/news/braking-systemshistory-6933.html

Engineering innovations in braking systems and their effect on people's lives

Early in the 19th century the lack of reliable, low-cost transportation was a major barrier to industrial development. The most common form of transportation was the horse-drawn coach. Unfortunately it was slow (travelling at just six kilometres an hour), cumbersome and uncomfortable for passengers. Prior to effective brake development, many different forms of carts and wagons were built relying on animal power to both accelerate and decelerate the vehicle.

The internal combustion engine continued to replace the horse as the preferred means of transport, but as roads improved and increasingly heavier cars began to be driven at higher speeds, the problem of safely stopping automobiles became critical to their success. Just as cars became more technologically sophisticated, so too did their braking systems.

In an effort to compare existing and newly developed brake systems, Ransom Olds arranged a comparative test in 1902 on an unpaved road in New York City. The test compared the newly developed band-brake (a single flexible stainless-steel band wrapped around a drum on the rear axle), against the tyre-brake of a four-horse coach and the internal drum brake of a Victorian horseless carriage.

Olds had entered his car in the Blue Ribbon Contest (a 100-mile race) and wanted to be sure his external brake was a match for the Victorian expanding-shoe internal drum design and the coach's tyre brake (a pad that was applied to the tyre by a long lever).

From a speed of 24 kph, the Oldsmobile stopped in 7 metres, the Victoria in 11 metres and the horses (which may not have been going 22 kph but had no engine braking to aid them) in 21 metres.

This public display and the winning of two of nine blue ribbons made such an impression on other manufacturers that by 1903 most had adopted this system of braking.

Environmental implications from the use of materials in braking systems

Before the introduction of disc brakes, most brake linings contained asbestos fibre. Since the late 1980s attempts have been made to discontinue the use of asbestos in brake linings due to health concerns.

Asbestos is the name applied to a group of six different minerals (amosite, chrysotile, tremolite, actinolite, anthophyllite and crocidolite) occurring naturally in the environment. The most common mineral type is white, also known as chrysotile. Asbestos is characterised by long, thin fibres appearing similar to fibreglass. Asbestos fibres are strong and are resistant to heat and chemicals. These properties make asbestos suitable for a wide range of products including building materials, friction products and heat-resistant fabrics. Because the fibres are so resistant to chemical attack they are also very stable in the environment: they do not evaporate in air or dissolve in water, and are not broken down over time.

Medical research has shown that asbestos fibres can lodge in the lungs and induce adverse respiratory conditions such as mesothelioma (cancer of the thin membrane that surrounds the lung and other internal organs). In the USA, the Environmental Protection Agency announced a proposed ban on asbestos use (1986).

The ban would have required all new vehicles to have non-asbestos brakes by 1993, and the aftermarket would also have to convert to non-asbestos materials.

Even though the EPA's proposed ban was overturned in the Federal Court there was a major shift away from asbestos by vehicle manufacturers. However, asbestos brake products are still used even though it is commonly believed asbestos was replaced by non-asbestos organics years ago.

Despite health concerns, asbestos is still used because it is an economical fibre for low temperature brake applications. Asbestos-related brake lining health risks include those from manufacturing, usage and replacement. Inhalation of asbestos fibres is the type of exposure that is most likely to cause adverse health effects for people. Inhalation of fibres may occur if:

- workers in industries that use raw materials or products containing chrysotile (e.g. manufacture of friction materials) inhale fibres suspended in the air

- family members are exposed to chrysotile fibres when workers carry fibres home on their clothes

- people living or working near chrysotile-related operations inhale fibres that enter the environment during the production process

- fibres are swallowed when eating in areas where chrysotile fibres are in the air or drinking water contaminated with fibres.

The benefits associated with the prohibition of chrysotile (white asbestos) in brake friction materials are based around the reduction of health risks for workers engaged in the processing of chrysotile or in the maintenance of vehicle braking systems. Within the European Union (EU) chrysotile has been assigned the highest category of carcinogen.

Literally hundreds of different natural and synthetic fibres are now used in brake linings. The use of substitute fibres in brake linings has prompted engineers to design vehicles with 'safe' brakes using non-asbestos brake linings. This has involved 'balancing' existing brake systems for the new brake lining compositions, and even designing new brake assemblies

In 1993, the World Health Organization (WHO) Environmental Health Criteria 151 reported that, 'all fibres that are respirable and bio-persistent must undergo testing for toxicity and carcinogenicity.'

Many fibres used in non-asbestos brake linings have been flagged at WHO meetings as 'probably or possibly carcinogenic.' These include refractory ceramic fibres, Kevlar pulp, mineral wool, glass fibres, phosphate fibres and carbon fibres. Disposal of dust and linings 'hard waste' in labelled and sealed bags is done by arrangement with the local authorities who have strict regulations for disposal.

A significant numbers of brake pads currently in use also contain copper. Breathing of copper particles (such as those dust particles produced during braking) has been known to cause disruption of the body's normal enzymatic activity. Copper-containing dust entering the environment can also find its way into the water table either via stormwater or airborne particle deposition.

Many manufacturers of anti-lock braking systems have also removed or redesigned their mechanisms to remove the reliance on mercury switches.

3.2 Engineering mechanics and hydraulics

Static friction

Our ability to move in a controlled manner relies on friction. Walking or any form of purposeful transport, short of rocket propulsion, would be impossible.

Whenever one surface moves over another a resistance is set up opposing its motion. This resisting force is called friction. The frictional force opposes the direction of an applied force (whether the object is moving or stationary) or motion.

Even though contacting surfaces may look smooth, at the microscopic level they are actually quite uneven. It is these surface irregularities (peaks and troughs) that catch and interlock, causing a resistance to movement between surfaces.

The contacting surfaces remain immovable until the applied force overcomes the surface resistance and one surface either abrades or rides up over the irregularities. For this reason it usually takes more force to initiate movement than it does to keep an object moving. These forces relative to static or dynamic situations generate appropriate coefficients of friction μ_s and μ_k.

The following rules apply to friction.

- Frictional force always acts opposite to the direction in which a body tends to move.

- Friction cannot exceed a certain value (limiting friction) for two surfaces.

- The coefficient of friction (μ) varies according to the materials in contact and the relative roughness of their surfaces.

- The coefficient of friction is independent of the area of contact.

- Coefficients of friction may be reduced by a thin film of appropriate liquid between surfaces in contact.

- The coefficient of kinetic or sliding friction (μ_k) is less than the coefficient of static friction (μ_s).

In addition to the types of materials in contact, the physical state of the contacting surfaces also affects their frictional resistance. Materials that have had their surfaces smoothed or polished will have lower coefficients of friction than when in their original or roughened state. Frictional resistance will also vary if the surfaces are wet, dry, icy or oily. Clearly road surface conditions as well as brake pad and disc combinations all affect the frictional performance of braking in cars.

Calculating friction

The force resisting friction (F_R) is expressed as a relationship between the mass of the object and the coefficient of friction. Mathematically it can be expressed as:

$F_R = \mu N$ where

F_R = force resisting friction

N = force normal to the surface

μ = coefficient of friction.

A direct consequence of this relationship is that as the weight of an object increases so does the frictional resisting force. The perpendicular force F_N is often expressed as N for simplicity as shown in Figure 3. 2.1. As demonstrated in Figure 3.2.1 and shown in the calculation below, if the coefficient were 0.3 then it would take 60 newtons of force to slide the 20 kg block.

$$F_R = \mu N$$

$$F_R = 0.3 \times 200$$

$$F_R = 60 \text{ N}$$

Data
mg = 20 × 10
= 200 N

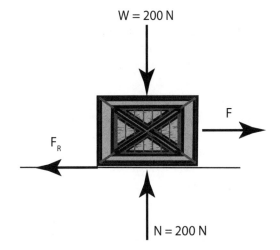

Figure 3.2.1 Sliding block and frictional resistance

If the resultant of the normal reaction and the friction force is found then the true reaction between the block and the surface is obtained. From Figure 3.2.2 it can be seen that the reaction is now at angle φ.

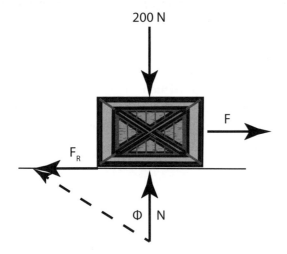

Figure 3.2.2 Angle of friction

Using trigonometry:

$$\tan \phi = F_R \div N$$

$$\therefore F_R = \tan \phi \times N$$

$$\text{but } F_R = \mu N$$

$$\therefore \tan \phi = \mu$$

The Greek letter φ (phi) is used to identify the angle of friction while tan φ generates the coefficient of friction (μ).

Stress and strain

Stress is defined as the internal force exerted by one part of an elastic body upon the adjoining part. Strain relates to the deformation or change in dimensional size or form occasioned by the stressing forces.

Young's modulus of elasticity is used to measure the stiffness of a material and as a measurement in engineering of the capacity of metals and other materials to withstand stress and strain.

Tension and compression

When a body is subjected to a pulling or stretching force it is said to be in tension, or undergoing tensile stress. Bodies subjected to pushing or squashing forces are said to be in compression or undergoing compressive stress.

Shear, or shearing stress, results when a force tends to weaken or break a body in a cross-sectional form. Torsion, or torsional stresses, occur when the external forces tend to twist a body around an axis.

Stress (σ) is the relationship between an applied load and a material's cross-sectional area and is measured in N/mm² or megapascals (MPa).

$$\text{Stress} = \text{load} / \text{area}$$

Stress therefore has the units of N/m² or N/mm² where:

$$1 \text{ N/m}^2 = 1 \text{ pascal (Pa) and}$$
$$1 \text{ N/mm}^2 = 1 \text{ MPa}$$

Strain (ε) is an engineering quantity that measures the change in length of a body (extension) relative to its original length when subjected to a load:

$$\text{Strain} = \Delta \text{ length} \div \text{original length}$$

Strain is a dimensionless quantity because the units in the numerator and denominator are the same and therefore cancel each other out.

Tensile stresses are those produced by forces trying to pull apart or lengthen a material.

Compressive stresses are those produced by forces trying to compress or reduce the length of a material.

Shear stresses are those produced by forces trying to slide one part of the material over the other. Shear stresses may be single, double or punching. Figure 3.2.3 displays the three fundamental types of stress.

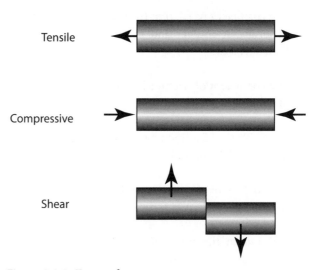

Figure 3.2.3 Types of stress

Calculations involving stress (σ) and strain (ε)

Note: The standard unit for stress in the SI system is the pascal, which is defined as 1 N/m^2. In the following calculations areas are calculated in mm^2 because of their size. Calculations performed using N/mm^2 directly translate as megapascals i.e. $1 \text{ N/mm}^2 = 1 \text{ MPa}$.

Tensile stress

Calculate the stress (σ) created in a 10 mm diameter brake rod if it is subjected to a load of 1.1 kN when the brake is applied.

$$\text{Data}$$
$$\text{Load} = 1.1 \times 10^3 \text{ N}$$
$$\text{Diameter} = 10 \text{ mm}$$
$$\text{Area} = \pi \times 10^2 \div 4$$
$$= 78.54 \text{ mm}^2$$

$$\sigma = \text{load} \div \text{area}$$
$$= 1.1 \times 10^3 \div 78.54$$
$$= 14 \text{ N/mm}^2$$
$$= 14 \text{ MPa}$$

Compressive stress

A force of 12 kN is applied to a 1 cm diameter punch used to create holes in a 8 mm thick steel plate used for brake shoes. Calculate the shear stress in the plate and the compressive stress in the punch.

Note: When punching a hole, the shear area is not the cross-sectional area but the area defined by the perimeter of the punch (πd, where the shearing action takes place) multiplied by the thickness of the material to be sheared.

$$\text{Data}$$
$$\text{Load} = 12{,}000 \text{ N}$$
$$\text{Diameter} = 10 \text{ mm}$$
$$\text{Plate thickness} = 8 \text{ mm}$$
$$\text{Shear area} = \pi \times d \times h$$
$$= 251.33 \text{ mm}^2$$
$$\text{Punch area} = \pi \times 10^2 \div 4$$
$$= 78.54 \text{ mm}^2$$

$$\sigma_S = \text{load} \div \text{area of shear}$$
$$= 12 \times 10^3 \div 251.33$$
$$= 47.75 \text{ N/mm}^2 \text{ or } 47.75 \text{ MPa}$$

$$\sigma_C = \text{load} \div \text{area}$$
$$= 12 \times 10^3 \div 78.54$$
$$= 152.7 \text{ N/mm}^2 \text{ or } 152.7 \text{ MPa}$$

Strain

The identical 10 mm brake rod mentioned above is exactly 2 m long and under load extends 1.5 mm. Calculate the strain present in the rod.

$$\text{Data}$$
$$\text{Length} = 2 \times 10^3 \text{ mm}$$
$$\text{Extension} = 1.5 \text{ mm}$$
$$\text{Diameter} = 10 \text{ mm}$$

$$\text{Strain} = \text{extension} \div \text{original length}$$
$$= 1.5 \div 2.0 \times 10^3$$
$$= 0.00075$$
$$= 75 \times 10^{-5} \text{ or } 7.5 \times 10^{-4}$$

As long as the units used are consistent there is no need to convert millimetres into metres. These calculations are just as appropriate for compressive strain.

Single shear stress

In this situation (see Figure 3.2.4) a load of 23 kN is attempting to shear a 12 mm rivet holding a brake pad/backing plate assembly together. The area in shear is the cross-sectional area of the rivet.

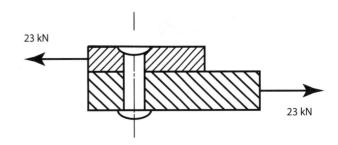

Figure 3.2.4 Pin in single shear

$$\text{Data}$$
$$\text{Pin diameter} = 12 \text{ mm}$$

$$\text{Shear area} = \pi \times 12^2 \div 4$$
$$= 113.1 \text{ mm}^2$$

$$\text{Shear stress} = \text{load} \div \text{area}$$
$$= 23 \times 10^3 \div 113.1$$
$$= 203.36 \text{ N/mm}^2$$
$$= 203.36 \text{ MPa}$$

Loads and extension

Testing of sample pieces to destruction in either tension or compression will produce data that can be plotted to produce a curve better known as a load-extension diagram. A universal testing machine such as the one shown in Figure 3.2.5 is used to produce this information.

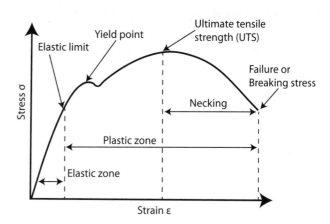

Figure 3.2.6 Typical stress-strain diagram

Ultimate tensile stress

When stress passes the limit of a material's elasticity it continues into the plastic zone. Within the plastic zone all deformation is permanent. When the stress-strain curve reaches the maximum height, this point is called the ultimate tensile strength (UTS).

Ductile materials often 'neck' (reduce in cross-sectional area) while continuing to elongate before fracture (Figure 3.2.7). Both elongation and reduction of area are measures of ductility.

Temperature also affects tensile properties: as environmental temperature increases, tensile values decrease.

Figure 3.2.5 Universal testing machine

Tension and compression

Tensile and compressive loads may be transferred through the universal testing machine. Under these conditions many of the mechanical properties of a material can be obtained from its load/extension diagram, including but not limited to:

- breaking force

- modulus of stiffness

- ultimate tensile strength

- toughness (area under the graph).

Load/extension diagram

Data gathered from this test may later be translated into a stress-strain diagram such as the diagram shown for low carbon steel in Figure 3.2.6.

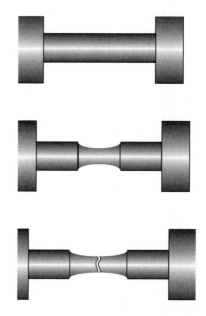

Figure 3.2.7 Progressive tensile test samples showing necking and failure

Failure

The force required to break the test piece from ductile materials such as mild steel is much less than the UTS due to the effects of necking.

Toughness

A material's toughness can be gauged by the area under the stress-strain curve. The greater the area, the tougher the material, and the greater the amount of energy required before failure.

Hooke's law

Hooke's law states; 'stress is directly proportional to strain within the proportional limit.' From this, the mathematical relationship can be expressed as:

$$Stress = k \times Strain$$

or

$$k = Stress/Strain$$

where k is a constant of proportionality. This constant is known as Young's modulus (E) and has the units of gigapascals (GPa) or 10^3 megapascals (MPa).

Young's modulus

The modulus of elasticity provides an indication of the stiffness of a material. The gradient of the straight-line section (elastic region) of the stress-strain curve indicates the relative stiffness of the material i.e. the steeper the gradient the stiffer the material. Figure 3.2.8 shows examples of typical curves showing distinct properties:

a) elastic material obeying Hooke's law

b) ductile material displaying plastic deformation.

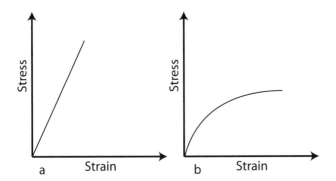

Figure 3.2.8 Typical stress-strain curves

True stress vs. engineering stress

'Engineering stress' is calculated using the ratio of the applied load to the undeformed (original) cross-sectional area. This method ceases to be an accurate measure when large amounts of deformation take place.

'True stress' is defined as the ratio of the applied load (L) to the instantaneous cross-sectional area (A). True stress and strain are practically indistinguishable from engineering stress and strain at small deformations, yet as shown in Figure 3.2.9 it can be seen that as the strain becomes large and the cross-sectional area of the specimen decreases, the true stress becomes much larger than the engineering stress.

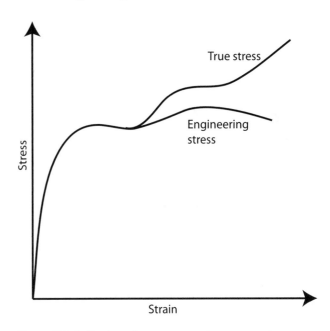

Figure 3.2.9 Engineering stress-strain curve vs. true stress-strain curve

Work, power, energy, principle of the conservation of energy

Energy is the ability to do work. Kinetic energy (like all forms of energy) is measured in joules. Kinetic energy is calculated using the formula:

$$KE = \tfrac{1}{2}\,mv^2$$

From this formula it can be seen that the two factors in the creation of a car's kinetic energy are the car's velocity and the car's mass. To see the relationship between these variables a series of data points have been plotted.

Figure 3.2.10 shows an energy versus mass graph. This graph shows the relationship between the mass of a car and the total kinetic energy that the car produces when the velocity is held at a constant 22.2 metres per second. Plotted against this is a range of test vehicles whose masses vary from 800 to 2100 kg.

The trend for this graph (Figure 3.2.10) is a constant gradient showing the growth in kinetic energy produced through the increasing mass of the car.

Alternatively, the energy versus velocity graph shown in Figure 3.2.11 shows how changing velocities while maintaining a constant mass affects kinetic energy.

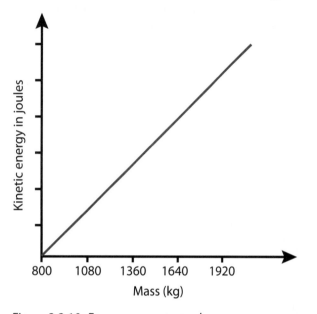

Figure 3.2.10 Energy vs. mass graph

The trend for the graph (Figure 3.2.11) shows non-linear growth in the amount of kinetic energy produced as the velocity of the vehicle increases.

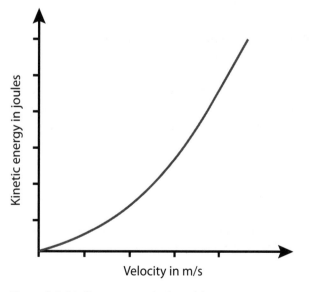

Figure 3.2.11 Energy vs. velocity with constant mass

Comparing Figures 3.2.10 and 3.2.11 it can be seen that the kinetic energy of a car is more greatly affected by changes in velocity than changes to its mass. Engineers take these relationships into account when designing both cars and braking systems.

Conservation of energy, velocity and heat

Brakes convert the energy of motion (kinetic energy) into thermal or heat energy. This is a direct application of the law of conservation of energy i.e. 'energy is neither created nor destroyed simply converted from one form to another.'

Because energy can be neither created nor destroyed, all of the kinetic energy (KE) from the car must be almost completely turned into heat (Q). Since the enemy of all braking systems is excessive heat it is important for engineers to be able to calculate heat generated by braking so they can attempt to reduce its effects:

$$KE = \tfrac{1}{2}\, mv^2$$

$$KE = (\tfrac{1}{2}) \times (\text{vehicle mass}) \times (\text{velocity of the vehicle})^2$$

From the above equations the velocity of the vehicle squared will be proportional to the temperature rise in the brakes.

A simple calculation will show that as the velocity of the vehicle increases so does the energy or work required to stop the vehicle.

Data
Vehicle mass = 1.2 t or 1200 kg
velocity or v_1 = 60 km/h or 16.66 m/s
v_2 = 90 km/h or 25 m/s

$$KE = \tfrac{1}{2}\, mv_1^2$$

$$= \tfrac{1}{2} \times 1200 \times (16.66)^2$$

$$= 166\ 533.36 \text{ J or } 166.53 \text{ kJ}$$

$$KE = \tfrac{1}{2}\, mv_2^2$$

$$= \tfrac{1}{2} \times 1200 \times (25)^2$$

$$= 375\ 000 \text{ J or } 375 \text{ kJ}$$

The simple calculations shown above indicate a 50% change in velocity (e.g. 60 km/h to 90 km/h). The energy (work) required will be transformed into heat energy. It should be noted that a 50% increase in velocity causes a 125% increase in energy. This heat energy is the work done by the brakes. The actual temperatures generated will be determined by how hard the brakes are applied and the duration of the braking. It can be seen that the velocity of a vehicle has a huge impact on the work required to bring a vehicle to a stop and brake temperatures and therefore performance and longevity.

Work

When work is done upon an object by an external force, the total mechanical energy (KE + PE) of that object is changed. If the work is 'positive work', then the object will gain energy. If the work is 'negative work', then the object will lose energy. The gain or loss in energy can be in the form of potential energy, kinetic energy or both. Under such circumstances, the work done will be equal to the change in mechanical energy of the object.

Worked example 1

Calculate the energy required to accelerate a 1200 kg car from 0 to 100 km/h in 8 seconds.

Data
$m = 1200$ kg
$t = 8$ s
$v_I = 0$
$v_F = 100$ km/h or 27.8 m/s

The work done by the car engine is equal to the change in kinetic energy of the car therefore:

$$\text{Work} = \text{Final KE} - \text{Initial KE}$$

$$= \tfrac{1}{2}\,mv_F^2 - \tfrac{1}{2}\,mv_I^2$$

$$= \tfrac{1}{2} \times 1200 \times (27.8)^2 - \tfrac{1}{2} \times 1200 \times (0)^2$$

$$= 600 \times 772.84 - 0$$

$$= 463\,704 \text{ J} \quad\text{or}\quad 463.7 \text{ kJ}$$

Worked example 2

Calculate the work done by a car's brakes in bringing a 1.25 tonne vehicle to a stop from a speed of 60 km/h.

Data
$m = 1250$ kg
$v_I = 0$
$v_F = 60$ km/h or 16.67 m/s

$$\text{Work done} = \text{Final KE} - \text{Initial KE}$$

$$= \tfrac{1}{2}\,mv_F^2 - \tfrac{1}{2}\,mv_I^2$$

$$= \tfrac{1}{2} \times 1250 \times (0)^2 - \tfrac{1}{2}\,1250 \times (16.67)^2$$

$$= 0 - 173\,680.5625$$

$$= 173\,680.56 \text{ J or } 173.68 \text{ kJ}$$

Note: Work done when braking a vehicle produces a negative work result as energy is removed from the system in the form of heat.

Power

Power (P) is the rate of doing work and is measured in watts.

$$P = W \div t$$

$$1 \text{ Watt} = 1 \text{ Joule/s}$$

On occasions, depending on the data provided, the formula $P = F \times s \div t$ may be used. This equation is applicable because $F \times s = W$.

Similarly $P = F \times v$ may also be used because velocity is equal to displacement divided by time.

Worked example

Calculate how much power is needed to accelerate an 1100 kg car from 60 km/h to 100 km/h in 20 seconds.

Data
$m = 1100$ kg
$t = 20$ s
$v_I = 60$ km/h 16.7 m/s
$v_F = 100$ km/h or 27.8 m/s

$$\text{Work} = \text{Final KE} - \text{Initial KE}$$

$$= \tfrac{1}{2}\,mv_F^2 - \tfrac{1}{2}\,mv_I^2$$

$$= \tfrac{1}{2} \times 1100 \times (27.8)^2 - \tfrac{1}{2} \times 1100 \times (16.7)^2$$

$$= 550 \times 772.84 - 550 \times 278.89$$

$$= 425\,062 - 153\,389.5$$

$$= 271\,672.5 \text{ J or } 271.67 \text{ kJ}$$

Mechanics of braking systems

In braking systems the function of the brake pedal assembly is to harness and multiply the force exerted by the driver's foot. It achieves this through the use of a simple lever. In the situation shown below (Figure 3.2.12) the pivot is at the top of the lever arm while the pedal is at the opposite end. The output (whether it be cable, rod or hydraulic line) is located somewhere in-between. Figure 3.2.12 shows a driver exerting a force of 300 N on the pedal and generating an output force of 900 N through the leverage created. The mechanical advantage of this system is 3:1.

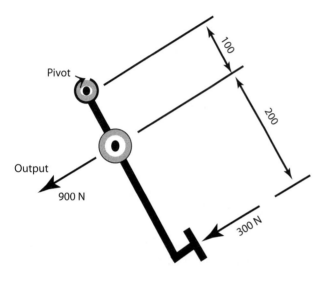

Figure 3.2.12 Brake pedal lever

Worked example

If the input force were changed to 250 N and the lever arm ratios stayed the same the calculation would appear:

Data
Force out = F_O
Force input = F_I = 250 N
Perpendicular distance = d_1 = 100
Perpendicular distance = d_2 = 300

$$F_O \times d_1 = F_I \times d_2$$

$$F_O \times 100 = 250 \times 300$$

$$F_O = 250 \times 0.3 \div 0.1$$

$$F_O = 750 \text{ N}$$

To generate the forces required for braking, a greater mechanical advantage is required than can be

produced through a simple lever arrangement (Figure 3.2.13). Lengthening the pedal lever arm would prove impractical, so another system is required to amplify the pedal pressure greater than can be achieved by the lever alone.

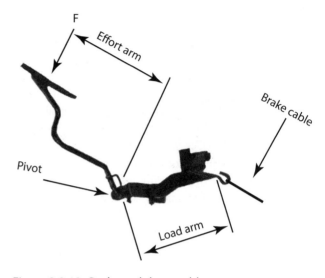

Figure 3.2.13 Brake pedal assembly

Mechanical advantage can be greatly increased through the use of a hydraulic system. Vehicle braking systems also have some physical principles common to all hydraulic designs (Figure 3.2.14).

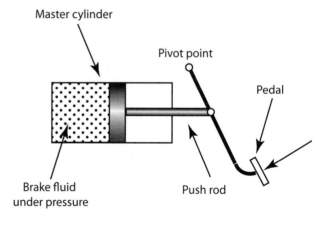

Figure 3.2.14 Brake master cylinder

Fluid mechanics

Pascal's principle

A fluid is a collection of randomly arranged molecules held together by weak cohesive forces and the forces exerted by the walls of a container. Both gases and liquids are fluids. Fluid systems are a means of transmitting power from one location to another.

Hydraulic systems use liquids as their basis because liquids are fluids that cannot be compressed and they obey Pascal's principle which states:

'any change in pressure applied to a completely enclosed fluid is transmitted undiminished to all parts of the fluid and the enclosing walls.'

Pascal's principle applies to all hydraulic systems no matter what the shape of the container or system.

Hydrostatic pressure and applications to braking systems

Hydraulic braking systems work because they rely on the fact that when the pedal is depressed, force on the master cylinder piston distributes pressure equally throughout the system. The size of the hydraulic pistons at the wheels relative to the master cylinder determines how much force the pressure in the system can apply at the wheel.

The basic functioning of an hydraulic braking system can best be explained through Figure 3.2.15. Hydraulic systems produce large amplifications of force simply by translating pressure from a smaller (diameter) input cylinder to a larger (diameter) output cylinder. Due to Pascal's principle and the fact that the pressure is the same everywhere in the fluid, the larger area generates a much larger total output force. In simpler terms the force per unit area (pressure) is the same throughout the fluid but in the larger cylinder is now distributed over a larger area and therefore increased. This is represented by rearranging the pressure formula:

$$P = F \div A \text{ to } F = PA$$

Because the pressure stayed the same in the second cylinder but area was increased, a larger resultant force was generated, inducing a mechanical advantage. Pascal's principle allows braking systems to generate large amounts of force from the application of a much smaller force. The greater the differences in the areas of the cylinders, the greater the potential force output of the big cylinder.

Note: Pascal's principle is independent of the shape and size of the container and therefore the size of the connecting tubing also has no relevance other than the fact that it must be unobstructed to allow full delivery of pressure equivalence. Hydraulic systems can also be thought of in terms of levers. Since the force is multiplied, the mechanical advantage can be found by arranging terms in the following fashion.

$$MA = D_2^2 \div D_1^2 \text{ or } A_2 \div A_1$$

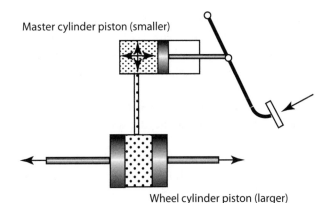

Master cylinder piston (smaller)

Wheel cylinder piston (larger)

Figure 3.2.15 Brake master cylinder

Hydraulic pressure allows wheels on opposite sides of the car to get equal braking. This assists the car to stop in a straight line without pulling to one side (Figure 3.2.16).

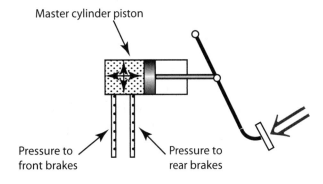

Master cylinder piston

Pressure to front brakes

Pressure to rear brakes

Figure 3.2.16 Hydraulic distribution

Worked example

If the foot pedal shown in Figure 3.2.16 applies a mechanical advantage of 5 to the master cylinder (Ø50), which in turn is connected to the brake cylinder (Ø75), determine the force applied at the pads if 30 N is applied at the foot pedal.

Hydraulic MA = $D_2^2 \div D_1^2$ Pedal MA = 5

$$= 75^2 \div 50^2 = 2.25$$

Total MA = 5 × 2.25 = 11.25 N

$$MA = \frac{L}{E} \text{ or } L = MA \times E$$

11.25 × 30 = 337.5 N at the pads

3.3 Engineering materials

Materials for braking systems

History records the use of many kinds of materials for brakes. The earliest spoon brakes used wooden blocks, sometimes supplemented with leather lining, whereas today high technology carbon composites are regularly employed. It is not just the development and introduction of new friction materials that has seen the evolution of braking systems but also the development of production methods and computer monitoring systems.

Herbert Frood and his company Ferodo started experimenting with friction materials for brakes in the late 19th century in England. Using a water wheel powered friction test machine, Frood tested a variety of materials and bonding agents. Through his pioneering experiments the manufacture of woven cotton brakes impregnated with a bitumen solution was used for both wagon wheels as well as early automobiles. However, with the advent of the new motorised vehicles, there was a realisation that harder-wearing and heavier duty brakes were needed and in 1908 he tested resin-impregnated woven asbestos reinforced with brass wire.

Even though the first brake lining materials were woven they were soon replaced (1920s) by moulded materials that contained chrysotile asbestos fibres. Although the earliest drum brake systems had iron shoes against steel, some strange materials were also used such as walrus hide linings in the English Wolseley.

Even today many brake materials still contain organic-based materials, like polymers and plant fibres. A derivative of the cashew nut known as friction dust has the ability to absorb the heat created by friction while retaining braking efficiency. It also improves resilience in the binding matrix and reduces brake noise. There are literally thousands of brake material additives and limitless combinations. Automotive engineers often combine five to 20 different material ingredients to form complex composite friction materials. The role of additives is to provide enhanced:

- durability

- wear control

- friction stability

- noise and vibration minimisation.

Friction stability refers to the brake pad's friction coefficient ability to remain high under hot, cold, wet and dry conditions at various braking speeds.

The functional properties additives provide are determined by more than composition since individual constituent form, distribution and particle size effects friction performance and wear behaviour. Nevertheless, brake materials and additives can be grouped according to their function, as outlined below.

- Fillers and reinforcements.

- Binding materials, often a phenolic matrix to hold the constituents together.

- Abrasives help maintain the cleanliness of mating surfaces and control the build-up of friction films (generated by surfaces in contact). Examples include aluminium oxide, iron oxides, quartz, silica, and zirconium silicate.

- Friction modifiers raise friction, lubricate or react with oxygen and help to control friction films. Examples include brass, graphite, copper, ceramic 'microspheres', 'friction dust', lead oxide, magnetite and various metal sulphides (Cu_2S, Sb_2S_3, PbS).

Steels and cast irons

Steels and cast irons are both primarily iron with carbon as the main alloying element. Steels contain less than 2% and more usually less than 1% carbon.

All cast irons contain more than 2% carbon. As the carbon content in steel increases so too does strength and hardness. However, ductility and weldability decrease.

Carbon steels may be classified by:

- chemical composition

- mechanical properties

- method of deoxidation

- thermal treatment (and the resulting microstructure).

Steel

Low-carbon steel is often employed for brake pad backing plates. The function of the plate is to distribute forces from the caliper pistons evenly to the friction pad. Due to the high conductivity of steel an insulating material is often sandwiched between the pad and the backing plate. A photomicrograph of a typical, annealed low carbon (hypoeutectoid) steel is shown below. This microstructure typically displays grains of ferrite and pearlite.

Figure 3.3.1 Hypoeutectoid steel

Cast irons

Two percent is approximately the greatest concentration of carbon at which iron can solidify as a single-phase alloy with all the carbon in solution in austenite. Because of this, cast irons solidify as heterogeneous alloys and always have more than one constituent in their microstructure. Cast irons must also contain silicon (usually from 1 to 3%) and are in reality iron–carbon–silicon alloys.

Early brake drums and discs were made of cast iron consisting of flake graphite in a ferritic matrix. While such a matrix was advantageous in terms of thermal conductivity it is inherently soft and did not resist wear well. In order to increase the inherent abrasion, ferrous mating surfaces needed to register a moderate hardness of at least 150–200 Brinell hardness number for heavy duty applications. A cast iron containing flake graphite in a pearlitic matrix was subsequently adopted, as shown in Figure 3.3.2.

Today automotive and truck discs and drums are typically produced using grey cast iron with graphite (appearing as flakes of a uniform distribution and random orientation) within a pearlitic matrix. Graphitic carbon also improves the thermal conductivity of cast iron, improving the performance and life of brake pads.

Figure 3.3.2 Pearlitic grey cast iron

Wear of grey cast iron in brake applications occurs mostly through abrasion and oxidisation. In an effort to reduce the effects of corrosion and prolong brake wear, motorcycle disc brakes (which are exposed much more to the weather) are usually stainless steel, whereas after-market racing component brake discs (where longevity is less of an issue) are still made from cast iron for the improved friction qualities.

The high-carbon and silicon content in grey cast irons give them a unique range of properties, including:

- more fluidity than molten steel

- less reactivity with moulding materials

- high compressive strength and resistance to fatigue

- good thermal conductivity and excellent castability

- melting temperatures appreciably lower than those of steel

- excellent machinability (even at wear-resisting hardness levels)

- vibration dampening graphite also provides lubrication on wearing surfaces.

Disadvantages associated with cast irons include low ductility discounting rolling and forging as forming processes. To increase the hardness of cast iron for abrasive-wear applications, alloying elements can be added to promote the formation of carbides in the matrix, or the iron may be heat-treated to obtain a martensitic matrix. Cast iron can also be hardened by flame or induction methods.

Composites—applications, manufacturing and forming

Composite materials are most often formed by the combination of two or more materials to achieve properties that are superior to those of its individual constituents. Composite materials are as diverse as porcelain enamel products (glass-coated metal), polymer, metal-laminated corrugated paper, fibreglass strengthened cement, fibre reinforced plastics and steel reinforced rubber (tyres).

The earliest use of composite materials date back to before biblical times with the Egyptians using straw to strengthen sun-dried clay bricks. Since that time composite materials have continued to develop. Engineers generally classify composites into one of four categories:

- polymer matrix composites

- metal matrix composites

- ceramic matrix composites

- carbon matrix composites.

The largest tonnage application for composite materials is in civil engineering structures such as roadways, bridges and buildings where ceramic (cement) matrix composite materials are used extensively.

With respect to domestic applications, reinforced plastics comprise 90% of the market and are based on glass fibre reinforcements. The thermosetting resin matrix is mainly unsaturated polyesters and their derivatives.

Fibre reinforced polymers (FRP) have generally been used to replace traditional materials such as wood, aluminium and steel. Significant advantages over these traditional materials include:

- lighter weight

- dimensional stability

- higher dielectric strength

- increased design flexibility

- greater corrosion resistance

- higher strength to weight ratio.

Due to the range of engineering properties, service conditions and environmental considerations, most brake materials are not composed of single elements or compounds but rather are composites of many materials.

Asbestos

Asbestos is hydrated magnesium silicate $Mg_3Si_2O_5(OH)_4$. The most common type of asbestos is fibrous chrysotile (white asbestos). The image shown in Figure 3.3.3, generated by a scanning electron microscope (SEM), shows the features typical of asbestos fibres: straight or curled and variable in length.

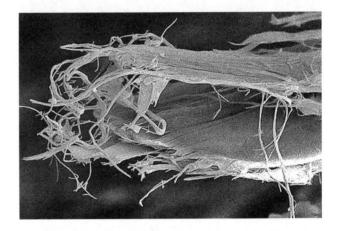

Figure 3.3.3 SEM image of fibrous chrysotile or white asbestos

The positive engineering properties of asbestos include:

- ease of processing

- thermal insulation

- excellent wear characteristics

- very stable in the environment

- resistant to heat and chemical attack

- regeneration of the friction surface during use

- thermal stability to 500 °C above which it produces silicates

- silicates produced by asbestos are harder and more abrasive than asbestos

- a kinetic coefficient of friction, (μ_k), of ~ 0.80 against clean iron.

As well as the health hazards associated with asbestos, the determining factors in the change to other materials for brake linings are performance based.

Since the early days of hydraulic brakes the lining materials were mostly the same for all applications no matter the make of car. It was essentially a mixture consisting of 30–70% asbestos and various other binder materials. In modern applications the disadvantages of using asbestos over alternative materials include:

- increased wear at high temperatures

- losses of up to 65% of its coefficient of friction when wet

- the formation of a surface glaze at as low a temperature as 121 °C, reducing its coefficient of friction

- insulative properties preventing heat transfer, making it harder for the drum or rotor to shed heat

- designs using smaller brakes, working harder at almost every pedal application, require the ability to shed heat quickly.

Possible replacements for asbestos in brakes include wollastonite (calcium silicate), vermiculite (hydrated calcium aluminium silicate), mica (aluminium silicate), basalt fibre, rock wool, ceramic fibre, polyacrylonitrile (PAN), polyester, chopped glass fibre and aramid fibres.

None of the materials listed performs exactly like asbestos but they offer some similar or improved performance characteristics.

Friction brake materials are most often classified as organics or semi-metallics.

Performance variations occur both within and between these brake material categories. Some of these variations include:

- wear rates

- noise levels

- appearance

- braking properties.

Non-asbestos organic materials

Organic pads are most often a light shade of grey and have a smooth surface texture. Organic formulations may contain fibreglass, aramid fibres (Kevlar), ceramics and carbon. Organic brake pads may also contain small amounts of copper.

Of all of the fibres, glass fibre may be the most common due to its strength, temperature resistance, friction qualities and relatively low cost. As expected, the softer materials provide better coefficients of friction but wear more quickly whereas the harder organics and man-made materials improve service life.

Ceramics by their nature can withstand extreme temperatures (as high as 1650 °C) and are often used as a sintering (heated to the point of flowing together in a mixture) partner with hard metals.

Carbon–carbon fibre composites make up a group of materials composed of a carbon matrix reinforced by long carbon fibres that can withstand high temperatures and are very resistant to wear. Under service conditions brakes made from such composites are:

- more reliable

- reduce vehicle vibration

- cause less pollution than traditional brakes.

Application of the high temperature use of carbon–carbon composites is most evident on the space shuttle were they are used in the nose cap, protecting the craft from the extreme temperatures generated during re-entry.

Unfortunately carbon–carbon fibre brakes only perform at the elevated temperatures found in racing conditions and do not get hot enough to work effectively in street applications.

Carbon fibre composite discs gripped by carbon fibre pads were once common in Formula One motorcycles and cars. In the 1990s they were outlawed by the respective racing organisations due to unexpected and spectacular catastrophic failure.

Aircraft brakes primarily consist of resin/steel metallic linings and carbon–carbon fibre (C–C) combinations. Commercial aircraft like the Airbus 319, Boeing 767 and 777 use C–C brakes while military aircraft like the

F-15E, F-18, F-22 and Joint Strike Fighter also employ C–C brakes systems.

By adjusting the composition of fibres, their form and binding matrices, a wide variety of properties peculiar to C–C can be produced.

As an example of this manipulation, some C–C discs are made with fine-scale needle-like fibres oriented perpendicular to the plane of the disc. These needles are perpendicular to another structural matte or woven layer of fibres that lie parallel to the disc face. This particular arrangement is employed because carbon fibres generally exhibit varying degrees of anisotropy. In this case heat transport is generally much higher longitudinally than transversely in the fibre axis. This structure is designed to enhance heat flow.

In addition to friction and wear behaviour, engineering properties important in C–C composite brakes include:

- density

- shear strength

- tensile strength

- flexural strength

- impact strength

- compressive strength

- thermal conductivity.

Semi-metallics

Resin-bonded metallic linings were introduced in the 1950s, and by the 1960s so-called semi-metallics were developed. Semi-metallics are a mixture of chopped, powdered or sintered metal bound together with phenolic resins and other binder or filler materials.

Semi-metallic brake pads are visibly different from organics in that they are darker in colour with visible metallic fibres and have a rough surface texture.

Semi-metallic pads are generally composed of ferrous metals in the form of chopped steel-wool fibre and finely powdered iron but they may also contain copper, graphite and lesser amounts of inorganic fillers and friction modifiers.

Lead has been gradually removed from brake pad formulations under stricter health regulations. Both organic and semi-metallic pads may contain copper due to its ability to dissipate heat generated during braking.

In recent years research has been conducted into using aluminium-based metal matrix composites (MMCs) for both brake discs and drum materials. Metal matrix composites are receiving wider attention due to the engineering properties characterising these materials, including:

- reduction in component weights

- increased service life

- reduced system maintenance.

Aluminium-based composites containing 20–30% silicon-carbide (SiC) have been proposed as substitutes for grey cast iron in the fabrication of vehicle brake discs and/or drums. The use of these materials instead of cast iron allows for:

- increased wear resistance

- weight reductions of 40–50%

- thermal conductivity approximately three times higher than cast iron

- lower brake disc operating temperatures through better heat dissipation.

The processing of Al-MMC brake components can be performed by forging or casting. In order to further reduce fabrication costs, in the case of casting, greater importance is being placed on recycling foundry scrap. This has the added advantage of reducing production and environmental costs. While much lighter than cast iron, they are not as resistant to high temperatures and are occasionally used on the rear axles of automobiles where energy dissipation requirements are not as severe compared with the front axle. Overall, the future for using Al-MMC materials for discs is not clear. While they reduce weight, they tend to be more expensive to produce than conventional grey cast iron.

Testing of materials

Hardness tests

Hardness refers to the resistance of a material to scratching or abrasion. It may also refer to resistance to indentation, penetration or cutting. The number of definitions for hardness indicates that hardness may not be a fundamental property of a material but rather a composite one including yield strength, work hardening, true tensile strength, modulus of elasticity, and others.

Hardness is routinely used as an indication of material condition. As a general guide, the greater the hardness of a material, the greater resistance it has to deformation and wear. As might be expected, a variety of tests have been developed to measure hardness. These tests fall into three broad groups consisting of:

- scratch hardness (Mohs, Bierbaum, Pencil)

- static indentation hardness (Brinell, Rockwell, Vickers, Knoop, Janka, Durometer)

- dynamic hardness (Scleroscope, Leeb).

A selection of commonly used hardness tests are described below and the indentors used for some of these tests are shown in Figure 3.3.5. The requirements for surface preparation varies but all necessitate some preparation of the surface to ensure it is clean and free of debris.

Scratch hardness

As the name implies, scratch hardness tests involve the scratching of the test surface with a stylus/indentor.

The German mineralogist Friedrich Mohs developed one of the earliest measures of material hardness in 1812. The Mohs hardness test as it has come to be known, is defined by how well a substance will resist scratching by another substance of known or defined hardness and a ranking from 1 to 10 assigned. The scale contains ten minerals that Mohs proposed as exemplars of each position on the scale, starting with the mineral talc at position 1, which can be scratched by a fingernail, to diamond at 10 (see Figure 3.3.4). The Mohs scale, therefore, is not linear, i.e. each increment in the scale does not indicate a proportional increase in hardness. For instance, the progression from calcite to fluorite (from 3 to 4 on the Mohs scale) reflects an increase in hardness of approximately 25%, while the progression

from corundum to diamond, on the other hand, (9 to 10 on the Mohs scale) reflects a hardness increase of more than 300%. The identification of minerals in the field, is not suitable for accurately gauging the hardness of most materials, particularly industrial materials such as steel or ceramics.

Mohs hardness	Mineral
1	Talc
2	Gypsum
3	Calcite
4	Flourite
5	Apatite
6	Orthoclase
7	Quartz
8	Topaz
9	Corundum
10	Diamond

Figure 3.3.4 Mohs hardness scale

The Bierbaum test uses a standardised diamond indentor that is dragged across the test surface and the width of the scratch produced measured. This test is suited to a variety of materials, particularly plastics.

The pencil test uses a set of twenty pencils ranging from grades 9B to 9H. A pencil is placed in a holder at an angle of 45° to the test surface and the holder moved across the surface under a fixed force of 7.5N. The test is repeated until a pencil grade that just scratches/indents the surface is found and that grade recorded as the hardness. This test has found use in the testing of polymer coatings.

Static indentation hardness

Static hardness tests typically involve the penetration of an indentor into the test surface using low loading rates. The Barcol hardness test uses a cone-shaped steel indentor that is pushed into the test surface until a spring is completely depressed, resulting in the application of a fixed load. The depth to which the indentor has penetrated the surface is then read off a dial gauge calibrated from 0 to 100. This test is often used to determine the degree to which plastic resin has cured.

Brinell tests use a hardened steel or tungsten carbide ball, typically of 10 mm diameter, to produce an indentation in the surface of the material using a standard load. The diameter of the impression is measured with a small portable microscope and the Brinell hardness read from a conversion table.

Figure 3.3.5 Commonly used indentors for hardness testing: Rockwell (top), Brinell (middle), Vickers (bottom)

Rockwell tests use either a small steel ball or a diamond indentor ground to form a cone of 120° to form an impression. Several Rockwell hardness scales are available (A, B, C, etc.) using various combinations of indentor and applied load, depending on the material to be tested. The depth of the impression is related to a Rockwell hardness that is read off a dial gauge or LCD.

Vickers tests use variable loads and a diamond pyramid indentor. Because the same indentor is used and only the applied load varied, a comparable hardness is obtained when testing a range of materials. Because of this, the Vickers test is the standard method for the reliable measurement of metal and ceramic hardness. The impression diagonals are measured and related to a Vickers hardness number by reference to a table selected based on the applied load used in the test.

Knoop tests explore microhardness by making rhombohedral indentations (one long and one short diagonal) with a pyramidal diamond indentor. The aspect ratio of the impression diagonals allows impressions to be placed closer together without concerns of previous impressions affecting later hardness results.

The Brinell, Rockwell, Vickers and Knoop hardness testers use a standardised indentor and fixed load to determine hardness and are used extensively in the testing of metals.

Dynamic hardness

Dynamic hardness tests are rebound tests in which an indentor falls from a standard height and the change in height on rebound measured. These tests depend on elastic recovery of the test surface and use high rates of loading.

The Scleroscope or Shore Scleroscope tests measure the loss in kinetic energy from a falling diamond-tipped metal 'tup'. The tup is enclosed within a glass-fronted graduated column and the bottom of the column placed against the surface to be tested. When the tup is released from the top of the column the tup falls, hits the test surface and rebounds. The height of rebound is recorded as the hardness (HSc). The test equipment is light and portable but must be held vertically and test access is restricted by the height of the column.

The Leeb rebound hardness test (see Figure 3.3.6) uses a small pen-shaped device containing a spring-loaded impact body. During testing a small permanent magnet within the impact body passes through a coil in the impact device, inducing a voltage proportional to the velocity. The hardness calculated is a ratio of the velocities before and after rebound. Values can be displayed as Leeb hardness (HL) or more usually displayed as a Vickers, Rockwell or Brinell equivalent.

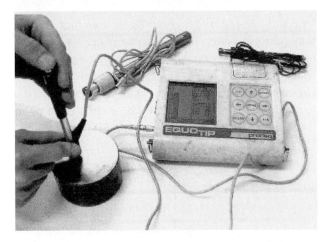

Many conversion tables are available that allow hardness measurements, undertaken with one method, to be compared with hardnesses obtained with a different method and to be equated approximately with tensile strength. These tables are developed from test data for materials such as steel or aluminium and cannot be extrapolated to include other materials not tested.

A comparison summary of commonly used hardness tests appears in Figure 3.3.7.

Figure 3.3.6 Equotip™ hardness tester used to determine Leeb hardness

Load	Test type	Test	Indentor	Measurement	Metal	Ceramic	Wood	Polymer	Minerals
Fixed load		Brinell	10mm ø steel or WC ball	Area	X				
		Rockwell	5 mm steel ball or diamond cone	Depth	X				
		Vickers	Diamond pyramid	Area	X	X			
		Knoop	Diamond pyramid	Area	X	X			
		Barcol	Steel cone	Depth				X	
		Pencil	Pencils	Scratch				X	
		Bierbaum	Diamond	Scratch width		X		X	
		Sclerescope	Diamond	Rebound height	X				
		Leeb	WC ball	Velocity change					
		Janka	11.28mm ø steel ball	Force			X		
Variable load	Static	Durometer	Steel rod	Depth				X	
		Mohs	Various	Scratch		X			X
	Dynamic								

Figure 3.3.7 Commonly used hardness tests

Figure 3.3.8 shows a hypoeutectoid steel of approximately 0.06wt% C exhibiting a normalised structure of ferrite.

The square-shaped impression left from the Vickers indentor (shown in the photomicrograph) is carefully measured with a microscope. The hardness value here is 131HV5, indicating a relatively soft material.

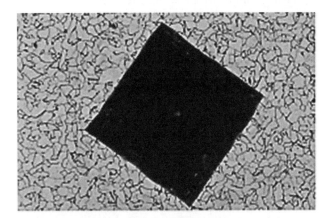

Figure 3.3.8 0.06 wt% C Steel Hardness test × 100

Figure 3.3.9 shows a micrograph of a steel plate, approximately 0.08wt% C exhibiting a structure of ferrite and pearlite with approximately 30% cold rolling. The cold rolling is evidenced by the elongated and distorted grain pattern. This level of cold working appreciably hardens the parent material. The smaller impression left from the Vickers hardness test indentor indicates the greater hardness of this sample, a direct result of the cold working. On close examination additional disturbance to the microstructure is visible around the perimeter of the indentation, caused by the conducting of the test.

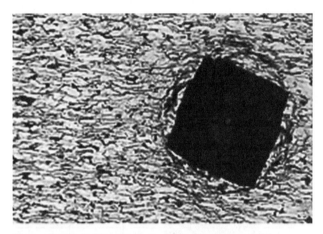

Figure 3.3.9   0.08 wt% C steel hardness test ×100

Wear testing

Wear testing of composite materials is regularly conducted to determine the best composition for brake pads. Samples of a specified size are rigidly clamped against the disc of a grinding machine for a predetermined period of time. Samples are then weighed to determine the amount of abraded material removed.

Tensile and compressive testing of materials

Engineering properties of materials may be determined by tensile, compressive and shear testing.

The data obtained from tensile testing is vital to engineers. Load-extension diagrams produced from tensile tests provide information relating to toughness, ductility, stiffness, ultimate tensile strength and more. The transition from elastic to plastic strain is a valuable piece of data. The point where plastic or permanent deformation commences (known as the yield point) is often of far more importance to engineers than final breaking force or ultimate tensile strengths of materials.

Most metals and polymers are tested under tension while materials such as concretes, glasses and ceramics

tend to be tested under compressive conditions where they perform better. Because these materials are most often employed in situations where compressive strength is required, they are generally not tested in tension. However, if a tensile strength figure for these materials is required it is often tested as a beam in a three point loading arrangement.

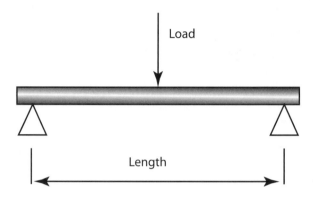

Figure 3.3.10   Flexural testing of a beam

The beam tested in Figure 3.3.10 undergoes both compressive (upper surface) and tensile (lower surface) forces. Tested in a flexural testing rig, brittle materials fail on the lower surface under tension, relative to the load applied.

3.4 Communication

CAD, pictorial, orthogonal and exploded drawings using Australian Standard AS1100

The computer-aided drawing of a brake pad shown in Figure 3.4.1 shows a multiview orthographic comprising of a front view and full-section side view.

The single piece sectioned part is cross-hatched in one direction only, indicating use of a single material. The front and side views, including dimensions, contain sufficient information appropriate for manufacture.

The rendered isometric shown in Figure 3.4.1 provides a pictorial representation of how the part would look in real life. One of the advantages of CAD packages is that any changes or updates made to the original sketch or features on the isometric drawing are immediately transferred to their orthographic counterparts.

All of the CAD orthographic drawings in Chapters 2, 3 and 4 comply with AS1100 drawing standards.

Figure 3.4.1 Multiview orthographic drawing

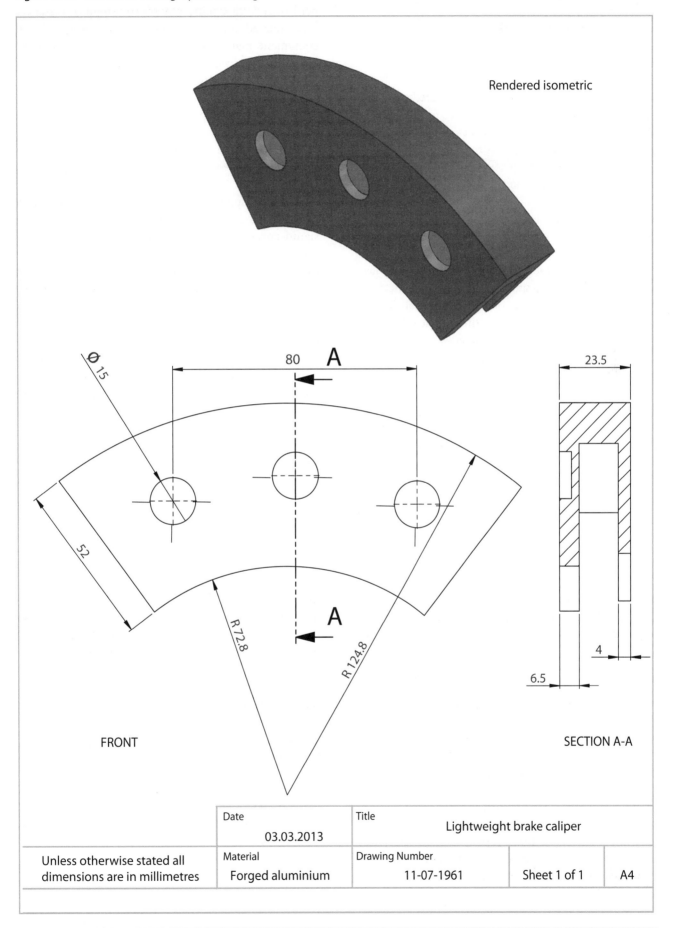

Rendered isometric

Ø 15

80 A

23.5

52

R 72.8

R 124.8

A

4

6.5

FRONT

SECTION A-A

Date		Title			
03.03.2013		Lightweight brake caliper			
Unless otherwise stated all dimensions are in millimetres	Material	Drawing Number			
	Forged aluminium	11-07-1961		Sheet 1 of 1	A4

Engineering report writing

Copper replacement in brake pads

Introduction

Brake pads are a complex mix of many ingredients. They are designed to create a friction surface to slow vehicles down and provide good wear resistance also reducing vibration and noise. Copper is regularly used in brake pads to improve these properties and efficiently conduct heat away from the friction surfaces.

However, as individuals, communities and governments become more aware of the environmental and health consequences associated with the use of certain materials, forward-looking legislators are passing laws reducing and/or restricting the use of specific materials in brake pads. Asbestos is one such material that has been reduced or eliminated over time and legislators are now turning their attention to copper.

Research

In the state of Washington in the USA researchers claim 'About 50% of the copper entering Puget Sound comes from brake pads' (People for Puget Sound, 2010).

Copper in the form of friction dust enters waterways and oceans through stormwater runoff from roads. Once in the marine environment, copper kills algae which, at the bottom of the food chain, supports all life at higher levels. Copper also negatively affects fish populations. In California, city officials were have trouble meeting *Clean Water Act* requirements and as early as the 1990s legislators have been looking at ways of limiting copper in brake pads. Other states are set to follow this legislative requirement as well as federal mandates in the US and Canada.

One approach to the problem is to eliminate dust as a by-product of braking. Pure Forge™ employs an 'atomic forging' process involving the treating of brake rotors and pads in a high energy plasma environment to modify the surface of components. The final product has an extremely dense surface at an atomic level. The end result of this process is a layer of ultra-dense exotic material that is fused to the surface of the rotor, creating a surface that is extremely hard and tough. Controlled testing conducted by the company showed little wear and even improved performance when compared to existing technologies:

'The vehicles equipped with PureForge™ rotors performed with significantly shorter stopping distances as compared to the vehicles equipped with original equipment manufacturers (OEM) rotors' (Pureforge™ 2012). Reduced wear not only reduces harmful dust but also suggests extended product life cycles.

Discs employing pureforge technology examined after 45 000 km showed less wear and scoring than comparable discs examined after only travelling one fifth of the distance.

In a different approach other manufacturers have chosen to replace copper with graphite. Graphite is already a significant constituent of existing brake pad composition due to its properties of wear resistance and its ability to provide and stabilise an appropriate coefficient of friction. Some manufacturers are attempting to replace copper with graphite and are testing it in its various forms to see which types perform the best. Limited research is available into the wide range of properties graphite additions may be able to provide. Significant testing will need to be conducted over graphite types, purities, crystallinity, particle size and shape, texture and thermal conductivity variants.

Already graphite incorporated in resin–bonded brake pads offers improved thermal conductivity which also affects heat dissipation, vibration and wear, and has a positive effect on noise reduction (squealing).

Conclusion

Both California and Washington in the United States have passed legislation that will require the reduction, then the removal of copper from brake pads, both in new vehicles and in aftermarket supplies. While these bans will not come into place until the mid 2020s, it is an indication of just how difficult it will be to re-engineer brake pads minus copper.

Collaborative work practices

Notes on collaborative work practices appear in the Communications sections 1.5 and 2.6 of Chapters 1 and 2 respectively.

3.5 Sample Preliminary questions and answers

Objective-response questions

1. To have kinetic energy an object must be

    A   in motion.
    B   at an elevated position.
    C   travelling at constant velocity.
    D   accelerating.

2. Figure 3.5.1 shows the fluid principle of

    A   Pascal.
    B   Archimedes.
    C   transmissibility.
    D   equilibrium.

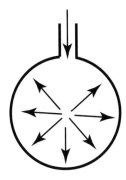

Figure 3.5.1 Fluid diagram

3. Given that the modulus of elasticity of a 0.85 m long brake cable is 190 GPa, calculate the extension if a load of 0.5 kN is applied to the 3 mm diameter cable.

    A   0.316 mm
    B 2.966×10^{-4} mm
    C   0.2248 mm
    D 2.248×10^{-4} mm

4. The yield point on a stress-strain diagram marks

    A   an increase in stress relative to strain.
    B   the beginning of the elastic phase.
    C   an increase in strain relative to stress.
    D   the toughness of a material.

5. True stress is

    A   mostly larger than engineering stress.
    B   the elastic modulus divided by strain.
    C   without units.
    D   also known as strength.

6. Which of these statements about friction is untrue?

    A   Friction between two surfaces depends on the nature of the surfaces in contact.
    B   Friction is dependent on the area of the surfaces in contact.
    C   Friction is directly proportional to the reaction between the surfaces.
    D   Friction always opposes motion.

7. If the velocity ratio of a 100% efficient machine is 20 and the load is restricted to a movement of 20 mm, how far will the effort move?

    A   0 mm
    B   1 mm
    C   20 mm
    D   400 mm

8. As the carbon content in steel increases

    A   ductility and weldability increase, while strength and hardness decrease.
    B   strength and ductility increase, while hardness and weldability decrease.
    C   strength and hardness increase, while ductility and weldability decrease.
    D   weldability and hardness increase, while ductility and strength decrease.

9. Brittle materials when compression tested often fail

    A   through fatigue.
    B   due to torsion.
    C   due to bending stresses.
    D   in shear at an angle of 45° to the axis of stress.

10. 'True stress' is calculated through

    A   use of the original cross-sectional area.
    B   final cross-sectional area.
    C   changing cross-sectional areas.
    D   cross-sectional area at necking.

11. The performance characteristics of carbon composite brake pads are not suitable for standard street cars because they

    A   are too expensive.
    B   they are only used in aircraft.
    C   generate more pollutants than traditional brakes.
    D   perform at temperatures beyond those found in commercial steet car applications.

Short-answer questions

1. If the tangential force generated between the brake drum and the internal expanding shoe is 300 kN and the normal force between the surfaces is 700 kN calculate the coefficient of friction. (2 marks)

2. A handbrake (Figure 3.5.2) operates through a cable system. Calculate the force delivered through the secondary cables if the force applied through the main cable is 600 N. (2 marks)

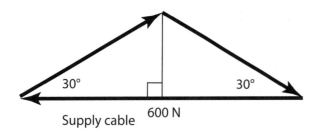

Figure 3.5.2 Handbrake cable

3. A braking bicycle of total mass 87 kg slows its speed from 28 km/h to 15 km/h. How much energy is absorbed by the brakes during this process? (3 marks)

4. Calculate the mechanical advantage gained through use of a master cylinder of diameter 40 mm and a brake cylinder of diameter 65 mm. Assume 100% efficiency. (2 marks)

5. Discuss THREE ways in which composites may be manipulated to vary their engineering properties. (3 marks)

6. Explain why parking brakes still use a mechanical or cable system instead of hydraulics. (2 marks)

Longer-answer questions

1. Explain the use of the non-destructive shore sclerescope test and where it is most commonly used. (3 marks)

2. Identify THREE reasons why fibre reinforced plastics (FRP) have been used to replace traditional materials such as wood, aluminium and steel. (3 marks)

3. Discuss the use of aluminium-based composites as substitutes for grey cast iron in the fabrication of vehicle brake discs and/or drums. (2 marks)

4. Determine the moment generated at the pivot point of the brake arm (Figure 3.5.3). (4 marks)

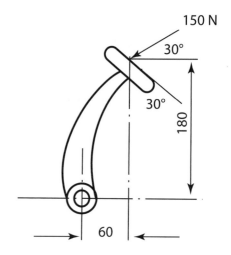

Figure 3.5.3 Brake arm

5. If a force of 30 N acts on the foot pedal of the brake arrangement shown in Figure 3.5.4, determine the torque acting on the brake drum if the coefficient of friction is 0.72. (4 marks)

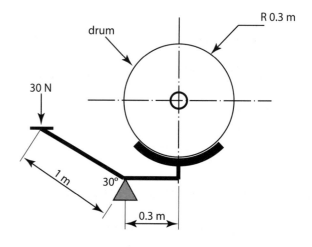

Figure 3.5.4 Foot pedal

Answers to objective-response questions

1. **A** An object must be in motion to have kinetic energy and it must be under constant velocity or undergoing acceleration. The object's position in space is not relevant.

2. **A** Pascal's principle states that any externally applied pressure is transmitted through all parts of an enclosed fluid, undiminished in every direction.

3. **A**
$$E = \frac{F \times L}{e \times A}$$

$$e = \frac{500 \times 850}{190 \times 10^3 \times 7.068}$$

$$e = 0.316 \text{ mm}$$

4. **C** The yield point indicates the point from which strain increases without a corresponding increase in stress.

5. **A** True stress is always greater than engineering stress due to the reduction in the cross-sectional area. B is wrong because true stress is not the Young's modulus divided by strain. C is wrong because stress is measured in megapascals and D is wrong because strength is measured as the maximum stress a material can withstand.

6. **B** is false. Friction is not dependent on the area of the surfaces in contact. Statements A, C and D are true.

7. **D**
$$VR = \frac{d_E}{d_L}$$

$$20 = \frac{d_E}{20}$$

$$d_E = 400 \text{ mm}$$

8. **C**

9. **D** In compression brittle materials fail in shear at an angle of 45° to the axis of stress. Simple compression tests do not induce torsion or bending stresses and are conducted until failure, so fatigue is not relevant.

10. **C** True stress-strain data is obtained by taking into account changes in cross-sectional area. Engineering or apparent stress uses the original cross-sectional area.

11. **D** Expense is not a measure of performamnce and carbon brakes are used in applications other than aircraft. Commercial streetcar operations do not reach the temperatures at which carbon brakes perform their best.

Answers to short-answer questions

1. $F_R = \mu N$ where N = 700 kN

    μ = coefficient of friction and F_R = 300 kN

    $300 = 700 \mu$

    $\mu = 300 \div 700$

    $\mu = 0.43$

2. Handbrake force diagram (Figure 3.5.5).

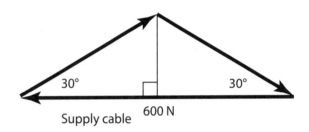

Figure 3.5.5 Force diagram

Force in cables = $\dfrac{300}{\cos 30°}$

Force in cables = 346 N

3. Energy before braking – Energy after braking = Energy absorbed (EA)

    $$KE = \tfrac{1}{2} mv^2$$

    $$\tfrac{1}{2} mv^2_{before} - \tfrac{1}{2} mv^2_{after} = EA$$

    28 km/h = 7.78 m/s   15 km/h = 4.17 m/s

    $$\tfrac{1}{2} \times 87 \times 7.78^2 - \tfrac{1}{2} \times 87 \times 4.17^2 = EA$$

    $$2\,632.9854 - 756.41715 = 1\,876.6 \text{ J}$$

    $$= 1.88 \text{ kJ}$$

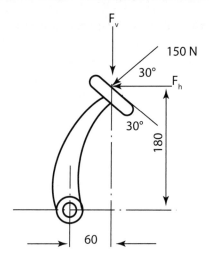

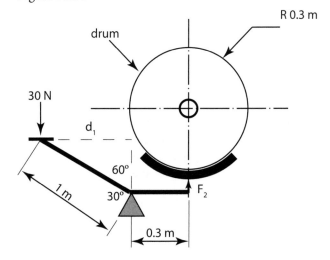

4. $MA = d_2^2/d_1^2$

   $= 65^2 \div 40^2$

   $= 2.64$

5. Composites may be manipulated by varying fibre composition, size, distribution, form, alignment and relative ratio to the binding matrix.

6. Parking brakes use levers and cables rather than hydraulics to activate, allowing them to continue to operate in the event of a total hydraulic failure. The parking brake may also need to be used as an emergency brake to stop the vehicle. Hydraulic brakes require the motor to be running to provide power assistance.

Answers to longer-answer questions

1. The Shore Sclerescope is a dynamic hardness test involving the use of a free-falling ball or 'tup'. The rebound height is read from a scale thus generating a relative measure of hardness, that is, the harder the material the greater the rebound height. This type of test is best suited to extremely hard materials or field testing.

2. Composites provide higher strength to weight ratios, lighter weights, greater corrosion resistance and greater dimensional stability.

3. Aluminium-based composites offer the following benefits over cast iron: weight reductions of up to 40–50%, increased wear resistance, thermal conductivity approximately three times higher than cast iron, lower brake disc operating temperatures through better heat dissipation, may be cast or forged. Disadvantages associated with the use of aluminium-based composites include their reduced resistance to high temperatures.

4. Resolve 150 N angled force into vertical and horizontal components as shown in Figure 3.5.6.

   $M\circlearrowleft - M\circlearrowright$ = Resultant at fulcrum

   $M = F_H \times 180 - F_V \times 60$

   $M = (150 \cos 30) \times 0.180 - (150 \sin 30) \times 0.06$

   $M = 23.383 - 4.5$

   $M = 18.883$ Nm $\circlearrowleft$

Figure 3.5.6 Brake pedal forces

5. Important to the solving of this problem is the calculation of the perpendicular distance as shown in Figure 3.5.7.

Figure 3.5.7 Foot pedal solution

   $F_1 \times d_1 = F_2 \times d_2$

   $30 \times d_1 = F_2 \times 0.3$

where:

   $d_1 = \sin 60$

   $F_2 = (30 \times \sin 60) \div 0.3$

   $F_2 = 86.6$ N = normal reaction

Frictional resistance at the pad = μN

   $F_R = 0.72 \times 86.6$ N

   $F_R = 62.352$ N

   Torque = $F \times d$

   Torque = $62.352 \times 0.3 = 18.7$ Nm

3.6 Glossary

Amorphous

Amorphous materials are usually characterised by certain areas of short-range order. A long-range order, as in crystals, does not exist in amorphous substances. The terms *amorphous*, *non-crystalline* and *glassy* are interchangeable.

Anisotropy

The engineering property of being anisotropic refers to having a different value when measured in different directions.

Asbestos

Asbestos is hydrated magnesium silicate $Mg_3Si_2O_5(OH)_4$. The most common type of asbestos is fibrous chrysotile (white asbestos). Asbestos fibres are variable in length and may be straight or curled.

Austenite

A face-centred cubic (FCC) phase in the iron-carbon phase diagram designated as gamma (γ) phase, austenite consists of a non-magnetic solid solution of carbon in iron.

Band brake

Early version of brake involving an external contracting band wrapped around a hub

Castability

The relative ease with which a material may be cast

Cast iron

Cast iron is an alloy of iron and carbon in which the carbon is in excess of the amount that can be retained in solid solution in austenite at the eutectic temperature. Carbon is usually present in the range of approximately 2% to 4.5%. In addition, silicon, manganese, sulphur and phosphorus are contained in varying amounts.

Ceramic

A multi-phase material containing phases composed of compounds of metals and non-metals, ceramics are typically hard and good insulators

Coefficient of friction

A ratio of the forces between two surfaces in contact calculated using the formula $F_R = \mu N$ where the Greek letter mu (μ) denotes the coefficient of friction

Composites

Composites are multi-phase materials formed from a combination of materials which differ in composition or form. Remaining bonded together these individual components of composites combine to improve upon the original properties of the component materials. Composites include fibrous, laminar and particulate materials or combinations of any of the above.

Compression

Applying pressure to an object to reduce its size or make smaller, a pushing or squeezing force

Corrosion

Corrosion is a chemical reaction that results in the conversion of metallic materials into oxides, salts or other compounds. Metals undergoing corrosion lose their strength, ductility and other important mechanical properties.

Ductility

The ease with which a material deforms plastically while undergoing tensile forces such as drawing

Elastic limit

The portion of the stress-strain relationship within which a material when loaded and then unloaded will return to its original un-deformed shape; this also equates to the end of the straight line portion of the stress-strain curve

Energy

Energy is the ability to do work and is measured in joules (J).

Engineering stress	Engineering stress is calculated using the ratio of the applied load (L) to the undeformed (original) cross-sectional area (A).
Friction	Friction is a force generated between surfaces opposite to the direction of motion (whether the object is moving or stationary) or motion.
Friction dust	Friction dust is a granular, free-flowing polymerised resin derived from cashew nut shell liquid (CNSL). The main component in processed CNSL is cardanol. Cardanol is a naturally occurring material, hydrophobic in nature, and remains flexible and liquid at very low temperatures.
Hooke's law	Hooke's law states that 'stress is directly proportional to strain within a material's proportional limit'.
Hydraulics	Hydraulics is that branch of science that deals with the study and use of liquids, as related to the mechanical aspects of physics. It studies the flow of fluids (liquids) for which there is virtually no density change.
Kinetic energy	Kinetic energy is the capacity to do work due to a particle's motion.
Matrix	A surrounding substance within which something else originates, develops or is contained
Normal	A force applied at 90° to a surface
Plasticity	The ability of a material to withstand permanent deformation without failure
Power	Power is a measure of work done over a period of time. Power is measured in watts, where one watt is the power used to perform one joule of work in one second.
Pearlite	A phase of carbon steel and cast iron consisting of ferrite and cementite formed into distinct alternating layers (or lamellae) on slow cooling from austenite; pearlite is a tough phase responsible for the mechanical properties of unhardened steel.
Shear	Shear is when one section of a body tends to slide over a neighbouring section.
Sintering	Most often associated with powder metallurgy, sintering involves heating compressed parts in a controlled-atmosphere furnace. The pressed powder particles fuse together (at temperatures below their melting point), forming metallurgical bonds.
Strain	Strain is defined as the amount of deformation an object experiences compared to its original size. Note that strain is expressed most often as a ratio and is therefore dimensionless.
Steel	Generally defined as a metallic product whose principal element is iron and where the carbon content is not more than 2%
Tension	A force tending to stretch or elongate something, a pulling force
Torsion	Torsion is the result of twisting forces produced in engine crankshafts while the engine is running. Forces causing torsion produce torque or turning moments.

Toughness	Toughness is the extent to which a material absorbs energy without fracture. It is usually measured in impact tests (Izod or Charpy) as energy absorbed. The area under a stress-strain diagram is also a measure of toughness.
True stress	True stress is defined as the ratio of the applied load (L) to the instantaneous cross-sectional area (A).
Ultimate tensile strength (UTS)	Ultimate tensile strength or UTS is the maximum stress a material can withstand before failing.
Weldability	Weldability is the ease with which a material is able to be welded. It is most often referred to in the case of steels.
Young's modulus	Young's modulus is the ratio of stress to strain within the elastic region of the stress-strain curve (prior to the yield point).

BIOMEDICAL ENGINEERING

CONTENTS

STUDENT OUTCOMES

A student:

- identifies the scope of engineering and recognises current innovations.

- explains the relationship between properties, structure, uses and applications of materials in engineering.

- describes the nature of engineering in specific fields and its importance to society.

- uses mathematical, scientific and graphical methods to solve problems of engineering practice.

- develops written, oral and presentation skills and applies these to engineering reports.

- applies graphics as a communication tool.

- describes developments in technology and their impact on engineering products.

- identifies the social, environmental and cultural implications of technological change in engineering.

- demonstrates the ability to work both individually and in teams.

- applies management and planning skills related to engineering.

- applies knowledge and skills in research and problem-solving related to engineering.

© 2011 NSW Education Standards Authority

KEY TERMS AND CONCEPTS

Amorphous	Nitinol
Antiseptic	Parallel circuit
Aseptic	Passivate
Binary code	PIC
Bioactive	Plasma spray
Biocompatible	Prosthesis
Bioinert	Resorb
Biomedical	Scaffold
Ceramic	Sepsis
Composite	Series circuit
Corrosion	Shape memory alloy
Fulcrum	Sintering
Glass	Stainless steel
Hydroxyapatite	Titanium
Investment casting	Torque
Lever	Transcutaneous charging
Logic gate	Truth table
	Weld decay

4.1 Scope of the profession

Nature and range of the work of biomedical engineers

Many definitions of bioengineering are possible. In its broadest sense, bioengineering can be defined as human intervention in biological systems. As such, bioengineering could include fields such as genetic engineering and the selective breeding of plants and animals, bioleaching of ore bodies, ecologically sustainable development, waste management, human health, biometric security systems and many more. A definition more focused on the traditional engineering disciplines might suggest that bioengineering utilises the disciplines of mathematics and engineering to replace, augment and design or repair biological systems.

These activities in many instances have of course historically incorporated contributions from people with training in traditional engineering fields such as mechanical, chemical, civil, electrical and metallurgical engineering. Developments such as the plough, water-wheel, horse-shoe, automatic milking machine, anaesthetics, orthopaedic shoes, eye glasses and the study of ergonomics can in a broad sense all be considered the result of bioengineering, although such a description was not necessarily thought of when some of these developments occurred.

As a recognised discipline, bioengineering is one of the newest areas of study and comes about due to the dual necessities of ever increasing specialisation combined with the need for multidisciplinary knowledge to solve complicated problems in engineering and science. Within bioengineering, professionals can still specialise in the traditional fields of engineering with special reference to biological systems and identify as a:

- biomechanical engineer

- biochemical engineer

- bioelectrical engineer, and more recently as a

- biomedical engineer.

It is the field of biomedical engineering, which broadly encompasses the application of engineering to medical issues, that the remainder of this chapter will be concerned with.

Biomedical engineering may involve the development of monitoring equipment or surgical instruments and artificial alternatives to biological materials and functions. It is easy to see from this brief list that the disciplines which may contribute to such endeavours are wide and that biomedical engineers may begin their training in a number of engineering disciplines.

Further reading

'What is biomedical engineering?' (n.d), retrieved 24 May 2013 from Engineers Australia website www.engineersaustralia.org.au/biomedical-college/whatbiomedical-engineering

Current projects and innovations

Biomedical engineering is one of the fastest growing areas of research and development.

The investigation of new materials and designs is underway into a vast array of products, such as:

- synthetic blood

- synthetic skin and tubing for blood vessels

- electronic devices to restore sight (bionic eye)

- retractable syringe to prevent needlestick injuries and the reuse of needles

- expandable implants for the femur bone to allow the normal growth of a child's leg affected by surgery

- nano-engineering to produce injectable machines capable of detecting and correcting anomalies on a cellular level

- injectable, biodegradable cement to heal bone fractures

- new drug delivery systems such as microneedle-based vaccine patches designed to deliver mass vaccinations to populations without the need for medical training

- development of a virtual patient to assist in the training of medical practitioners, allowing the consequences of various responses to symptoms to be simulated.

Work continues into the development of artificial organs that would provide hope for many sufferers of disease who currently must rely on the availability of a compatible donor organ. These developments rely on a thorough understanding of engineering principles such as fluid dynamics and material properties along with biological processes. The end-point requirement by which success will ultimately be judged, however, is the quality of life of potential recipients. Quality of life issues will take into consideration:

- portability

- absence of pain

- restrictions in life style

- passive/active transitions

- lifetime of artificial device

- reliability of device operation

- intrusiveness of maintenance procedures.

Assistive technologies, that is technologies that while not capable of correcting a condition can assist in improving quality of life, have a long history and include devices such as the walking stick, artificial limb and wheel chair.

Recent developments in assistive technologies include:

- the 'Hall walker' that allows children with cerebral palsy to walk

- the development of an artificial limb attached to a titanium implant secured in the bone

- computer software that assists people with conditions such as motor neurone disease (MND) to communicate.

Motor neurone disease (MND) is a disease of the central nervous system that gradually destroys the ability to control movement and speech. MND was previously known as amyotrophic lateral sclerosis (ALS) or in the USA more commonly as Lou Gehrig's disease after a famous American baseball player who developed the disease in the 1940s.

The most famous person to have MND today is probably the physicist Stephen Hawking. Biomedical engineering through computer software and voice synthesising technology has allowed Professor Hawking to continue his work and communicate with a relative independence previously impossible.

3D printing

3D printing is already transforming the dental industry. Inter-oral scanning of the mouth can produce highly accurate digital images that may then be transmitted to computers and then 'printed' out to produce implants, bridges and crowns. A variety of materials may be formed from plastics to ceramics with high degrees of accuracy and rapid cycle times. This technology banishes the older and often unpleasant and sometimes inaccurate method of taking impressions of the teeth manually.

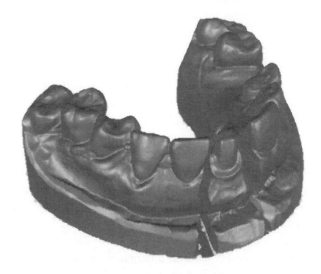

Figure 4.1.1 Inter-oral scan of mouth, image courtesy of WYSIWYG3D, www.wysiwyg3d.com.au/case-studies/case-studies-dental/

The same technology is being applied to the construction of artificial limbs. Accurate scans of patient limbs provide better data for the development and manufacture of prosthetic devices. Remaining limbs may also be scanned to give medical staff a clearer idea of the limb they are attempting to match and then 'mirror'.

In 2012, in the Netherlands, a 3D printed replacement jaw was fitted to an elderly woman's face. Produced from titanium powder, heated and fused togther using a laser beam, the implant was built up layer by layer from a complex computer model sent directly to the printer. The final product only took a couple of hours to print and was covered in a bioceramic coating before insertion.

Bioprinters are the latest development in this rapidly evolving field. Using the patients own genetic material replacement organs may be printed from an individual's own DNA.

At this point, simpler tissues such as skin, heart muscle patches and blood vessels are capable of reproduction, although the hope is more complex organs like complete hearts and livers will be possible in the future.

3D scanning

The use of 3D scanning in engineering applications is increasing as the acceptance of the technology becomes more widespread. Scanning of people or casts of people's parts as shown in Figure 4.1.1 can be used by designers to design better fitting products such as helmets and face masks. Scanning can also be used to create datasets of human sizes for anthropometric applications. A complete scene can also be scanned to assess a work environment for health and safety issues.

Breakthrough Australian technologies

HypoMon

In 2011, HypoMon was awarded an Australian International Design Award for excellence in design and innovation. Designed as a non-invasive hypoglycemia (low blood glucose) monitor for children and young adults with Type 1 diabetics, HypoMon eliminates the need for a finger prick blood sample and monitors individuals even while they sleep. Through the use of a sensor, monitor and wireless transmitter, signals may be sent to an alarm, waking the wearer and allowing for treatment to take place for a reaction that may have previously gone undetected.

AtomRapid™

In 2012, AtomRapid™ won the Engineer's Australia Bradfield Award for its simple, low-cost, accurate blood collection instrument for use in the field.

It is hoped AtomRapid™ will reduce the number of errors and false positives while at the same time provide a fast service for blood sampling in remote areas. Still under development pending results from clinical trials, it is anticipated that AtomRapid™ will assist in the fast and accurate diagnosis of diseases such as HIV and malaria.

Health and safety matters

Biomedical engineering is intimately involved in issues of health and safety. Biomedical engineers are constantly searching for safer and more efficient ways of performing tasks and producing products. Extensive testing is required of biomedical systems, materials and equipment to ensure that they perform reliably in the intended manner and do not cause unintended consequences. The need to ensure long-term reliable operation and the high standards of quality control contribute to making many of these products expensive. Consequently, the availability of the latest equipment is often restricted to the wealthy industrialised nations and communities.

The availability of magnetic resonance imaging (MRI), positron emission tomography (PET) and radiation therapies may be available at only a few locations within a country or at major teaching hospitals within a capital city. In less developed countries, intensive care equipment and basic X-ray facilities may be in short supply.

Training for the profession

Biomedical engineering is unique within the engineering profession in the requirement to combine both a thorough understanding of engineering and an understanding of biology, particularly in relation to human health. This training creates professionals fluent in the technical jargon of both the engineering and medical fields.

Biomedical engineering is changing from a post-graduate to an undergraduate system as more and more universities establish biomedical engineering courses to meet market demand. Within Australia, several universities offer undergraduate training in biomedical engineering including:

- RMIT: Bachelor of Engineering (Biomedical)
- University of Sydney: Bachelor of Engineering (Biomedical)
- University of Melbourne: Bachelor of Biomedicine (Bioengineering)
- Griffith University: Bachelor of Engineering (Sport and Biomedical).

Career prospects

The career opportunities in biomedical engineering are particularly bright at present as the market for biomedical products and services continues to expand. Some estimates have suggested that the growth in the number of jobs within this sector is likely to be up to twice that in other fields of engineering in coming years.

Opportunities exist in a number of areas such as the pharmaceutical industry, academia, biomedical/ biotechnology research and development, medical equipment development, sales, health services or in government and consulting.

Further reading

Auckland Bioengineering Institute (n.d), retrieved 24 May 2013, from University of Auckland website, www. abi.auckland.ac.nz/uoa/

'Biomedical engineering' (n.d), retrieved 24 May 2013 from University of NSW website, www.handbook. unsw.edu.au/undergraduate/specialisations/2012/ BiomedicalEngineering.html

Department of Engineering (n.d), retrieved 24 May 2013 from Imperial College London website, www.3.imperial. ac.uk/bioengineering

Gerwin, V, 'Biomedicine meets engineering', *Nature*, vol. 425, pp. 324–325, September 2003, www.readcube.com/ articles/10.1038/nj6955-324a

Relations with the community

While the field of biomedical engineering as a profession is a rapidly growing one, it is probably true to say that its recognition within the community at large as a distinct field of study is relatively weak. This is no doubt due to the history of biomedical developments occurring in the traditional engineering fields with subsequent adaptation to a medical situation and the strong association of medical equipment with the medical profession itself.

This is perhaps best illustrated by the work of Arnold Beckman, an American chemist, who developed an electronic pH meter in 1934 in response to a request for an accurate means of measuring the pH of lemons.

An electronic pH meter is now standard equipment in most chemical and biological laboratories around the world. At the heart of the pH meter, Beckman devised a precision electrical resistance device called a helical potentiometer. The Helipot™, as it came to be known, forms a vital part of the control system in electronic games today, but at the time played an important part in the development of radar in WWII.

Beckman founded the National Technical Laboratories to manufacture his devices, later changing its name to Beckman Instruments. Over the years, Beckman developed many instruments that have become vital parts of biomedical equipment. Developments include the spectrophotometer (1940), which allowed the investigation of the structure of vitamins. This instrument later played a vital role in determining the structure of penicillin to assist in its mass production. By the 1960s, Beckman Instruments had become an important source of clinical instruments, including devices for peptide sequencing and analysis. Today, as Beckman–Coulter, it operates in over 120 countries, supplying automated equipment for biological analysis.

Technologies unique to the profession

Many of the imaging and monitoring technologies used in modern medicine today were specifically designed for medical use or found their greatest expression in this field.

X-rays were introduced into medical use soon after their discovery, and have become a mainstay of modern medicine. Today, through computerised axial tomography (CAT) scans, a 3D image can be obtained by combining a number of X-rays taken as a scanner circles the body.

Three-dimensional images can also be obtained using magnetic resonance imaging (MRI) in which the patient is placed at the centre of a strong magnetic field while being exposed to radio frequency (RF) pulses of energy. Computer systems analyse changes in energy levels within the body as it responds to the RF pulses to form an image.

Further reading

Arnold Beckman, PhD, biography (n.d), retrieved 24 May 2013 from Arnold and Mabel Beckman Foundation website, www.beckman-foundation.com/beckman.html

Harris, T, 'How CAT scans work' (n.d), retrieved 24 May 2013 from How Stuff Works website, www.science. howstuffworks.com/cat-scan.htm

Hornak, JP, PhD, 'The basics of MRI' (n.d), retrieved from The Basics of MRI website, www.cis.rit.edu/htbooks/mri/

'Products' (n.d), retrieved 24 May 2013 from Infinite Biomedical Technologies website, www.i-biomed.com/products/

Ethics and engineering

Many ethical and philosophical questions are raised by our increasing ability to intervene in the operation of the human body. Monitoring support equipment such as ventilators, dialysis machines, defibrillators and heart monitors allow body functions to be maintained while healing occurs. The availability of such machines, however, has resulted in intense debate at various times about when death occurs and the value versus quality of life. No answers will be found in this text, although a discussion of some of these issues within the classroom might prove useful.

Bioethics departments are now common in universities and hospitals around the world in order to advise on the ethics of research programs and practices. Indeed, the study of philosophy has been enlivened by the rise of bioengineering.

The use of animals as biological models in the development of medicines and operating procedures has been a standard practice for centuries. William Harvey pioneered work determining that the heart acted as a pump to circulate blood through the body. Published in 1628, Harvey's work was achieved through experiments on dogs. Operations such as hip replacements and the biocompatibility of many metals were originally performed on animals.

Today experiments must first pass a rigorous process of review by a bioethics panel before they can proceed. These panels review not only the expected outcomes of the research and how it is to be performed but also, using ethical guidelines, decide whether it should be undertaken. Special provisions are made for the informed consent of human patients while animal subjects must be maintained in a humane manner and only used when a viable alternative is not available and in a manner that does not result in unnecessary suffering.

Engineers as managers

The nature of engineering education is to define a problem and to look for practical solutions in a logical, methodical manner. This training also places great emphasis on teamwork and the efficient marshalling of resources.

Efficiency engineer FB Gilbreth revolutionised surgical procedure in the early 1900s by filming and analysing surgical procedures. He found that much inefficiency was caused by the practice of surgeons interrupting the operation to obtain the instrument needed. Gilbreth introduced the concept, common today, of a surgery assistant who provides instruments to the surgeon's outstretched hand while the surgeon concentrates on the operation. In so doing, the time taken to perform surgery was dramatically reduced. The skills of analysis Gilbreth brought to the operating theatre were equally as effective in analysing practices as in bricklaying and other industries of such disparate nature. Gilbreth was immortalised in popular culture by the book *Cheaper by the Dozen*, later made into a film of the same name in 1950. Gilbreth was essentially a researcher and consultant, a role in which good communication skills are essential. The effective implementation and acceptance of his results were left to others charged with managing the business concerned.

Because of their skills in problem solving and organisation, many senior engineers progress their careers into areas of management, particularly in technically-based organisations. These positions may even take them to industries well removed from their initial area of training. In order to prepare for such careers, post-graduate courses in management are often used to supplement engineering knowledge with skills in human resources. Increasingly, engineering courses themselves are placing greater emphasis on broader communication and interpersonal skills in preparation for the challenges of modern engineering and society.

Further reading

Karr, CL, 'Instructor's guide to written communication' (n.d), retrieved 25 May 2013 from University of Alabama website, www.foundationcoalition.org/home/FCVersion2/communication/420/instructor-guide.pdf

Beder, S, 'Towards a more representative engineering education', *International Journal of Applied Engineering Education*, vol. 5(2), pp. 173–182, 1989

4.2 Historical and societal influences

Historical background to biomedical engineering

The historical background to bioengineering is impossibly diverse for adequate treatment here, but might be appreciated by a brief examination of three product areas of biomedical engineering:

- surgical instruments

- prosthetics and implants

- monitoring devices.

Historical developments of products

Surgical instruments

The need for rudimentary surgical treatment, such as the removal of foreign objects from wounds and the separation of the umbilical cord following birth, have been required since before recorded history. These functions were no doubt initially performed using fingers and teeth. As tools were developed they were included in such procedures, increasing the facility and reducing the time required. These instruments were by necessity made using materials and techniques available at the time.

Early surgical instruments were therefore fashioned from sharpened stone (such as flint), wood, shell and bone and were articles that served general domestic and military roles such as knives, needles and scrapers.

The design of instruments was expanded and refined as the sophistication of surgery increased. By Greco-Roman times, around the 6th century BCE, instruments designed specifically for medical use were available, although knowledge of surgery, and anatomy in general in these societies progressed largely through the necessities of treating wounds incurred in battle.

At this time, instruments were made from materials common to the age such as bronze and iron. The precious metals such as gold and silver also achieved limited use for probes and tubes due to their corrosion resistance and malleability.

Few examples of these early instruments have survived. Bronze (an alloy of copper and tin) was widely used in surgical instruments but its value and wide application

in ancient times often resulted in the re-melting of these instruments for other purposes. Iron instruments were also widely used, principally as knives and forceps, although few remain due to the ravages of corrosion. One of the most famous archaeological collections of surgical instruments are those found in the ruins of a house in the Roman city of Pompeii, buried in 97 CE as a result of the eruption of Mt. Vesuvius. A selection of these instruments is shown in Figure 4.2.1.

Figure 4.2.1 Surgical instruments dating from 97 CE, found during the excavation of the ruins of Pompeii

Images of surgical instruments are also found in ancient Egyptian reliefs (note the scales in the bottom right corner), such as the one from the Kom Ombo Temple shown in Figure 4.2.2

Figure 4.2.2 Egyptian relief, image by Ad Meskens (own work), CC-BY-SA-3.0, via Wikimedia Commons

The manufacture of instruments for surgery was usually performed by craftsmen skilled in metal working, such as blacksmiths, armourers and cutlers.

By the 18th century, specialists in the manufacture of surgical instruments were appearing, as was the introduction of catalogues from which instruments could be purchased. Many of these instruments still incorporated a bronze blade although wrought iron became increasingly common. The instruments available at this time can be divided into the six basic groups recognised today.

1. Point (needle, drill)
2. Flatten (spatula, knife, saw)
3. Probe (dissector)
4. Fold (hook, tweezers, shears)
5. Canalise (cannula-tube, syringe, hollow bore needle)
6. Pivot (clamp, scissors, retractor)

Some of these instruments are shown in Figure 4.2.3.

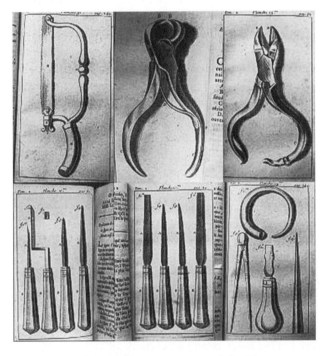

Figure 4.2.3 Surgical instruments made by Pierre Fauchard during the 18th century

By the 19th century wrought iron blades were gradually supplanted by steel. The handles of surgical instruments, however, continued to be commonly manufactured from materials such as wood, ebony, ivory or tortoiseshell until the introduction of aseptic surgery and sterilisation during the period 1885–1910.

Anaesthetic, in the form of ether, was introduced to the operating theatre for the first time in a Boston hospital in 1846. Up until then, operations were performed on conscious patients restrained to a table or chair.

Attempts at dulling the pain fell into three basic groups: chemical (using opium or alcohol), physical (such as bleeding to induce unconsciousness or the use of ice to numb the region) and psychological (positive thinking or in some instances hypnosis). Outside of these was panic and resignation to pain. A surgeon's skill was measured largely by the speed with which cutting could be concluded. The most common operation in these pre-penicillin days was amputation. If a patient survived surgery, ultimate recovery was dependent on the likelihood of post-operative infection as a result of sepsis (germs). The causes of infection remained unknown, however, until the discoveries of Louis Pasteur (1822–1895) and his germ theory in 1865. Although Ignaz Semmelweiss (1818–1865) had shown the importance of cleanliness in reducing infection in 1848 he had been largely ignored. Instruments at this time were used over and over again with little in the way of cleaning, with the exception of the handles which needed to be cleaned to ensure a firm grip. Other parts of the instrument, such as blades of knives and saws, were often left uncleaned.

The British surgeon Joseph Lister (1827–1912), influenced by Pasteur's germ theory, introduced antiseptic (against germs) procedures in 1865 with the use of carbolic acid. Lister insisted on hands, instruments and dressings being washed in a solution of carbolic acid. Similarly, surgery was performed in a fine spray of the solution to prevent contamination of the wound by airborne germs. These practices were later revised with the introduction of sterilisation or aseptic (without germs) techniques.

The requirements of cleaning to protect against infection had a profound effect on instrument design. Many instruments such as scissors and forceps were redesigned to allow separation to facilitate cleaning, while the handles of many instruments were redesigned to allow detachment for similar reasons.

Materials that did not react well to the sterilisation process such as ebony, which was prone to warping, were abandoned as was the use of elaborate designs that although providing increased grip when wetted by bodily fluids were difficult to adequately clean. Designs were therefore changed to simpler styles containing broader scalloped and fluted surfaces that provided grip while reducing the presence of hard-to-clean recesses and grooves. This change in design took some time to occur, however, and instruments with difficult to clean surfaces were still available at the beginning of the 20th century (see Figure 4.2.4).

Figure 4.2.4 Hey's saw, image by Medical History Museum, the University of Melbourne

Similarly, instruments that operated using a pivot mechanism such as scissors, clamps and forceps needed to be capable of easy separation and reattachment without loss of function over time. The design that was to become the most successful, known as the 'Aesculap' lock or 'box lock,' achieved dominance largely through its compatibility with machine drop forge operations, allowing quick and cheap manufacture and stability and reliability in service (see Figure 4.2.5).

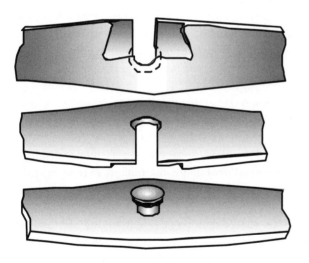

Figure 4.2.5 'Aesculap' lock or 'box lock'

The necessity of design change to meet the requirements of aseptic surgery led to a flurry of activity on behalf of manufacturers eager to develop and patent new instruments in the knowledge that every surgeon in the world would need to replace their existing equipment. Most of the new designs were created by instrument makers themselves rather than surgeons, due to a belief among the medical establishment of the time that to hold a patent was contrary to professional character.

With the increased concerns of eliminating germs from surgery, the presence of corrosion on instruments also became a focus of attention. Plating of instruments was a common response to such concerns, with silver plating and later nickel and chromium plating being introduced to prevent corrosion. While these materials provided some resistance to the corrosion of plain carbon steel implements, they were prone to peeling, particularly at pivot points. Corrosion of carbon steel, therefore, remained a problem until the introduction of stainless steel in the early 20th century. By 1925, stainless steel dominated surgical instruments, although disposable carbon steel scalpel blades are still preferred by many surgeons today due to their higher hardness and superior edge retention.

Despite these changes, instrument design and manufacture remained a largely boutique industry based on the individual requirements and designs of client surgeons until the mid 20th century, when some standardisation of quality requirements was introduced to regulate manufacture. Even today, however, the design of some reusable instruments pose problems of sterilisation and require special precautions and methods of inspection to ensure cleanliness.

Plastic was only introduced after WWII but is now used widely. The introduction of plastic also ushered in the concept of single use disposable equipment that was meant to largely eliminate many of the problems associated with cleaning. Tubing, syringes and instrument handles, particularly for disposable items, are often manufactured from polymers.

Further reading

Davis, AD, 'Medical technology' in Williams, TI (ed), *A History of Technology: c1900 to c1950, Part II*, vol. 2, pp. 1317–1361, Clarendon, Oxford, 1978

Edmonson, J M, 'Asepsis and the transformation of surgical instruments', *Transactions and Studies of the College of Physicians of Philadelphia*, vol. 13(1), pp. 75–91, 1991

Fenster, JM, *Ether day*, Perennial, New York, 2002

Kirkup, J, 'From flint to stainless steel: Observations on surgical instrument composition', *Annals of The Royal College of Surgeons of England*, vol. 75(5), pp. 365–374, 1993

Prosthetics and implants

A prosthetic device or prosthesis is an artificial part used to replace a damaged or diseased body part. These devices may therefore be attached to the body as either an external prosthetic, such as an artificial limb, or as an internal prosthetic, often referred to as an implant, such as an artificial hip joint.

Prosthetic devices have been used for centuries. Dentistry in particular has used gold for over 2000 years to repair teeth, while teeth made of wood or ivory have an extensive history. Glass eyes and prosthetic limbs made of wood or ivory have also been common. Evidence of a prosthetic wooden toe has been found. Figure 4.2.6 shows part of an ancient Egyptian female mummy buried near Luxor and now held in the Cairo Museum, dated at approximately 1000 BCE. The image clearly shows the big toe, carved from wood and attached to the foot by a sewn leather wrapping.

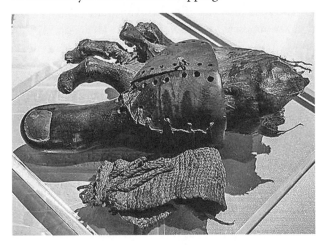

Figure 4.2.6 Wooden toe prosthetic from Egyptian mummy, c1000 BCE

While a need for such artificial limbs has existed for centuries, the industry remained relatively small until the introduction of modern warfare and the ability of artillery to inflict massive injuries on a large number of people. The demand for artificial limbs, therefore, rose dramatically with major conflicts such as the American Civil War, Crimean War and, later, WWI. Over this period the need for a large number of prosthetics (35 000 during the American Civil War alone) drove the need for design standardisation. Duralumin (an alloy of aluminium and copper) was also introduced during this period, while plastic limbs were introduced in the 1950s.

The use of internal prosthetics or implants has a shorter history and dates back approximately 440 years to 1565 when a gold plate was used to repair a cleft palate.

Restrictions to the use of implants resulted not only from ignorance of the basic functions of the human body and the limited availability of suitable materials, but by the unhygienic conditions under which surgery was performed.

Iron and brass wires, for example, were used for the stabilisation of bone fractures in 1775. However, the high rates of infection associated with injury at the time made identification of the implant as a contributing factor in failure difficult to establish. There is no doubt, however, that the poor corrosion resistance of these materials in the body would have proved detrimental.

Internal implants may be permanent, as is the case for hip or knee replacements, or temporary, such as plates and screws used to secure broken bones while healing occurs.

Metal plates for the repair of bone fractures secured by nails were first trialled in 1886 and were common by the 1900s. A number of metals, such as copper, aluminium, and silver, were experimented with and all but steel were found to be unsuitable. Even steel was found to have a life of less than six weeks if staining of adjacent tissue with corrosion products was to be avoided. From the mid 1920s studies increasingly focused on the effects of implant materials on adjacent tissues and on the process of bone repair. The austenitic stainless steel Type 304, consisting of 18wt% Cr and 8wt% Ni, was found to have superior properties to those metals previously used and gained wide acceptance. Problems with corrosion of this grade in the saline (chloride containing) environment of the body remained however.

In 1934, a cobalt-based alloy known commercially as Vitallium™, previously used in orthodontics (dentistry) and consisting of cobalt, chromium and molybdenum (CoCrMo), was trialled and found to be superior in all respects to previously implanted metals. It was however very expensive.

Type 316 stainless steel was trialled in 1938 and was much cheaper than the CoCrMo alloy. Type 316 stainless steel is a variant of the 18/8 Type 304 grade and contains a 2–3 wt% molybdenum addition that greatly increases its resistance to corrosion in saline environments. For some time stainless steel was the material of choice for implants because of its greater availability and cost. Today, stainless steel is used primarily for temporary implants such as bone plates and screws as some corrosion and adverse tissue reactions can still occur over time, especially where crevice corrosion is a possibility.

Titanium was investigated in 1954 and has gained wide acceptance due to its excellent combination of corrosion resistance, biocompatibility and mechanical properties, including its strength to weight ratio.

In 1962, the first total hip replacement was performed by the British surgeon John Charnley. In this operation the natural ball and socket joint of the hip is replaced by an implant. The top of the femur containing the ball is removed and a space in the bone reamed to accommodate the stem of the implant. Fixation of the stem within the bone is commonly accomplished by filling with the polymer cement polymethylmethacrylate (PMMA) although cement-less fixation is also used. The socket half of the joint consists of a cup-like pad, which is secured to the appropriate position in the hip bone.

Charnley originally used the polymer Teflon (PTFE) for the cup due to its low coefficient of friction. This was soon changed to HMWPE (high molecular weight polyethylene) as Teflon was found to deteriorate, shedding flakes of Teflon into the surrounding tissue. A number of alternative designs have been developed since Charnley, although they all exhibit similar features.

Figure 4.2.7 is an X-ray of a pelvis showing a total hip joint replacement. The right hip joint (on the left in the photograph) has been replaced. A metal prostheses is cemented in the top of the right femur and the head of the femur has been replaced by the rounded head of the prosthesis. A white plastic cup is cemented into the acetabulum to complete the two surfaces of the artificial 'ball and socket' joint.

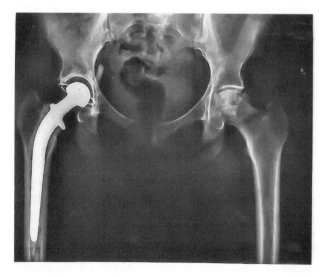

Figure 4.2.7 Total hip replacement

The Australian Orthopaedics Association (AOA) monitors the outcomes from all joint replacement operations and maintains a National Joint Replacement Registry, similar to registries maintained in other countries, in order to establish best practice.

In 2011 over 700 000 hip and knee joint replacement procedures were performed in Australia, using a wide variety of materials, designs and techniques (AOA Annual Report 2012).

Further reading

Bliquez LJ, 'Prosthetics in classical antiquity: Greek, Etruscan and Roman prosthetics', in Haase, W and Temporini, H, (eds), *Aufstieg und niedergang der Römischen welt II*, pp. 2640–2676, Walter de Gruyter, Berlin and New York, 1996

Fischer, LP, Planchamp, W, Fischer, B and Chauvin, F, 'The first total hip prostheses in man (1890–1960)', *Histoire des sciences médicales*, vol. 34(1), pp. 57–70, 2000

Guyatt, M, 'Better legs: Artificial limbs for British veterans of the first world war', *Journal of Design History*, vol. 14(4), pp. 307–325, 2001

Kalyani, N, 'Developments in mechanical heart valve prostheses', *Sadhana*, vol. 28, pp. 575–587, 2003

Kusy, RP, 'Orthodontic biomaterials: From the past to the present' (2002), *Angle Orthodontist*, vol. 72(6), pp. 501–509, 2002

Murphy, WB, 'Spare parts', Twenty-First Century Books, Brookfield, 2001

Nerlich et al, 'Ancient Egyptian prosthesis of the big toe', *The Lancet*, vol. 356, pp. 2176–2179, PubMed, 2000

Norton, KM, 'A brief history of prosthetics', *Motion*, vol. 17(7), November/December 2007

Reeves, N, 'New light on ancient Egyptian prosthetic medicine', Davies, V, (ed), *Studies in honour of Egyptian antiquities: a tribute to T G H James*, British Museum Press, London, 1999

Sonstegard, DA et al, 'The surgical replacement of the human knee joint', *Scientific American*, vol. 238(1), pp. 44–51, 1978

Monitoring devices and aids

Modern medicine today uses a multitude of devices to assist in the monitoring, testing and treating of patients. Some suggested sources of information on a few of these instruments are provided at the end of this section. Many of these devices are complex and expensive machines, some of which are unique to medicine. Figure 4.2.8, however, shows a stethoscope and demonstrates relative simplicity while showing development of design and materials over time. It is also one of the few pieces of equipment that has been developed largely by physicians themselves, at least until recently.

The stethoscope

The stethoscope (from the Greek *stethos*, meaning 'to observe') is probably the most immediately recognisable symbol of the medical profession, yet its history extends back to only the beginning of the 19th century. It marks the beginning of the use of equipment to augment the senses of the physician in the diagnosis of illness and monitoring of patient health.

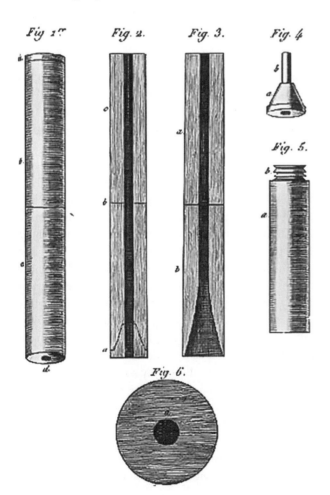

Figure 4.2.8 Laennec stethoscope drawings, 1819

The French physician Rene Laennec is credited with the invention of the stethoscope in 1816 when he used a pasteboard roll to assist in the amplification of sound from the lungs of a patient. Later versions were manufactured from wood drilled through, with a bell-shaped opening at one end. The Laennec stethoscope became an almost immediate success following the publication of Laennec's work in 1819. Later, modifications were made in materials and design by a number of physicians and instrument makers.

Modifications largely maintained the one ear or 'monaural' design. Pierre Piorry, for example, developed a trumpet-like design in 1826, which became the basis for most of the subsequent monaural designs.

The Piorry model (see Figure 4.2.9) was made of wood, was of much thinner wall thickness and approximately half the length of Laennec's stethoscope. Some models incorporated a removable ivory earpiece and chest piece. Various modifications based on the Piorry design were available in wood, ivory or silver-plated metal.

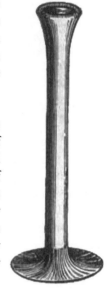

4.2.9 Piorry stethoscope design, 1851

Flexible monaural designs were available by the 1830s, consisting of a bell-shaped chest piece and an earpiece connected by a flexible tube constructed of a coiled spring covered in woven silk. The tube was restricted to a length of approximately 0.5 m (about the length of a physician's arm) to avoid excessive length and the need to coil the tube, which might reduce sensitivity. The discovery of the vulcanisation of rubber by Dunlop further improved the options for flexible tubing, leading to designs incorporating rubber cloth lined with a spiral and elastic iron wire. The stethoscope, however, remained largely a monaural device.

The photo shown in Figure 4.2.10 is a unique Piorry flexible stethoscope. This monaural device consisted of ivory chest and ear pieces. The flexible tubing allowed for passing between physicians without disturbing the placement of the chest bell.

Figure 4.2.10 Piorry flexible stethoscope, 1835

Binaural designs were slow to gain favour until that of the American physician George Camman in 1855. The Camman stethoscope used two flexible metal tubes fabricated from copper or tin and held together by a hinged joint as shown in Figure 4.2.11 Tension between the tubes was maintained by a rubber band. The tubes joined with a ball that was provided to amplify any sound coming from the bell-shaped chest piece. The bell was originally made of ebony while the earpieces at the end of the flexible tubes were ivory. This stethoscope largely superseded the monaural designs and is very similar to that used today.

Figure 4.2.11 Camman stethoscope, 1855

The bell design is particularly suited to the reception of low frequency sounds. High frequency sounds are better heard with a flat diaphragm type head, which was often accomplished with the use of an inset that could fit snugly into the bell. The diaphragm was manufactured from any number of materials such as hard rubber, silk, mica or metal.

The modern stethoscope incorporates both a bell and diaphragm design to allow the reception of both high and low frequency sounds, as shown in Figure 4.2.12.

Figure 4.2.12 Modern binaural stethoscope

Further reading

Blaxford, MD, 'An ear to the chest: an illustrated history of the evolution of the stethoscope', Parthenon, London, 2002

Reiser, SJ, 'The medical influence of the stethoscope', *Scientific American*, vol. 240(2),pp. 114–118 and 121–122, 1979

The effect of biomedical engineering on people's lives

The loss of a limb can have a dramatic impact on quality of life, both in terms of dignity and in terms of ability to find work. The provision of an artificial limb can go a long way to restoring independence and productivity. The cost of such appliances, however, is often high and availability low in countries most in need, such as those affected by war. Land mines claim many new victims every year, both young and old. With a life of over fifty years, mines can remain active well past the end of any conflict, so that the impact on human life can go on for decades. The victims of such devices are often children. A child who has lost a limb may need a new prosthetic every six months to accommodate growth. Biomedical engineers in many countries have worked to provide low-cost prosthetics that can return the hope of an active and productive life. In communities affected by war, the availability of such technology has an impact not only on the individual but also on the health of the local economy.

Biomedical engineering also affects a large portion of the community every day in less dramatic fashion. These influences include the design and manufacture of devices to assist in daily life such as:

- special utensils that allow the opening of a bottle or can by people with arthritis

- programs that allow the hearing impaired to use a telephone

- modification of eating utensils to allow their use by the physically impaired

- improvements in mobility by the design of wheel chairs, walkers, car steering

- design of monitoring equipment that allows treatment at home rather than in a hospital

- design of protective equipment such as safety helmets and mouth protectors.

These and many other examples serve to illustrate the wide influence biomedical engineering can have on the lives of individuals and communities.

Not all biomedical developments have been without controversy, however, with some leading to intense debate about their appropriateness. This is perhaps no better illustrated than by the reaction of the deaf community to the introduction of the cochlear implant and concerns about damage to their unique culture.

Similarly, controversy over the effects of silicone breast implants on the health of recipients following leakage of silicone to surrounding tissue led to extensive legal action and large settlements against Dow Chemicals in the 1980s.

Because of the potential to produce dramatic improvements in quality of life there are particularly high expectations placed on the field of biomedical engineering. These include the professional standards of practitioners and the integrity and quality of the testing, validation, production and supply processes for equipment.

Further reading

'The cochlear implant' (n.d), retrieved 26 May 2013 from Powerhouse Museum website, www.powerhousemuseum.com/hsc/cochlear/the_cochlear.htm

Drewry Jr, RD, 'What man devised that he might see' (n.d), retrieved from Teagle Optometry website, www.teagleoptometry.com/history.htm

'Getting an artificial leg up', retrieved 26 May 2013 from ABC News website, www.abc.net.au/science/slab/leg/default.htm

Grossman, J, 'Rebuilding limbs and lives', *Rush Record*, pp. 2–5, Fall/Winter 2002–2003

Lawrence, M, 'Rehabilitation engineers work to perfect artificial limbs', summer 1997, retrieved 26 May 2013 from The Mission website, www.uthscsa.edu/mission/summer97/rehab.html

Lloyd, K, 'Cochlear implants—the AAD view', *Vicdeaf News*, October 2001

McGirk, T, 'Heroes of medicine: the $28 foot', *Time*, October 1997

NAD Cochlear Implant Committee, 'Cochlear implants', retrieved 26 May 2013 from National Association of the Deaf website, www.nad.org/issues/technology/assistive-listening/cochlear-implants

'Overseas' (n.d), retrieved 26 May 2013 from the Fred Hollows Foundation website, www.hollows.org.au/Fred-Hollows/overseas/

Pence, J, 'It's like being born again', *The Lutheran*, April 1996

4.3 Engineering mechanics and hydraulics

Mechanical advantage, velocity ratio and efficiency

Mechanical advantage (MA) is the actual benefit obtained using simple machines such as levers and is directly calculated using the relationship between the load (resistance) and the effort. That is, it represents the amount to which the machine amplifies effort.

For example, if by using a simple machine a 500 N object can be moved by applying an effort of only 10 N, a mechanical advantage of 50 was obtained. Since both the load and effort are measured in newtons they cancel each other out so that MA is a dimensionless number:

$$MA = \frac{load}{effort}$$

The velocity ratio (VR) is the ratio of the distance moved by the effort compared with the distance moved by the load:

$$VR = \frac{distance\ moved\ by\ effort}{distance\ moved\ by\ load}$$

Values of VR greater than 1 indicate there is a magnification of effort operating, while values less than 1 indicate that a diminution of effort exists. Again, since both the figures in this equation have common units, they cancel out to produce a dimensionless result.

Efficiency (η) is a measure of the effectiveness, expressed as a percentage, with which the effort supplied is translated by the machine into work, or a measure of the output compared with the input:

$$\eta = \frac{work\ output}{work\ input} \times 100$$

since Work = Force × distance

$$= \frac{load \times distance\ moved\ by\ load\ arm \times 100}{effort \times distance\ moved\ by\ efort\ arm}$$

$$= \frac{MA}{VR}$$

For an ideal machine, where no energy losses occur due to friction or gravity, the efficiency is 100%.

Most first and second-class levers would be expected to provide a VR > 1, although a VR < 1 for a first-class lever is still possible. In this arrangement, a diminution of effort results in a magnification of movement and since the load is made to move a greater distance than the effort in the same time, a greater velocity is achieved. This arrangement was the basis of the trebuchet (illustrated in Figure 4.3.1), a medieval war machine used to hurl missiles. When a weighted basket was allowed to fall under gravity the beam rotated about the fulcrum accelerating the load (missile), which was projected towards the opposition.

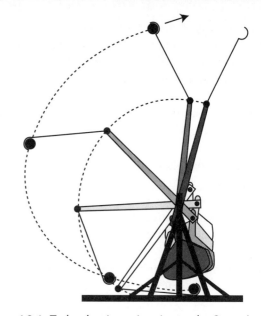

Figure 4.3.1 Trebuchet in action, image by Onno (own work) via Wikimedia Commons

Many first-class levers evident in the human body are not magnifiers of effort but are magnifiers of motion and have a VR < 1. Third-class levers always have a VR< 1. Although instruments such as the tweezers (shown in Figure 4.3.2) essentially consist of two opposing levers, one is considered to be stationary with respect to the other for the purposes of analysis.

Worked example of a third-class lever

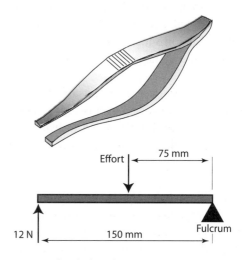

Figure 4.3.2 Third-class lever—surgical tweezers

$$\Sigma\ moments = 0$$

$$(effort \times effort\ arm) - (load \times load\ arm) = 0$$

$$(E \times 0.075) - (12 \times 0.15) = 0$$

$$E = 24\ N$$

In another surgical instrument that utilises levers, scissors, the position of the load continuously changes during operation. With this change, the angle at which forces act relative to the lever can also vary. A simple example of this is shown in Figure 4.3.3. In this case, two first-class levers work in opposition. As the scissors close, the position of cutting (load) moves away from the fulcrum and as it does so the effort required to continue cutting increases. Note also the change in the angle at which the forces act relative to the levers depicted.

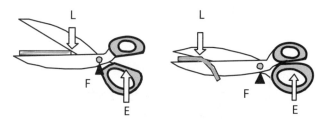

Figure 4.3.3 Changing position of the load during the use of a pair of scissors

Orders of levers

A significant development in the study of levers occurred with the analysis of their operation within the human body. Italian scientist Giovanni Alfonso Borelli (1608–1679) is credited with the application of the mechanics of the lever to the study of human movement.

Movement is derived by the action of muscles on the bones of the skeleton, particularly the long bones, which act as the levers while the joints serve as the fulcrum. Although this observation was made by both Aristotle and later in the second century by the Roman physician Galen (130–210 CE), the true nature of lever systems within the human body were not appreciated. Galen assumed that human movement was the result of long lever arms allowing weak muscles to overcome large resistive loads.

This assertion went largely unquestioned until Borelli's analysis, which showed that because the muscle attachments which convey the effort are located close to the joints, the levers of the human body were primarily magnifiers of motion rather than force. This meant that a greater effort must be exerted than the resistive load the lever is trying to overcome. The treatise detailing his work was published in 1680 following his death, and was appropriately titled *De Motu Animalium (On the movement of animals),* the same as Aristotles' study of the mechanics of animal movement written over 1900 years earlier.

Because of his work on human movement Borrelli is considered by many to be the father of biomechanics.

First-class levers

There are several first-class levers in the human body, with the head being perhaps the most obvious example.

An adult human head weighs between 4.5 kg and 5 kg. The head pivots at the junction of the occipital bone of the skull with the atlas bone at the top of the spine. Movement is controlled by the sternocleidomastoid and trapezius muscles attached to the sides and rear of the skull. When the head is held upright and facing forward, as shown in Figure 4.3.4, the centre of gravity of the head lies over the atlanto-occipital joint. In this position the muscles of the neck can be considered to be at rest.

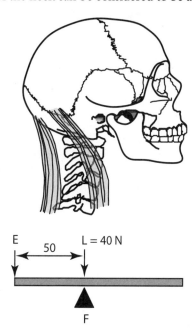

Figure 4.3.4 The head and neck as a first-class lever at rest, centre of gravity over the atlanto-occipital joint

$$\Sigma \text{ Moments} = 0$$

$$(\text{effort} \times \text{effort arm}) - (\text{load} \times \text{load arm}) = 0$$

$$(E \times 0.05) - (40 \times 0) = 0$$

$$E = 0$$

As the head is lowered, the centre of gravity moves away from the fulcrum and an opposing force must be applied by the neck muscles to hold the head in position. In the example shown in Figure 4.3.5 all distances are assumed to be effective lever arms for simplicity.

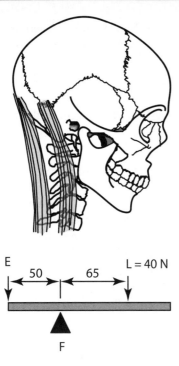

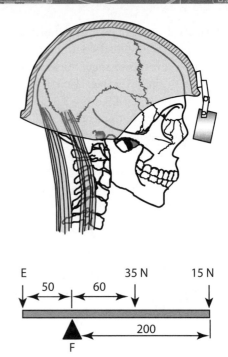

Figure 4.3.5 The head and neck as a first-class lever with the head lowered

Figure 4.3.6 Head and neck as a first-class lever with head slightly lowered plus additional loading

$$\Sigma \text{ Moments} = 0$$

$$(\text{effort} \times \text{effort arm}) - (\text{load} \times \text{load arm}) = 0$$

$$(E \times 0.05) - (40 \times 0.065) = 0$$

$$E = 52 \text{ N}$$

Therefore, the muscles would need to exert a force of 52 N to hold the head in equilibrium.

In many occupations and leisure activities some form of protective helmet must be worn which will add to the load that must be resisted by the muscles of the neck. This is of particular concern to sections of the armed services, and search and rescue, where extra equipment such as night-vision goggles or heads up display (HUD) units may be attached to the front of the helmet.

Worked example 1

In the example shown in Figure 4.3.6 the head is slightly tilted forward such that the centre of gravity is approximately 60 mm from the fulcrum and is exerting a load of 35 N (includes the weight of the helmet). The night-vision device attached to the front of the helmet weighs 1.5 kg and is approximately 200 mm from the fulcrum.

$$\Sigma \text{ moments} = 0$$

$$(\text{effort} \times \text{effort arm}) - (\text{load} \times \text{load arm}) = 0$$

$$(E \times 0.05) - [(35 \times 0.060) + (15 \times 0.20)] = 0$$

$$E = 102 \text{ N}$$

Worked example 2

Another example of a first-class lever is the action of the triceps on the bones of the forearm (Figure 4.3.7).

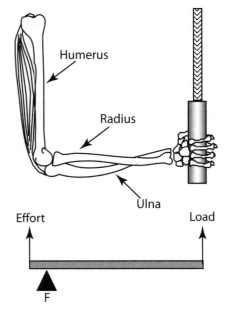

Figure 4.3.7 Forearm and triceps as a first-class lever

The triceps act as extensors allowing the forearm to straighten relative to the upper arm bone, the humerus. As may be seen in Figure 4.3.7, the triceps are attached to the ulna bone at a position close to the fulcrum represented by the elbow joint. The effort arm is therefore very short compared to the load arm, represented by the length of much of the ulna and the bones of the wrist (carpals) and hand (metacarpals).

Worked example 3

What effort would need to be exerted by the triceps to hold the bell-pull in place as shown in Figure 4.3.7, if the bell-pull offers a resistive force of 10 N? Assume the triceps insertion point in the ulna is 25 mm from the elbow, while the bell-pull held in the hand is 300 mm from the elbow. For the purpose of this exercise the weight of the forearm will be ignored.

$$\Sigma \text{ Moments} = 0$$

$$(\text{effort} \times \text{effort arm}) - (\text{load} \times \text{load arm}) = 0$$

$$(E \times 0.025) - (10 \times 0.300) = 0$$

$$E = 120 \text{ N}$$

Note: the large effort that the triceps must supply to overcome a relatively small resistive load due to the attachment position of the muscle. The real benefit of this arrangement is not in magnifying the force of the muscles but in magnifying the speed and distance moved by the arms and legs. Because of the difference in the lever arms, the muscles of the arms and legs need to contract over a relatively short distance to produce a large movement at the other end, as shown in Figure 4.3.8.

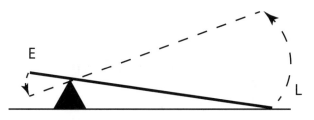

Figure 4.3.8 First-class lever as a magnifier of motion

Second-class levers

There are few second-class levers in the human body. One example of such a lever is the action of lifting the heel of the foot off the ground, as illustrated in Figure 4.3.9. The metatarsal heads act as the fulcrum while the weight of the body acts down through the tibia. The

heel bone (calcaneus) is raised by the contraction of the calf muscle, which is attached to the heel bone by the Achilles tendon.

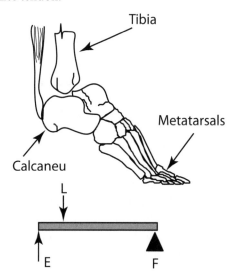

Figure 4.3.9 Lifting of the heel as an example of a second-class lever

The load arm is the distance from the head of the tibia at the ankle joint to the metatarsal heads, while the force arm is the distance between the attachment point of the calf muscle to the heel bone and the metatarsal heads.

Worked example 4

Determine the calf muscle force that must be exerted to hold the heel in the raised position shown in Figure 4.3.10 if the person weighs 60 kg.

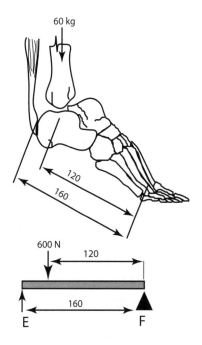

Figure 4.3.10 Lifting of the heel—a second-class lever

For the purpose of simplicity, assume the weight of the foot is negligible and all distances represent effective lever arms. Assume the person places all of their weight on one foot.

$$\Sigma \text{ moments} = 0$$

$$(\text{effort} \times \text{effort arm}) - (\text{load} \times \text{load arm}) = 0$$

$$(E \times 0.160) - (600 \times 0.120) = 0$$

$$E = 450 \text{ N}$$

Note: a variation of this problem would have been to represent the load force of the body as a ground reaction force or GRF. Since the body is being resisted by the ground at the fulcrum, the diagram could have been presented as shown in Figure 4.3.11.

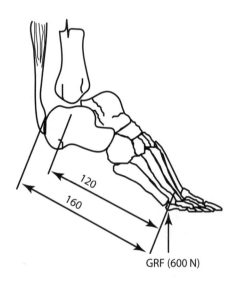

Figure 4.3.11 *Ground force reaction*

Third-class levers

The most easily recognised third-class lever in the human body is probably the action of the biceps muscle on the radius bone of the forearm. The biceps act as flexors, allowing the forearm to bend relative to the upper arm bone, the humerus. As may be seen in Figure 4.3.12 the biceps are attached to the radius bone at a position close to the fulcrum represented by the elbow joint.

The effort arm is therefore very short compared to the load arm, represented by the length of the radius and the bones of the wrist (carpals) and hand (metacarpals).

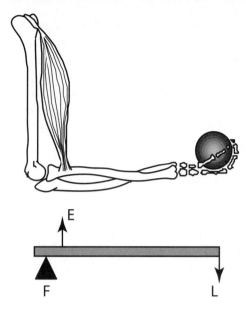

Figure 4.3.12 *Forearm and biceps—third-class lever*

Worked example 5

Determine the effort required to hold a steel ball of mass 2.6 kg in the hand as shown in Figure 4.3.13. Assume the weight of the forearm and hand is 11 N and acts through a centre of gravity 124 mm from the elbow.

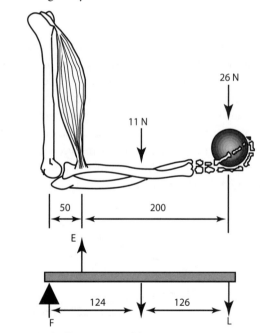

Figure 4.3.13 *Forearm problem*

$$\Sigma \text{ moments} = 0$$

$$(\text{effort} \times \text{effort arm}) - (\text{load} \times \text{load arm}) = 0$$

$$(E \times 0.05) - [(11 \times 0.124) + (26 \times 0.250)] = 0$$

$$E = 157.28 \text{ N}$$

An illustration of the variation in angle of the muscle and load to the lever arm that may be experienced during flexure of the biceps is represented in Figure 4.3.14.

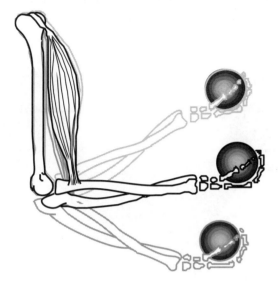

Figure 4.3.14 Illustration of the variation in angle the biceps make with the forearm in flexing

An accurate calculation of effort would therefore require consideration of the effective lever arms. Similarly, resolution of forces acting at an oblique angle to the lever arm into horizontal and vertical components would reveal a horizontal component that must be resisted by muscles at the joint (fulcrum).

Further reading

Martin, RB, (presenter), 'A genealogy of biomechanics', speech presented at 23rd Annual Conference of the American Society of Biomechanics, University of Pittsburgh, PA, 23 October 1999

Velocity ratio

A measure of the theoretical benefit obtained by using a lever can be represented by a measure known as the velocity ratio (VR). The VR compares the length of the effort arm to the length of the load arm by way of a simple ratio:

$$VR = \frac{\text{length of effort arm}}{\text{length of load arm}}$$

Values of VR greater than 1 indicate there is a magnification of effort operating, while values less than 1 indicate that a diminution of effort exists. Most first and second-class levers would be expected to provide a VR > 1, although as shown previously, many first-class

levers in the human body are not magnifiers of effort and have a VR < 1. Third-class levers always have a VR< 1.

Mechanical advantage (MA) is the actual benefit obtained using simple machines such as levers and is directly calculated using the relationship between the load and the effort:

$$MA = \frac{\text{load}}{\text{effort}}$$

or through the application of efficiency using the relationship:

$$\text{Efficiency} = \frac{MA}{VR}$$

Note that for systems of 100% efficiency MA = VR.

Worked example 6

Determine the velocity ratio of the first-class lever system shown in Figure 4.3.15.

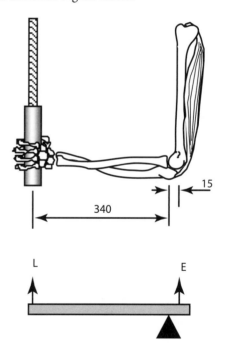

Figure 4.3.15 First-class lever problem

VR = 15 ÷ 340

= 0.044

In this case the MA is also less than 1 and force is not magnified in the system. Note that because MA is a ratio of two values with identical units, the units cancel so that mechanical advantage is a dimensionless figure.

4.4 Engineering materials

Forming methods

The manufacture of surgical instruments and prosthetic devices was a manual skill until the 20th century. Manufacture was undertaken by a number of specialist craftsmen such as carpenters, goldsmiths, blacksmiths, foundrymen, cutlers and armourers. The basic practices employed by these craftsmen continue today, although on a larger scale and with the assistance of automation and an understanding of material properties unknown in previous ages. Metals for specialised applications such as aerospace and biomedicine are commonly processed using vacuum melting and electro-slag refining (ESR) techniques to attain high levels of cleanliness, with very low inclusion contents.

Methods of forming, particularly when related to metals, can be divided into four basic groups of:

- plastic deformation (forging and rolling)

- casting

- cutting

- joining.

Plastic deformation

A number of processes involve plastic deformation in order to form an item. The majority of these processes are performed at elevated temperatures in order to reduce the amount of energy required for deformation. These processes include:

- forging

- rolling.

Forging

The forging processes involve the compression of material held at elevated temperature between flat or shaped surfaces known as dies in order to produce plastic flow.

Rapid blows result in the maximum forces to the material occurring as the forging hammer hits the surface. Deformation occurs primarily on the surface layers. Slower compression of the material by a forging press results in deeper penetration of the deformation zone.

Forged items display increased strength due to improved directional properties since metal flow occurs parallel to the surface, resulting in a favourable orientation of inclusions and grains. An example of the metal flow obtained in forging is illustrated in Figure 4.4.1.

Figure 4.4.1 Grain flow pattern developed forging, image courtesy of Glenn McKechnie (own work), CC-BY-SA-2.5, via Wikimedia Commons

The forging process is often defined by whether forging is performed between open or closed dies.

Open die forging

In open die forging the dies are generally of simple geometric shape and the material is not completely enclosed by the die (see Figure 4.4.2).

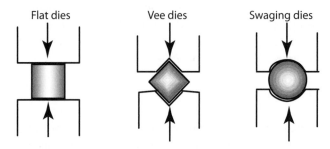

Figure 4.4.2 Schematic representation of the three basic forms of open die forging

Applications of open die forging include:

- simple shapes

- short order to delivery cycle

- quantity too small to justify closed die

- forgings that are too large for closed die

- products whose mechanical properties cannot be obtained by machining from billet.

Closed die forging

Closed die forging is performed using carefully machined dies that completely enclose the material between the die walls.

Marginally more material than required is supplied to the die to ensure complete filling of the cavity. Excess material is extracted into a thin cavity around the main cavity, creating a 'flash' that is later removed.

Metal flow occurs parallel to the surface, resulting in a favourable orientation of inclusions and grains (see Figures 4.4.1 and 4.4.3).

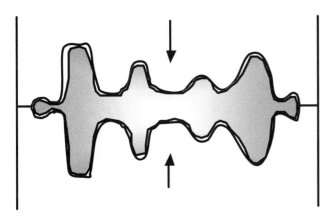

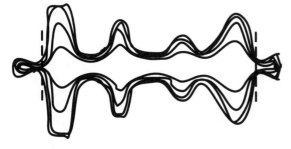

Figure 4.4.3 Schematic of closed die forging (top) and grain flow patterns following forging (bottom)

Applications of closed die forging include:

- high volume production

- complex shapes

- heavy reductions

- products where control of grain flow is important

- products with close dimensional tolerances

- objects requiring minimum subsequent machining.

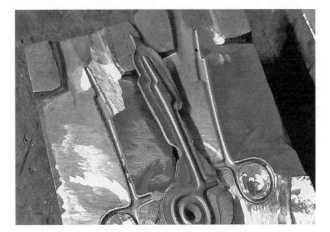

Figure 4.4.4 Forging and die, image by Dr Frigz, www. blog.frigzinternational.com/2011/11/30/surgical- instruments-forging-101/

Forging surgical instruments

After forging, surgical instruments are ground and milled to remove excess material (flash) from the forging. Additional features are also created at this point such as teeth, serration, etc. Machining operations may be conducted a number of times to fashion the instrument to the final shape. At this stage stainless steel instruments are tempered to remove any brittleness while still retaining hardness. Polishing is the next operation to provide a smooth finish, free of microscopic imperfections that may harbour organic debris. Figure 4.4.4 shows a forged instrument freshly released from the die.

Further reading

Akridge, J, 'Surgical instruments: From bones and stones to stainless steel and high technology' (n.d), retrieved 26 May 2013 from Surgical Instruments Guide website, www.hpnonline.com/inside/2004-03/surgical%20 instruments.htm

Rolling

The hypodermic needle, one of the most iconic of biomedical devices, is produced at least in part by rolling. The raw material for the manufacture of a needle is a flat strip of steel (usually 304 or 304 L austenitic stainless steel) that has been rolled to approximately 20 mm wide and 0.5mm thick. This strip is then formed into a tube by passing the strip through a series of rollers and the seam welded using either the gas tungsten arc welding (GTAW) or laser welding processes. This tube, which may be 6 mm in diameter at this initial stage, is subsequently annealed to soften it in preparation for drawing through a series of dies which will reduce the tube diameter and increase its length until the required diameter or gauge is obtained. The final drawing operation is typically performed cold to increase strength through cold work. Needle gauges in common use can range from 6 gauge (5 mm) to 36 gauge (0.10 mm). The tube so produced is then cut to length and one end ground to create the beveled needle point.

Further reading

'Hypo Tube Manufacturing' (n.d), Advanced Tube Solutions website www.advancedtube.com/5.html

Casting

Investment casting (lost wax casting)

Investment casting (also known as lost wax and precision casting), represents a sub-set of sand casting and is used extensively for the production of precision components such as hip and knees joints. In the investment casting process illustrated in Figure 4.4.5 a permanent mould or die (often made of metal) is used to produce an expendable wax pattern. The pattern may then be incorporated into an assembly with similar patterns, and attached to a wax feeding system. The whole assembly is subsequently dipped into a ceramic slurry to build up a coating. Fine sand is then added to form a strong shell and the assembly allowed to dry. The dry assembly is then placed in a mould flask and surrounded by a coarser sand/slurry mixture and dried. As an added assurance of internal quality, investment cast prosthetic components also undergo a hot isostatic pressing (HIP) treatment in which they are placed in a pressure vessel containing argon gas and exposed to elevated pressure and temperature. This treatment results in the closing of any internal voids in the casting, resulting in improved mechanical properties, approaching that of wrought components.

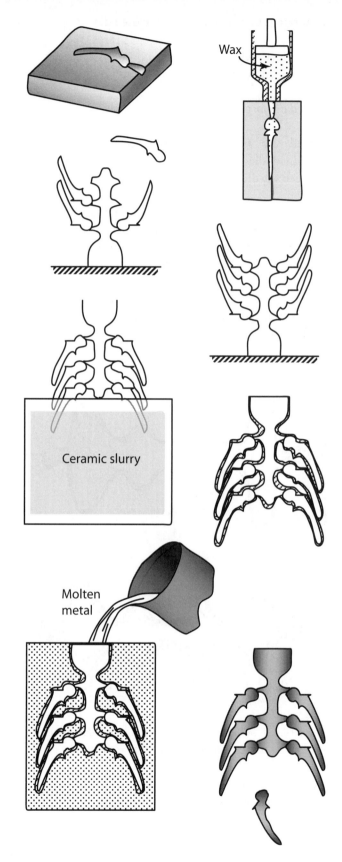

Figure 4.4.5 The investment casting process

Joining

Powder forming

Powder forming, also known as powder metallurgy (PM), is the process of first creating metal powders then blending and compacting the mixture in a die. The resultant shapes are then heated or 'sintered' in a controlled atmosphere furnace to bond the particles, as indicated in Figure 4.4.6.

During the sintering operation densification occurs, through which the particles change shape by plastic flow and diffusion, to agglomerate and reduce inter-particle voids. In multiphase systems such as WC–Co, the lower melting point material will form a layer around the higher melting point particles, filling voids and acting as a binder.

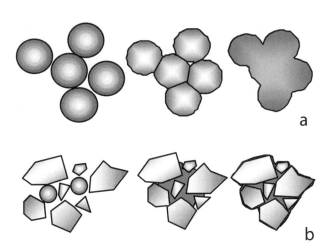

Figure 4.4.6 Sintering process for a) single phase material, b) multiphase material such as WC–Co

Materials produced by powder metallurgy

Many of the modern ceramics used in biomedical applications are formed by powered metallurgy techniques, including those listed below.

- Porous materials: the chief products in the group are filters and oil-retaining bearings, often referred to as self-lubricating bearings. These products cannot readily or satisfactorily be produced by alternative processes.

- Hard materials: producing a whole range of cutting tools and wear parts, such as tungsten carbide bonded with cobalt shown in Figure 4.4.7.

- Metals with very high melting points, that is, the refractory metals tungsten, molybdenum and tantalum are very difficult to produce by melting and casting.

- Composite materials: two or more metals which are insoluble even in the liquid state, or mixtures of metals with non-metallic substances such as oxides and other refractory materials.

Figure 4.4.7 Tungsten carbide particles in cobalt matrix

Welding and soldering

Tungsten carbide (WC) tips, jaws or cutting surfaces are often added as an insert to stainless steel instruments.

The WC provides exceptional wear properties on contacting surfaces but also maintains edge sharpness for greater periods of time. The WC insert is most often soldered to the stainless steel instrument, providing a firm bond but one that allows for future replacement of the insert. When a more permanent join is required welding is specified but this of course does not allow for the insert to be replaced over time.

Plates, screws, pins and staples

Plates, screws and nails find widespread use in the internal fixation of bone fractures. With the help of these components fractured bones are realigned and held in place until the body's natural processes of repair can heal the fractures.

Metal staples by contrast are often used in soft tissue wound closure.

Screws derive their fixation strength from a mechanical bond in which pull-out requires the shearing of material contained between the threads. As a screw is driven into an assembly, the joint is placed in compression when the head of the screw meets the surface. Many screws used in the body for bone fixation are cannulated, that is, they have a hollow bore along their longitudinal axis. This allows the screw to be guided down a positioning wire into the correct position. Once the screw is in position the wire is removed through the cannula.

A variety of metals are used for plates, screws, pins and staples. Austenitic stainless steel and titanium are possibly the most widely used.

Adhesives

Adhesives find extensive, although often unnoticed, use in bioengineering. The needle (cannula) used in hypodermic syringes is retained within the hub by an adhesive cured using ultraviolet light while a modified cyanoacrylate (super glue) is often used to close minor cuts in the skin without the need of stitches.

Cutting

Machining

Machining operations are routinely performed as a final operation on both cast and forged components to reach final tolerances and to drill holes. Many components are also routinely machined from bar stock through to finished product on a single numerically controlled (NC) machine. Computer control allows the programming of a sequence of operations along with the automatic repositioning of the component along multiple axes. Polymer parts are also often machined directly from bar stock.

In surgical instruments metal surfaces that are to form part of the articulating surface are polished to a fine finish to reduce the coefficient of friction and remove any possibility of trapping organic debris in an effort to reduce contamination sites.

Die shearing, restriking, machining

Surgical instruments or parts therof and implants often start their production process by the die shearing process. Product blanks are cut from cold rolled sheet, using hydraulic presses forcing matching dies together to cut metal under extreme pressure.

Restriking is used to modify the form and work harden the surface layers. Machining or milling cuts holes, recesses and openings. All surfaces are then polished to remove imperfections and irregularities. Tweezers, other instruments and implantable plates are regularly produced in this fashion.

Emerging technologies in biomedical engineering materials

Medical applications of 3D printing are increasing as prosthesis makers take advantage of this technology to create customised artificial limbs. New materials and manufacturing techniques have led to improvements in plastic fabrication, mouldings and the faster production of better artificial limbs.

Additive manufacturers have also managed to fashion sharp, durable, surgical instruments from a variety of materials that are able to be printed remotely onsite and emerge ready to use in a sterile form.

Surgeons are also able to more directly influence the customising of their own instruments based on their own physiological needs or preferred means of working.

Components as simple as springs and their compression rates can also be tailored to surgeons' preferences.

3D printing now extends to biological materials and recent breakthroughs have seen scientists develop a process called dynamic optical projection stereolithography, that allows them to rapidly print biological materials like blood vessels. The hope is one day to be able to produce more complex body organs that match a patient's DNA on demand.

Further reading

Lavi, Abraham, President-CEO Vilex, Inc., 'Technical training: Internal fixation', retrieved 26 May 2013 from Vilex website, www.vilex.com/vilex-surgicalproducts/technical-training/internal-fixation-paper.html

Tavakoli, M, 'The adhesive bonding of medical devices', retrieved 26 May 2013 from Medical Device and Diagnostic Industry website, www.mddionline.com/article/adhesive-bonding-medicaldevices

Structure and properties of materials

Material properties for biomedical equipment vary greatly depending on the intended function. The process of selection and testing required before a material is accepted for use is often long and rigorous. An example of the stages in such a process is indicated in the flow diagram shown in Figure 4.4.8.

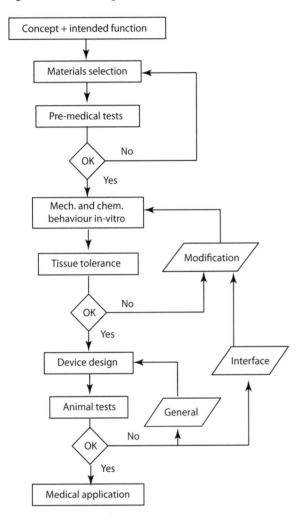

Figure 4.4.8 *Selection process, image modified from JA Helsen and H.J Breme 1998, Metals as Biomaterials, John Wiley & Sons*

Some of the properties that must be considered are:

• strength

• wear resistance

• fatigue resistance

• modulus of elasticity

• dimensional stability

• corrosion resistance

• sterilisation compatibility

• low toxicity and biocompatibility.

The body represents one of the greatest challenges in material selection. Not only must the material used possess the mechanical properties consistent with its function it must resist corrosion while not causing adverse reactions in its biological surroundings. This last requirement is known as being biocompatible.

Biocompatibility

Materials that come into contact with the body must be capable of sterilisation and exhibit a degree of biocompatibility consistent with the period over which contact is to be maintained.

Carbon steel can be used in scalpel blades for instance because they are disposable items that are in contact with bodily fluids for only the relatively short duration of the operation. Carbon steel would not be suitable for the extended contact with body fluids required of even temporary implant devices such as bone screws or plates, however, due to poor corrosion resistance. While corrosion would weaken the steel, failure would have occurred long before loss of mechanical properties caused concern. The reaction of surrounding tissue to the corrosion process would lead to inflammation and pain, requiring removal of the steel implant.

Materials intended for permanent or semi-permanent installation must have a much higher level of corrosion resistance and biocompatibility.

Biocompatibility covers a broad range of requirements but basically means that the material must be compatible with the continued health and function of the body tissue, bone and fluids in which it may come in contact. This includes not only the parent metal but also any corrosion product and wear debris that may form in service.

Corrosion

Corrosion rate depends on the reactivity of the material in the environment. For many materials this consists of the rate at which a protective oxide is formed at the surface. If a dense, tightly adherent oxide is formed it tends to protect the metal surface from continuing attack, leading to a condition in which the surface is said to be passivated. Porous, loosely adhering oxides allow continued corrosion by either allowing corrosive species through the oxide or by loss of the oxide, exposing the surface to further attack. A relative measure of resistance to corrosion can be gained from a determination of the electrical potential of the material in-situ. The electrical potential of a number of metals, in a simulated biological environment, is shown in Figure 4.4.9.

Metal	Anodic back Electromotive force (mv)
Magnesium	−1550
Zinc	−950
Aluminium	−600
Mild steel	−480
Brass	−110
Copper	−30
410 Stainless steel	+40
430 Stainless steel	+75
431 Stainless steel	+90
Silver	+110
Nickel	+200
302 Stainless steel	+300
316 Stainless steel	+480
Cobalt-based alloy	+650
Gold	+1000
Tantalum	+1650
Titanium	+3500

Biocompatible | Non-biocompatible

Figure 4.4.9 Electrical potential, image adapted from Clarke and Hickman, J Bone and Joint Surgery, vol. 35B, pp. 467–473, 1953

Included in the table is an indication of the threshold value, based on this parameter, at which the material could be considered biocompatible.

Strength

Strength is a generic term that can have a number of meanings. Two commonly used measures, obtained by performing a tensile test on a prepared sample, are the yield strength and ultimate tensile strength.

The yield strength represents the position on the stress–strain curve at which deformation changes from elastic to plastic (or permanent). For structural applications, the yield stress is an important property since once the yield point is passed the structure has deformed beyond acceptable limits.

If plastic deformation is to continue past the yield point, an increasing level of stress is required due to work hardening until a maximum point is attained. Beyond this position further plastic deformation is attained at lower levels of stress. This maximum in the stress–strain curve is known as the ultimate tensile strength (UTS) or just the tensile strength.

Fatigue resistance

Cracking of a component occurring under cyclic loading can occur at stresses well below yield stress. Cracking produced in this manner is called fatigue. Fatigue is the most common form of materials failure. It has been estimated that up to 80% of machinery failure is due to the mechanism of fatigue.

A fatigue fracture always starts as a small crack, which under repeated application of the stress grows in size with little macroscopic ductility or distortion. As the crack expands the load-carrying cross-section of the component is reduced, with the result that the stress on this section is raised. Failure, therefore, occurs progressively over a number of stress cycles and may take from several hours to years.

Indicative fatigue data on materials is obtained from standardised test pieces in a special test rig that applies a cyclic load. A diagram is subsequently built up of load cycles to failure for a variety of applied loads. This diagram is called an S/N diagram, where S is applied stress and N is the number of cycles. The form of the S/N curve typically seen for ferrous metals such as steel is shown in Figure 4..4.10. Steel samples exhibit a plateau in the S/N curve. This plateau represents a stress below which failure does not occur. This level is called the fatigue or endurance limit and is typically found with ferrous metals and titanium alloys.

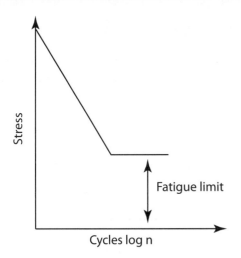

Figure 4.4.10 S/N curve for ferrous metals

Non-ferrous metals do not experience an endurance limit as shown in Figure 4.4.11.

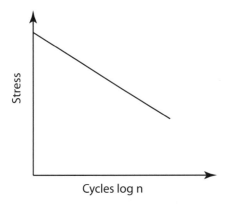

Figure 4.4.11 S/N curve for non-ferrous metals

The generation of S/N curves requires several specimens to be subjected to reversals of stress, each of different intensity, until failure occurs or 10 million cycles have been endured

Dimensional stability

Materials for biomedical applications need to be stable both within the body environment and during pre-surgical treatments such as sterilisation. This can be of concern for some polymers, which may be prone to swelling or degradation.

Sterilisation compatibility

All materials intended for use in surgery must be capable of undergoing at least one of the forms of sterilisation commonly performed, without degradation. This requirement can limit the suitability for service or the number of times that some materials, particularly polymers, may be used.

Modulus of elasticity

It should be remembered that the amount of elastic deformation that a material can sustain in tension or compression before it undergoes permanent plastic deformation is known as the modulus of elasticity or Young's modulus, and is represented by the capital letter E, having the units of GPa. It is determined during tensile testing and is visible on stress–strain diagrams as the straight-line section of the diagram prior to the yield point. The angle of the line (gradient) indicates the relative stiffness of the material and, therefore, also provides a measure of stiffness or resistance to bending. Generally when placed under stress, materials of higher modulus of elasticity will absorb the stress rather than passing it on to materials of lower modulus with which they are in contact.

Stress shielding

Under normal conditions the bones of the body act as structural components and serve two basic functions:

- provide shape to the body

- act as aids in locomotion (movement).

The long bones of the body in particular are under both static and dynamic loads. The bones in fact require exposure to a certain level of loading to develop normally and remain in good condition. Astronauts in an environment of prolonged weightlessness can suffer both weakening of the muscles and loss of bone density because they are not exposed to the normal loads of gravity. In a similar manner, problems can occasionally arise in hip and joint replacements due to a phenomenon known as stress shielding. The metals used in joint replacement typically have a modulus of stiffness far in excess of normal bone. Because of this, stresses are not passed on from the implant to the surrounding bone. The bone is said to have been shielded from the stress. As a consequence, the bone around the implant may be resorbed, leading to loosening and failure of the implant. In an ideal situation the Young's modulus of the implant material in contact with the bone should be as close as possible to that of cortical bone (ie $E = 10$–20 GPa). In order to overcome stress shielding, work is continuing into the use of composite implants combining a stem of low stiffness with frictional surfaces of high hardness and wear resistance. Porous coatings of various materials are also under development to act as an intermediary layer between the implant stem and the surrounding bone.

The porous layer serves two important functions as outlined below.

- It has a lower modulus of stiffness, allowing transfer of loads to the surrounding bone.

- It allows the in-growth of natural bone into the coating to improve fixation.

Allergic reactions

The body can produce an adverse reaction when exposed to a number of substances. This is commonly known as an allergic reaction and can vary in intensity from person to person, from local annoyance to life threatening.

Routine tests are performed before the implantation of material into the body to detect possible adverse allergic reactions. Nickel commonly produces an allergic reaction and for this reason nickel coatings are avoided on jewellery designed to come in contact with the skin.

Toxicity

The body needs a certain level of trace metals for good health. If these levels are exceeded, however, they can be toxic, leading to ill health and disease. All materials for implantation within the body are tested for toxicity before use is sanctioned by the relevant authority. The introduction of materials within the body is complex and can vary depending on the application and size of the component. Chromium ions, for example, can create a toxic reaction within the body. Chromium is also a major component of stainless steel and Co–Cr alloys extensively used for prosthetic devices. The high corrosion and wear resistance of stainless steels and Co–Cr alloys, however, means that few chromium ions are released into the surrounding tissue to cause problems.

Further reading

Helsen, JA, and Breme, HJ (eds), (1998), *Metals as biomaterials*, John Wiley & Sons, Chichester, England

Ludwigson DC, 'Requirements for metallic surgical implants and prosthetic devices', *Metals Engineering Quarterly*, pp. 1–6, August 1965

Classification of biomaterials

Tissue response is the major consideration when classifying biomedical materials. Generally speaking these categories are:

- inert materials eliciting little or no tissue response

- active materials encouraging bonding to surrounding tissue

- degradable or resorbable materials that are incorporated into the surrounding tissue or even dissolve completely over time.

Metals are mostly inert while ceramics may be inert, active or resorbable and polymers may be inert or resorbable. A sample of biomaterials is provided in Figure 4.4.12.

Metals	Ceramic	Polymers
316 S/Steel	Alumina	UHMWPE
Co–Cr alloys	Zirconia	Polyurethane
Titanium	Hydroxyapatite	

Figure 4.4.12 Some accepted biomaterials

Alloy steels such as stainless steel, titanium

Ferrous alloys

Because of the criteria previously listed, plain carbon steels see relatively little use in biomedical applications. Ferrous alloys with elevated contents of such elements as nickel and chromium are generally required, creating what is generally known as stainless steel.

Stainless steel

Note to students: the section of the syllabus on stainless steel requires students to generally appreciate the engineering properties and applications of stainless steels as a generic group. The reality is that stainless steels are a complex collection of a variety of materials with individual variations in composition, structure and application. More detail is provided here than is required for a basic knowledge of stainless steels, however, the additional information brings a deeper knowledge and understanding to the topic.

Stainless steel is an iron-based alloy that gets its name from its apparent resistance to discoloration by corrosion. This property was discovered in England in 1913 by Harry Bearley. The observed resistance to corrosion is the result of a relatively high chromium (Cr) content of somewhere between 13wt% and 30wt% depending on the grade. Chromium combines readily with oxygen to form a tightly adherent layer of chromium oxide (Cr_2O_3) at the surface. This oxide layer effectively shields the metal surface from further oxidation.

Chromium has another significant effect on iron: it alters the iron-carbon phase diagram such that the F.C.C. austenite region is contracted to the point that austenite is not formed at chromium contents above 13wt%. At chromium contents above 13wt% only the B.C.C. ferrite phase is present down to room temperature. Chromium is therefore considered to be a ferrite stabiliser. Other elements often found in stainless steel also act to varying degrees as ferrite stabilisers, such as molybdenum (Mo), silicon (Si), niobium (Nb) and titanium (Ti). The combined effect of these elements on the stability of ferrite can be determined by calculating a figure known as the chromium equivalent, which takes into account the effects of each of these elements relative to the effect of chromium.

The other major element added to some stainless steels is nickel (Ni). Nickel acts to increase the austenite region of the phase diagram and is therefore considered to be an austenite stabiliser. Similarly, other elements often found in stainless steel act to varying degrees as austenite stabilisers, such as carbon (C) and manganese (Mn). The combined effect of these elements on the stability of austenite can be determined by calculating a figure known as the nickel equivalent.

Stainless steels are generally classified by the matrix structure present at room temperature. It is therefore the interplay of ferrite and austenite stabilising elements which determines the type of stainless steels formed. Five basic categories of stainless steel exist, these being:

- ferritic

- martensitic

- austenitic

- duplex

- precipitation hardening.

As may be seen from Figure 4.4.13 stainless steel may be found either above or below the range of compatibility with the human body as an implant.

Ferritic stainless steel

Chromium content over 13% in iron suppresses the formation of austenite so that heating and cooling will occur purely within the ferrite phase. Carbon additions will take Cr out of solution to form chromium carbides. If sufficient chromium is present to account for the presence of carbon, and still maintain 13% Cr in solid solution, the structure will remain ferritic.

The ferritic stainless steels contain between 13% and 30% Cr and typically less than 0.12% C. They have a B.C.C. ferritic structure and exhibit good strength and moderate formability along with good corrosion resistance. A selection of typical ferritic grades is presented in Figure 4.4.13. Type 409 is typically used in automobile exhaust systems. The characteristics of ferritic stainless steels typically include:

- B.C.C. structure (magnetic)

- not hardenable by heat treatment

- good corrosion resistance in chlorides

- low work hardening and relatively brittle

- poor weldability unless carbides stabilised by Ti or Nb.

Grade	C	Mn	Si	Cr	Other
405	0.08	1.00	1.00	11.45–14.5	0.10–0.30 Al
409	0.80	1.00	1.00	10.5–11.75	6 × %C Ti
430	0.12	1.00	1.00	16.0–18.0	
442	0.12	1.00	1.00	18.0–23.0	
446	0.20	1.50	1.00	23.0–27.0	0.25 N

Figure 4.4.13 Ferritic grade stainless steels—single values indicate maximums

Martensitic stainless steel

Chromium has a high affinity for carbon and will readily combine with it to form chromium carbides. If carbon is not kept at a sufficiently low level enough chromium can be removed from the matrix to take the matrix content below 13wt%. If this occurs, the material will pass through the austenite region of the phase diagram during cooling before transforming to ferrite. Under these conditions martensite will form if cooling is rapid enough. In this instance, cooling in air is sufficient to obtain martensite in the microstructure.

Because low carbon levels (i.e. <0.1wt%C) were initially hard to achieve, the first stainless steel to be discovered was martensitic stainless. A typical microstructure of martensitic stainless steel is shown in Figure 4.4.14. The matrix has an acicular (needle-shaped) appearance with fine precipitated carbide particles.

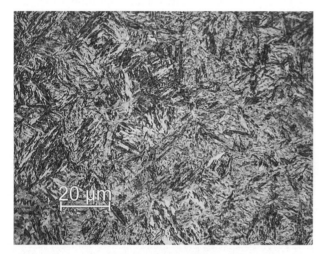

Figure 4.4.14 Type 410 Martensitic stainless steel exhibiting a microstructure of martensite and carbides

The martensitic stainless steels contain between 13% and 30% Cr, similar to ferritic stainless steel but with a carbon content typically greater than 0.12%C. Martensite has a body centred tetragonal (B.C.T.) structure, which represents distortion of the B.C.C. structure and is often designated as alpha prime (α').

The characteristics of martensitic stainless steels include:

- good corrosion resistance

- B.C.C. structure (magnetic)

- hardenable by heat treatment

- high strength but moderate formability.

A selection of typical martensitic grades is presented in Figure 4.4.15.

Grade	C	Mn	Si	Cr	Ni
410	0.15	1.00	1.00	11.50–13.0	
416	0.15	1.25	1.00	12.00–14.0	
420	0.15 min.	1.00	1.00	12.00–14.00	
431	0.20	1.00	1.00	15.0–17.00	1.25–2.50

Figure 4.4.15 Ferritic grade stainless steels—single values indicate maximums

Many surgical instruments are made from martensitic stainless steel to take advantage of its high strength. Because they do not spend any appreciable time in the body biocompatibility is not a concern, while corrosion resistance is sufficient to allow sterilisation by autoclaving.

Austenitic stainless steel

Austenitic stainless steels contain a chromium and nickel addition.

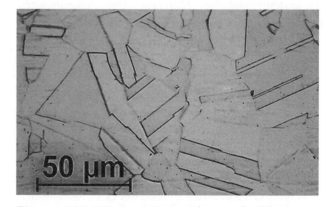

Figure 4.4.16 316 austenitic stainless steel exhibiting equiaxed austenite grains and annealing twins

The most readily recognised austenitic stainless steel contains 18% Cr and 8% Ni, resulting in the common designation as an 18/8 stainless steel. As previously indicated the nickel addition results in these alloys having an austenitic structure at room temperature (see Figure 4.4.16).

Many general articles such as basins and trays are made from type 304 or 304L stainless steel, which represents a standard 18/8 composition. The suffix 'L' indicates a low carbon version. Type 304 stainless steel was also used initially for bone plates and screws but has been superseded by type 316L and 317L, which contain a molybdenum addition that improves resistance to the chlorides found in bodily fluids. When required for service as implants, the chemistry range of these grades is restricted to a range that ensures that the Pitting Resistance Equivalent Number (PREN) meets a minimum requirement as indicated below:

$$PREN = \%Cr + 3.3(\%Mo) + 16(\%N) > 32$$

While this precaution guards against pitting corrosion, the austenitic stainless steels are also subject to crevice corrosion. Because of this they are not used for permanent implantation.

Examples of commonly used austenitic stainless steels are shown in Figure 4.4.17. Note that each of the alloys types contains 2% manganese.

Grade	C	Si	Cr	Ni	Other
302	0.15	2.0–3.0	17.0–19.0	8.0–10.0	
304	0.08	1.00	18.0–20.0	8.0–10.5	
304L	0.03	1.00	18.0–20.0	8.0–12.0	
310	0.25	1.50	24.0–26.0	19.0–22.0	
316	0.08	1.00	16.0–18.0	10.0–14.0	2–3 Mo
316L	0.03	1.00	16.0–18.0	10.0–14.0	2–3 Mo
317	0.08	1.00	18.0–20.0	11.0–15.0	3–4 Mo
321	0.08	2.00	17.0–19.0	9.0–12.0	5×C% Ti

Figure 4.4.17 Commonly used austenitic stainless steels

The austenitic stainless steel grades 316L and 317L are, however, routinely used for temporary implant devices such as plates, screws and nails used in the fixation of bone fractures. These grades are also used extensively in jewellery for body piercing.

Cheaper jewellery used in body piercing is occasionally found not to comply with the above requirements and can lead to failure.

Type 310 stainless steel, with elevated chromium and nickel contents, is typically used in high temperature service to resist oxidation.

Type 321 stainless steel has a titanium addition to stabilise the alloy against the formation of chromium carbides during welding by preferentially forming titanium carbides. In so doing, the depletion of chromium from the matrix is prevented that might have led to a localised zone adjacent to the weld, susceptible to corrosion. Localised corrosion in the heat-affected zone of welds, performed on austenitic stainless steel, is known as weld decay.

Characteristics of austenitic stainless steels include:

- very ductile
- non-magnetic
- F.C.C. structure
- work hardenable
- relatively low strength
- the ability to be deep drawn
- non-hardenable by heat treatment.

Duplex stainless steel

The duplex stainless steels contain a small nickel addition, sufficient to result in a structure containing both austenite and ferrite phases. The lower nickel grades have a ferrite matrix with islands of austenite, shown in Figure 4.4.18, while the higher nickel versions have an austenite matrix with islands of ferrite.

Despite their high strength and excellent resistance to stress corrosion cracking (SCC) these alloys are yet to see widespread use in the biomedical field. Some trials have been performed with 2507 for bone plates, with encouraging results, due to its superior performance with regard to pitting and crevice corrosion compared with Type 316L stainless steel.

The duplex stainless steels find wide use in the chemical industry for their high strength and corrosion resistance, particularly in chloride containing environments where the austenitic stainless steels are unsuitable.

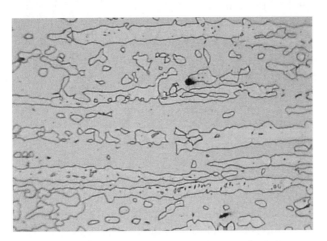

Figure 4.4.18 Type 329 duplex stainless steel exhibiting a microstructure of austenite in a ferrite matrix

The characteristics of duplex stainless steels include:

- magnetic

- high strength

- F.C.C. and B.C.C. structure

- resistance to SCC if ferritic matrix present.

A selection of typical duplex stainless grades is presented in Figure 4.4.19. Note each of the duplex stainless steel grades containes 2% manganese.

Grade	C	Cr	Ni	Mo	N	Mn
329	0.10	25.0–30.0	3.0–6.0	1.0–2.0	–	–
2304	0.03	23	4.5	–	0.1	1.2
2205	0.03	22	5.5	3.2	0.18	2.0
2507	0.02	25	7	4	0.3	1.2

Figure 4.4.19 Common duplex stainless steels

Precipitation hardening stainless steel

Precipitation hardening stainless steel grades are typically soft and ductile in the solution-annealed condition. They gain high strength through the precipitation of microscopic compounds of titanium, copper, aluminium or molybdenum. These alloys find wide application in valves and shafting where corrosion resistance and high strength is required. Biomedical applications are generally restricted to cutting tools. A selection of typical precipitation hardening grades is presented in Figure 4.4.20.

Grade	C	Cr	Ni	Other
PH13–8 Mo	0.05	12.25–13.25	7.5–8.5	2.0–2.5 Mo 0.9–1.2 Al
15–5PH	0.07	14.0–15.5	3.5–5.5	2.45–4.5 Cu 0.25–0.45 (Nb+Ta)
17–4PH	0.07	15.5–17.5	3.0–5.0	3.0–5.0 Cu 0.15–0.45 (Nb+Ta)
17–7PH	0.09	16.0–18.0	6.5–7.75	0.75–1.5 Al

Figure 4.4.20 Typical precipitation hardening grades

The characteristics of precipitation hardening stainless steels include:

- magnetic

- F.C.C. structure

- extremely high strength

- hardenable by aging heat treatment

- erosion resistance similar to type 304.

Further reading

Commonwealth Scientific and Industrial Research Organisation (CSIRO), 'Biomedical materials' brochure, 2012

Corces, A, (Calhoun, JH, ed), 'Metallic alloys', retrieved 26 May 2013 from Medscape website www.emedicine.medscape.com/article/1230554-overview

Newson, T, 'Stainless steel—A family of medical device materials', *Medical Devices Manufacturing and Technology*, pp. 1–3, London, 2002

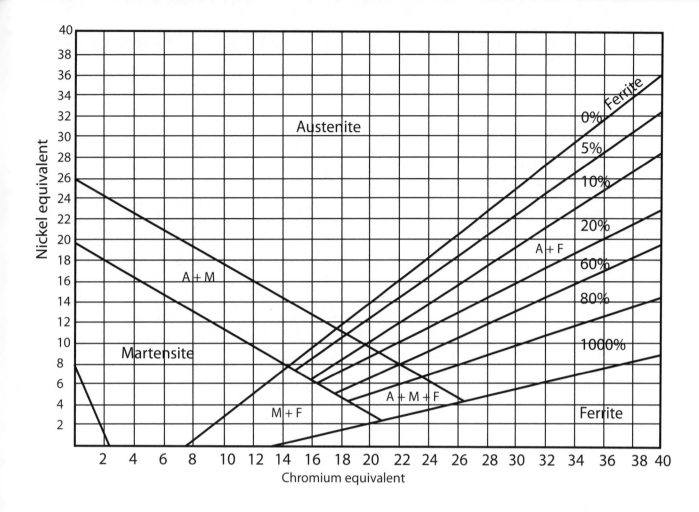

Figure 4.4.21 Schaeffler diagram

The Schaeffler diagram (Figure 4.4.21) provides a means of graphically summarising the effects of various austenite and ferrite stabilising elements in producing a particular stainless steel structure. The graph was developed to predict the structure of stainless steel welds and is strictly true only for materials cooled in air from molten to ambient temperatures at rates experienced by the weld bead. The graph does, however, provide a general guide to stainless steel phases based on chemistry.

The effects of individual elements are expressed in terms of the equivalence to the effect of either chromium or nickel. Carbon is therefore shown as having thirty times the effect of nickel, weight for weight i.e. its nickel equivalent is 30 C in the stabilisation of austenite, while silicon is one and a half times more effective as a ferrite stabiliser, weight for weight, than chromium, i.e. its chromium equivalent is 1.5 Si. For a typical chemistry of the austenitic stainless steel grade 316L shown in Figure 4.4.22 some δ ferrite could be expected if not properly solution annealed.

C	Si	Mn	Cr	Ni	Mo	Nb	Ti
0.02	0.50	1.6	18.5	9.2	2.4	–	–

Figure 4.4.22 316 stainless steel composition

Chromium equivalent (Cr equiv)

$$= 18.5 + 2.4 + 1.5 * (0.50) + 0 + 0 = 21.65$$

Nickel equivalent (Ni equiv)

$$= 9.2 + 30 * 0.02 + 0.5 * (1.60) = 10.6$$

Cobalt–chromium–molybdenum alloy

Cobalt–chromium alloys were first introduced in the 1920s by the Haynes Stellite Corporation for high temperature service such as turbine blades due to their high strength and resistance to oxidation. These alloys represent a non-ferrous cobalt based group of alloys with between 20–30 wt% Cr (see Figure 4.4.23).

The applicability to biomedical situations was first recognised in the 1930s when it was used in the manufacture of orthodontic (dental) components. In this application, the alloy was marketed as Vitallium. This alloy, with minor variations, is now available under a wide variety of brand names in both the cast and wrought condition. Although the designation of Vitallium related to a specific composition it became in some areas a general description for the Co–Cr group of alloys employed in biomedical applications, as an explosion of trade names from various suppliers entered the field. Today reference is more routinely made to the relevant national or international standards dealing with biomedical materials. These standards give a generic chemistry to which material of any particular grade group must conform before acceptance for biomedical use.

The Co–Cr group are austenitic alloys strengthened by the presence of complex alloy carbides containing chromium and either molybdenum (Mo) or tungsten (W).

They exhibit high tensile and fatigue strength with good ductility and wear resistance. The Co–Cr alloys do, however, have a relatively high modulus of elasticity. Biocompatibility is excellent and the high wear resistance of these alloys results in minimal wear debris in surrounding tissue. The Co–Cr alloys exhibit high corrosion resistance in chloride containing environments, particularly with respect to crevice corrosion.

		Cr	Mo	W	C	Ni
Cast	Stellite 21	27	5	–	0.25	3
	ASTM F799	26–30	5–7	–	0.35	1
	ASTM F75	28	6	–	0.25	9
Wrought	Stellite 25	15	–	15	0.10	10
	BS3531:1	19–21	–	14–16	0.15	9–11

Figure 4.4.23 Selection of typical Co–Cr grades

These alloys are typically solution annealed to produce a uniform structure for hip or knee replacement.

Castings are typically produced by investment casting techniques followed by hot isostatic pressing (HIP). Today, a plasma sprayed ceramic coating is often applied to that region of the implant that is to be in contact with bone to encourage bone ingrowth and reduce stress-shielding effects.

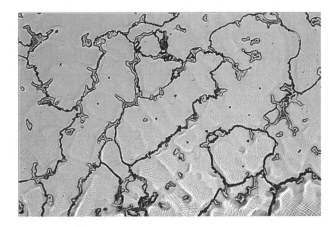

Figure 4.4.24 Cast Co–Cr–Mo alloy consisting of primary Mo7C3 particles in an alpha (FCC) matrix, image by Australian Surgical Design and Manufacture Pty Ltd

Further reading

Gibson, N, and Stamm, H, 'The use of alloys in prosthetic devices', *Medical Devices Manufacturing and Technology*, pp. 48–51, London, 2002

Titanium

Titanium is the ninth most abundant element in the Earth's crust, making up approximately 1% of the crust. The two most common commercial ores are the mineral sands ilmenite (FeTiO3) and rutile (TiO2). First discovered by the British clergyman the Rev William Gregor in 1791, titanium was rediscovered by the German chemist Heinrich Klaproth in 1795. Klaproth named the new element after the Titans (also known as the elder gods) who ruled Earth before the more commonly known Olympians overthrew them.

Klaproth also discovered uranium in pitchblende in 1789 and had named it after the most recently discovered planet at the time, Uranus.

Due to its high reactivity with oxygen and nitrogen, the pure metal was not produced on a laboratory scale until 1910. A commercial means of purifying titanium was not available until 1938 when Wilhelm Kroll developed a process subsequently known as the Kroll process. It is the highly reactive nature of titanium that results in the formation of a tight, dense, oxide coating, reducing susceptibility to corrosion.

Commercially pure titanium has a hexagonal close packed (HCP) crystal structure at room temperature. This structure consists of two planes of atoms arranged in a hexagonal pattern with atoms at each corner and at the centre of the hexagon. These planes are separated by a plane of three atoms, as represented in Figure 4.4.25.

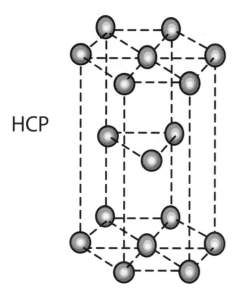

HCP

Figure 4.4.25 Hexagonal close packed structure

The HCP structure in titanium is known as the alpha (α) phase and is shown in Figure 4.4.26.

The characteristics of titanium include:

- H.C.P. structure

- excellent biocompatibility

- excellent corrosion resistance

- alloys readily with most metals

- relatively low modulus of elasticity.

On heating to temperatures above 882 °C titanium undergoes a phase change to a B.C.C. structure designated as the beta (β) phase. If quenched from this temperature a martensitic reaction similar to that found in steel can occur although the strengthening effect is negligible.

Strengthening of commercially pure titanium is usually attained by the addition of interstitial elements such as C, O, N and H. The beta phase can be extended to room temperature by appropriate alloy additions. Alloy additions are categorised depending on their effect in stabilising either the alpha or beta phases. Additions such as Al, O and N are alpha stabilisers while the beta stabilisers include Mo, V, W and Ta.

One of the most widely used titanium alloys is the alpha-beta alloy designated as Ti–6Al–4V in which 6wt% of the alpha stabilising element aluminium and 4wt% of the beta stabilising element vanadium are present. In the furnace-cooled condition, the Ti–6Al–4V structure consists of primary alpha phase in a beta phase matrix as shown in Figure 4.4.27.

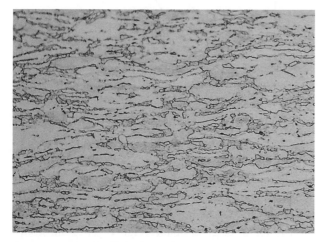

Figure 4.4.26 Unalloyed titanium consisting of alpha (α) grains, slightly elongated by cold work magnification

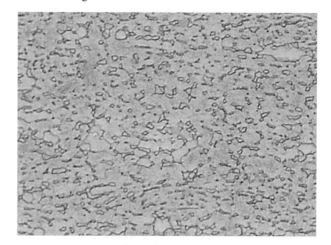

Figure 4.4.27 Photomicrograph of a Ti 6Al 4V alloy plate in the furnace-cooled condition consisting of alpha (α) phase slightly elongated due to cold work in a beta (β) phase matrix

Strengthening is by precipitation (or age) hardening, in which the Ti–6Al–4V alloy is initially solution annealed, by being heated above 955 °C to ensure complete transformation to beta, and then water quenched to retain the beta phase. In this condition, some of the beta is metastable meaning that it will transform to a more stable phase if given appropriate conditions. Aging at approximately 540 °C is then performed in order to precipitate the alpha phase by transforming some of the metastable beta.

Both pure titanium and the alloy Ti–6Al–4V are used in implant surgery. These alloys have excellent biocompatibility and good fatigue strength and strength to weight ratio.

The low modulus of elasticity of titanium makes it particularly suitable for bone implantation as it does not have the problems of stress shielding that can be associated with stainless steel and Co–Cr–Mo alloys. A selection of alloys and their relative Young's modulii and densities are shown in Figure 4.4.28.

Material	E (GPa)	ρ (g/cm^2)
Stainless steel	190–200	7.87
Ti (unalloyed)	105–110	4.5
Ti –6Al –4V	100–116	–
Haynes 25	130	9.13
NiTi Austenite	70–110	–
Martensite	21–69	–
Cortical bone	15–30	–

Figure 4.4.28 Young's modulus and density of selected alloys

Further reading

Bhadeshia, HK, 'Metallurgy of Titanium and its Alloys' (n.d), retrieved from University of Cambridge website, www.msm.cam.ac.uk/phase-trans/2004/titanium/titanium.html

Shape memory alloys

SMAs are metals that exhibit pseudo-elasticity and shape memory effect due to rearrangement of the atomic lattice. Discovered in the 1930s the shape memory alloys represent a group of materials that are capable of changing shape or size in a predetermined manner by undergoing a solid-state phase change at a defined temperature. Despite creating a great deal of interest, these alloys remained largely a laboratory curiosity until the 1960s when the NiTi alloy nitinol (an acronym of the Nickel and Titanium Naval Ordinance Laboratory) was produced. Due to its excellent mechanical properties and biocompatibility nitinol has since become one of the most widely used shape memory alloys. Nitinol is non-magnetic and consists of almost equal amounts of Ni and Ti in a simple cubic lattice arrangement.

One of the defining characteristics of the shape memory alloys is pseudo-elasticity. If a shape memory alloy is in the stable lattice arrangement of the austenite phase, and is exposed to a mechanical stress, slip can occur leading to distortion of the lattice and the formation of martensite. Normally a reduction in temperature would be required to achieve this change but under the influence of an applied stress martensite formation can occur without the involvement of a temperature change and is referred to as deformation martensite. This change in structure is accompanied by an apparent non-linear deformation, typically associated with plastic deformation.

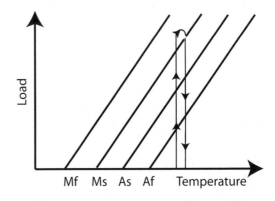

Figure 4.4.29 Load diagram of the pseudo-elastic effect (Ms/Mf Martensite start/finish, As/Af Austenite start/finish)

When the applied stress is removed, however, the atomic lattice returns to the austenite phase and the material returns to its original shape. Figure 4.4.29 illustrates this phenomenon in which an applied stress essentially increases the temperature at which martensite will form and shows the reversible change back to austenite on the removal of the applied stress.

Pseudo-elasticity can be expressed symbolically as:

Austenitic structure + force (stimulus)
leads to
martensitic structure – force (stimulus)
leads back to
austenitic structure

Some shape memory alloys exhibit a temperature controlled reversible martensite transformation. In this instance, removal of the applied stress does not result in the material returning to the austenite phase and its original shape. This change requires moderate heating up to approximately 100 °C.

At elevated temperatures these alloys have an austenitic structure that is relatively strong. On cooling these alloys undergo a phase transformation to martensite, which is relatively soft. The unique character of these alloys is seen when the alloy is formed to shape in the austenitic condition and then cooled to martensite. If another forming operation is then performed while it is in the martensitic condition, changing the shape of the material, it will maintain that shape until reheated to austenite at which time the alloy reverts to its previously formed shape.

Alloy	Transformation range °C	Transformation hysteresis °C
Ag-Cd	–190 to –50	~15
Cu-Al-Ni	–140 to –100	~35
Cu-Zn	–180 to –10	~10
Ni-Al	–180 to 100	~10
Ni-Ti	–50 to 110	~30
FeMnS	–200 to 150	~100

Figure 4.4.30 Transformation temperature ranges for a selection of SMA's, ASM handbook

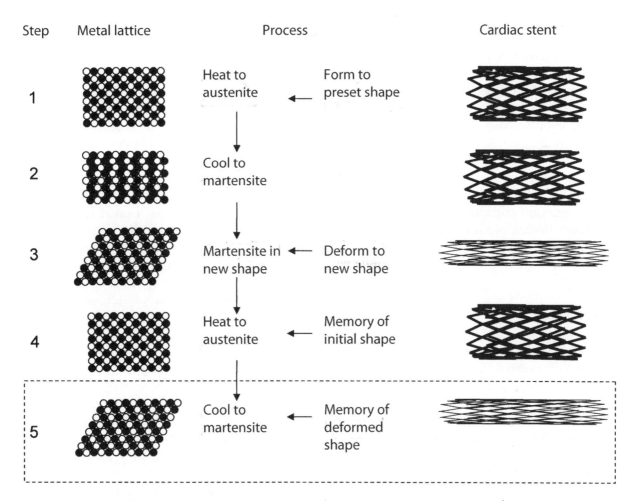

Figure 4.4.31 SMA. transformation stages: 1 to 4 a one-way shape memory, stage 5: two-way shape memory

---

Some alloys even have the ability to change back when the temperature has again been reduced resulting in a two-way memory effect. These alloys can therefore cycle between shapes with changes in temperature.

The transformation temperature in nitinol can be modified to some degree. The temperature may be 'fixed' in its original or parent shape by heating and holding the alloy at a temperature of about 500 °C. A number of shape memory alloys have been developed, which operate at a variety of different temperatures, as indicated in Figure 4.4.30. Precise control of the material composition is required to ensure the reliable reproduction of the transformation temperatures.

The shape memory affect can be illustrated as shown in Figure 4.4.31 in which the phase changes have been represented at each stage along with the changes that would be seen with an arterial stent made from the shape memory alloy nitinol. The excellent biocompatibility of nitinol combined with its non-magnetic nature and excellent mechanical properties have resulted in its extensive use in biomedical applications such as coronary stents but also medical staples, guide-wires, orthodontic arch-wires and components of eyeglass frames.

SMA's are considered to be passive response type devices, as they do not require separate sensors to operate but rather react directly in response to an external stimulus.

Shape memory alloys have also been used in products such as electrical connectors and safety taps to prevent hot water scalding children, and airflow controls.

Some use of SMA's has been made in passive dampening systems to mitigate earthquake damage. The roof of the St Francis basilica in Assisi has been joined to the wall with nitinol anchors consisting of wire bundles that stretch in response to vibrations, dissipating the seismic loads.

Further reading

Feninat, FE, Laroche, G, Fiset, M and Mantovani, D, 'Shape memory materials for biomedical applications', *Avanced Engineeing Materials*, vol. 4, no. 3, 2002

'Fundamental characteristics of nickeltitanium shape memory alloy' (literature review), retrieved 26 May 2013 from Oulu University Library website, www.herkules. oulu.fi/isbn9514252217/html/x317.html

Pelton, AR, Russell, SM and DiCello, J, 'The physical metallurgy of nitinol for medical application', *Journal of Metals*, vol. 55(5), pp. 33–37, 2003

Petrini, L, and Migliavacca, F, 'Biomedical applications of shape memory alloys', *Journal of Metallurgy*, vol. 2011, 2011

Poncet, PP, 'Nitinol medical device considerations' (n.d), Menlo Park, CA, Memry Corporation

Ceramics

Typically ceramics are a combination of one or more metallic elements with a non-metallic element. They form ionic/covalent bonds, giving them unique engineering properties. Ceramics are generally hard, brittle, chemically inert materials which may be present in either a crystalline or non-crystalline form. They are also good electrical insulators and exhibit high temperature resistance, making them popular as refractories. Common ceramics materials include aluminium oxide (Al_2O_3) and silica (SiO_2). Their inherent brittleness eliminates ceramics from many structural situations.

Ceramics display good compressive strength yet they have little tolerance for cracking, such that even microscopic defects can lead to failure well below their theoretical tensile strength. Processing techniques are therefore often directed to producing a compressive surface layer that must first be overcome before fracture will occur.

Alumina (Al_2O_3) and zirconia (ZrO) have found some use as spray coatings on femoral stems and as the femoral head of a composite construction implant. These ceramics are considered to be largely inert within the body, or bioinert. That is, they do not take part in the body's process of resorption and regrowth although a porous coating may be provided on femoral stems to promote bone ingrowth. These materials are not bioactive.

Hydroxyapatite (HA or HAp)

Hydroxyapatite ($Ca_{10}(PO_4)_6(OH)_2$ represents a material similar to the inorganic component of natural bone and is therefore compatible with the normal body processes of bone dissolution and growth. Materials that exhibit these features are said to be bioactive. Plasma sprayed coatings of HA are often applied to the surface of implants to encourage bone in-growth as an aid to fixation.

Glass

Glasses represent a group of non-crystalline (amorphous) ceramics in which the constituent atoms are stacked in an irregular or random pattern, that is, there is no long-range order. Until recently, glass was used almost exclusively outside of the body due to its relatively low strength in tension and brittleness.

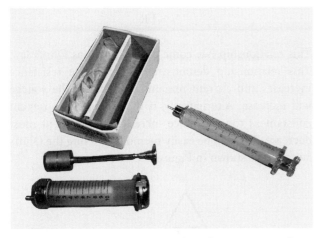

Figure 4.4.32 Glass syringes and packaging, image by Newcastle Regional Museum, Royal Newcastle Hospital collection

Until the introduction of plastic for disposable syringes glass was used extensively in this role (Figure 4.4.32). The optical properties of glass, and its general inertness to chemical reaction, make it ideally suited to visual inspection of cleanliness and long-term storage of biological samples.

Bioglass

Bioglass ($Na_2OCaOP_2O_3$–SiO), as the name implies, is also a bioactive material, containing the traditional glass forming oxides of sodium, silicon and calcium. This material is also applied to implants to encourage bone in-growth. Sodium oxide at the surface represents a form of water-glass that dissolves in the body, leaving behind pores for bone in-growth.

Polymers

Polymethylmethacrylate (PMMA)

Commonly known under the trade name Plexiglas®, PMMA belongs to a group of polymers known as acrylics. This group of thermoplastics is typically characterised as forming clear, rigid polymers and being well suited to injection moulding. PMMA was the first polymer to be used as a replacement for glass in reading glasses. Its low resistance to scratching, however, led to commercial failure in this application although it continues to be used in low-cost camera lenses and safety glasses. PMMA was also used in the first widely available contact lens but was limited in this application by its impermeability to oxygen. Wide biomedical use has, however, been made of PMMA for the manufacture of intraocular lenses (IOL) and as a grouting material in the cementing of hip and knee prosthesis since Charnley first used it in this application in 1964. As a grouting material, PMMA is supplied as a powder that is mixed just prior to use and which is trowelled around the femoral stem to fix it in position within the femur. Polymerisation of the PMMA occurs in-situ. This reaction is exothermic, reaching temperatures of up to 70 °C, so that great care must be taken by the surgeon to avoid tissue damage.

Ultra high molecular weight polyethylene (UHMWPE)

UHMWPE has a molecular weight about ten times higher than HMWPE. The higher molecular weight translates into superior scrape resistance and impact strength. As a thermoplastic, it finds wide use as the bearing cup surface in hip and knee joints against a metal articulation. UHMWPE provides a low coefficient of friction, essential if wear is to be maintained to a minium in artificial joints. In its bulk form UHMWPE has good biocompatibility, however, problems can arise from tissue reaction to fine particles liberated by wear. In recent times bioengineers have developed a radiation cross-linking technique that is expected to significantly reduce wear and improve the longevity of UHMWPE hip implants beyond ten years.

Polypropylene

A thermoplastic, commonly used for the manufacture of disposable syringes and non-absorbable sutures. Also finds use in finger joint prosthesis.

Polyamide (nylon 6,6)

A thermoplastic developed in the 1930s, it was widely used as a replacement for silk in parachutes in WWII and still finds use in non-absorbable sutures.

Polyvinyl chloride (PVC)

One of the most widely used thermoplastics available. PVC is used as electrical insulation on wires and hand tools and as agricultural piping and furniture. Varying degrees of plasticiser determine the flexibility/rigidity of the material. Biomedical applications include use for artificial limbs and disposable medical products such as blood bags, tubing and cardiac catheters.

Biodegradable polymers

Polylactic acid (PLA) and polyglycolic acid (PGA) represent two types of biodegradable polymer in common use. They find wide use as implantable drug delivery devices, which deliver a drug to the body as they degrade. PGA also finds use as an absorbable suture.

Hydrogels

Hydrogels contain up to 40% water within their polymer network. The hydrogels are soft flexible polymers with a high permeability to oxygen, resulting in extensive use today as soft contact lenses.

Cyanoacrylates

Cyanoacrylate, better known in layman's terms as 'super glue', is a group of polymers that have application as a topical skin adhesive. Fast curing cyanoacrylates have found application as single-solution skin adhesives for small incisions. Avoiding the use of suturing and providing a microbial barrier, cyanoacrylates are used for low load, linear incisions of less than 2 cm.

Of additional benefit is that the adhesive naturally sloughs from the skin after a period of seven days, thus requiring no follow-up treatment such as the removal of staples or sutures.

The use of cyanoacrylates in the above situations has proved to be not only fast but also cost effective.

Care, however, must be taken with the use of cyanoacrylates not to be used internally, to avoid contamination of the adhesive when applying and to monitor the patient for evidence of contact dermatitis.

Further reading

Ben-Nissan, B, 'Ceramics in orthopaedic applications—the use of alumina and zirconia in total hip replacements', retrieved 26 May 2013 from Azom website, www.azom.com/article.aspx?ArticleID=2162

Bonfield, W, and Tanner, E, 'Hydroxyapatite composite biomaterials—evolution and applications', *Materials World*, vol. 5(1), pp. 18–20, 1997

4.5 Electricity/electronics

Ohm's law

George Simon Ohm (1787–1854) determined by experimentation that a relationship existed between voltage, current and resistance that could be expressed by the simple equation:

$$V = I R$$

This relationship has come to be known as Ohm's law. This relationship demonstrates that if the resistance increases and current remains unchanged, the voltage will increase. Alternatively, if the voltage is to remain constant as the resistance increases, the current must decrease. This can be easily memorised using the Ohm's law triangle shown in Figure 4.5.1.

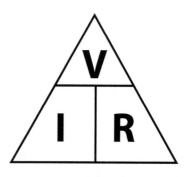

Figure 4.5.1 Ohm's law triangle

Series and parallel circuits

There are many ways to connect components in electrical circuits. Series and parallel are the two simplest methods. A simple series connection provides only one pathway for current to flow. Parallel circuits form multiple pathways or branches that enable a range of separate paths for current flow. Each of these approaches have their own characteristics.

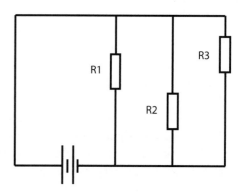

Figure 4.5.2 DC parallel circuit

In a DC parallel circuit equal voltage is distributed equally across every component, that is, three components connected in parallel to a 9 volt battery will each receive 9 volts. In a series circuit, when one of the components fails or one of the wires is left open or is broken, the entire circuit fails. The total resistance of a set of resistors in a parallel circuit is found by adding up the reciprocals of the resistance values and then taking the reciprocal of the total:

$$1/R_T = 1/R_1 + 1/R_2 + 1/R_3$$

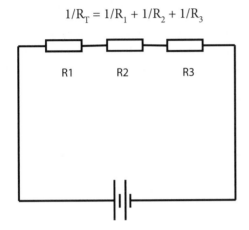

Figure 4.5.3   DC series circuit

In a DC series circuit, the amount of current is the same through any component in the circuit and the total resistance is equal to the sum of the individual resistances. Total voltage in a series circuit is equal to the sum of the individual voltage drops. The design of parallel circuits allows for branches of the circuit to function even if one or more other branches are broken or contain failed components.

Power sources

Engineered implants may be grouped into two different types, passive and active as outlined below.

- Passive implants include such devices as artificial joints, stents, valves, etc.

- Active implants include devices powered to assist or improve bodily functions and include devices such as cochlear implants, cardiac pacemakers or insulin pumps. Devices that require some form of power are yet again divided into two types: powered internally (batteries) or externally.

Batteries as a power supply include single use batteries, such as those containing lithium-metal anodes and rechargeable lithium ion batteries. The type of power source used varies significantly with the power demands of the particular device. As an example, a pacemaker divides its power requirements between cardiac stimulation and monitoring tasks such as data logging. Neither of these functions has high power requirements. A simple one amp-hour lithium ion cell can provide up to five years trouble free operation of this type of device. Compared to a similar volume lead-based cell the Li-ion battery provides more power with significant weight reduction.

The most important features of batteries for biomedical devices include:

- designed to be as small as practical

- production of no by-product during its service life

- a known and predicable service life with little or no drop in performance

- reliability—often hard-wired and sealed into devices, batteries must last the lifetime of the device.

Implantable devices are often manufactured in a round or elliptical shape to avoid sharp edges and the obvious dangers associated with insertion into the human body. Battery shapes most often imitate the shapes of the device they are held within to allow for ease of fitting.

Some implantable medical devices require more power than could be reliably supplied by batteries over an extended period of time. To reduce the need for additional surgeries and replacement of devices and/or batteries, some devices have their power provided from outside the body. To reduce the risk of infection, transcutaneous charging systems are non-invasive and require no penetration of the skin to deliver a charge. Unfortunately, this approach comes with its own set of problems. Power sources of this type may produce potentially harmful electromagnetic interferences (EMI) that may damage implanted devices or harm patients. Recent developments in this field include wireless charging of either embedded batteries or powering of the devices themselves. A prototype wireless charging device won the 2005 Jaime Filipe Engineer Award for the best innovative design. António Abreu in the USA also holds the patent for a non-invasive battery recharger for electronic cardiac implants.

Research continues into this technology for applications leading to high power electrical transmission and distribution systems such as those found in national electricity grids.

Microcircuits/integrated circuits

A programmable interface controller (PIC) is a small computer complete with input, output and memory that can be programmed to perform simple tasks. Input and output are typically in the form of voltage. Alternatively, these devices are known as peripheral interface controllers and trademarked as PIC chips by Arizona Microchip Technology.

Because the PIC is capable of storing and running a simple program many modern electronic devices incorporate PICs to provide various programmable options. The flexibility of PICs allows high performance and low cost.

Various laundry program options available in modern washing machines and microwave ovens are provided through PICs.

The flexibility of the PIC comes from the wide range of functions for which it can be utilised. In any one application where a PIC is suitable, however, this capacity is largely unnecessary. The use of a purpose-built controller for each and every application to ensure that full use of capability is made would be time consuming and expensive to build and maintain compared with the convenience of a single component that can satisfy a large number of different requirements albeit with redundant capabilities. PICs are popular with both designers and manufacturers because they:

- are compact
- are inexpensive
- are widely available
- are flexible in their use
- have flash memory advantages
- include access to free development tools.

The inclusion of PICs in a product can allow the reduction of other circuitry. Because PICs can replace many circuit components, stock levels can be reduced and assembly can be simplified. This reduction of component and simplification of assembly can lead to lower cost and greater product reliability. The ability to reprogram PICs also gives them an extended life.

Digital technology

Digital signals are made up of two basic conditions of being 'off' or 'on'. These conditions can be represented numerically as the numbers zero (0) and one (1) for 'off' and 'on' respectively.

Analog signals by contrast are continuously and infinitely variable between an upper and lower limit, and can include both positive and negative values.

A binary code is one based on two states such as 'on' or 'off', 'up' or 'down', 'true' or 'false'. If these two states are represented numerically, the two options are the digits '0' or '1'. Arithmetic based on these two digits is called base-2 arithmetic and is also known as binary arithmetic.

In the decimal (base 10) system the position of digits within a number represent powers of 10 as shown below.

The number 1549.25 may be shown in base 10 as:

$$1\times10^3 \quad 5\times10^2 \quad 4\times10^1 \quad 9\times10^0 \quad 2\times10^{-1} \quad 5\times10^{-2}$$

$$1000 + 500 + 40 + 9 + 0.2 + 0.05$$

$$= 1549.25$$

Similarly, in the binary (base 2) system the position of digits within a number represent powers of two as shown below.

The base 2 number 11000001101.01 may be shown in base 10 as:

$$1\times2^{10} \quad 1\times2^9 \quad 1\times2^3 \quad 1\times2^2 \quad 1\times2^0 \quad 1\times2^{-2}$$

$$1024 + 512 + 8 + 4 + 1 + 0.25$$

$$= 1549.25$$

Because electronic devices operate in a binary fashion, that is, current flows or doesn't, they are particularly suited to binary code.

Logic gates act as digital switches in which an output of '0' or '1' is produced. Depending on the combinations of logic gates used, various operations can be performed within a circuit. The common logic gates encountered are shown in Figure 4.5.4. Note that for every operation there is a logic gate that performs an inverse version of that operation. The symbols for both are similar with the exception of the inclusion of a small circle on the output side known as an 'inversion bubble'.

Logic gate	Traditional symbol	IEC symbol	Function
NOT		=1	Also known as an **inverter**. Output (Q) is opposite to input.
AND		&	Current output (Q=1) only if **both** inputs are equal to 1.
NAND		&	Current outputs opposite to **AND** gate.
OR		≥1	Current output (Q=1) if **any** input equals 1.
NOR		≥1	Current outputs opposite to **OR** gate.

Figure 4.5.4 Common logic gates

As may be seen from Figure 4.5.4 there are three basic gate symbols representing a NOT gate, an AND gate and an OR gate. The other gate functions are modifications of these symbols to represent some modification to the output that takes place.

Note that the NOT or inverted form of the gates is represented by the addition of the 'inversion bubble'.

The AND gate can be thought of as analogous to a simple electric circuit in which switches are present in series. If even one of the switches is open (input 0) no current flows. However, if both switches are closed (both inputs 1), current flows. Similarly, the OR gate can be thought of as analogous to a simple electric circuit in which switches are present in parallel. If even one of the switches is closed (input 1) current flows even if all of the other switches are open. Only if all switches are open (all inputs 0) will there be no current.

A truth table represents the output of a circuit under all possible combinations of input and output conditions. For n inputs there will be 2^n rows, each representing the output for a unique combination of input values. Each input value will be either a '0' or '1' as shown in Figure 4.5.5. By convention the output is labelled 'Q'.

Logic gate	Traditional symbol	Truth table		
NOT		A	Q	
		0	1	
		1	0	

Logic gate	Traditional symbol	A	B	Q
AND		0	0	0
		0	1	0
		1	0	0
		1	1	1
NAND		0	0	1
		0	1	1
		1	0	1
		1	1	0
OR		0	0	0
		0	1	1
		1	0	1
		1	1	1
NOR		0	0	1
		0	1	0
		1	0	0
		1	1	0

Figure 4.5.5 Logic gate truth tables

Example—Digital hearing aid

Human hearing is typically found to be able to detect sounds in the frequency range of 20 Hz to 20 000 Hz. As aging takes place, the response to the higher frequency end of the spectrum begins to deteriorate due to damage to the fine hairs of the cochlea. Hearing can also be compromised by exposure to loud noise over an extended period of time, which also damages the hairs. A hearing test or audiogram provides a measure of hearing acuity, detailing the extent to which hearing has been compromised.

A hearing aid can be used to regain some of the hearing that has been lost. Older analog style hearing aids operated by boosting the volume, which could have the effect of making some sounds too loud and others too soft. Modern digital devices, however, can be programmed based on the results of an audiogram to correct the specific frequencies affected.

Sounds entering the microphone of a digital hearing aid are converted to an analog electrical signal and then via an A/D (analog/digital) converter to a digital signal. This signal is then sent to the core where it is filtered into various bands, which are individually adjusted for volume based on the personalised program of the wearer. The adjusted signal is then sent to a D/A (digital/ analog) converter and on to a receiver to be converted to an acoustic signal.

The key elements of an electronic hearing aid include:

- microphone: converts acoustic signal to an analog electrical signal

- analog-to-digital (A/D) converter

- core: containing filters to separate frequency bands and processed to amplify certain frequency bands

- digital-to-analog (D/A) converter

- receiver: analog signal converted to an acoustic signal.

A programmable interface controller or PIC, a small computer complete with input, output and memory, may be programmed based on the results of an audiogram and incorporated into a hearing aid, thus customising the response of the hearing aid to the requirements of the user.

Figure 4.5.6 Cochlear implant

Hearing aids are often powered by 'zinc-air' batteries that are activated once they come in contact with oxygen. This type of battery is more correctly known as a zinc/potassium hydroxide/oxygen cell but 'zinc-air' is the name in common use.

Advantages directly associated with this type of power cell include:

- low operating cost

- constant output voltage

- long (sealed) shelf life—up to three years

- high energy density—up to five times that of alkaline and mercury systems

- environmentally safe as requires no special handling or disposal procedures

- large operating temperature range—0 °C to 50 °C

- safe—self-venting internally generated gases through air-access holes eliminates potential cell rupture or explosion.

Recent developments in the monitoring of implanted devices include wireless connectivity. This allows for constant real-time monitoring of the performance of the device and on-the-fly re-programming of the controller to maximise performance.

Further reading

Dondelinger, RM, 'Batteries: from alkaline to zinc-air', *Biomedical Instrumentation and Technology*, pp. 100–110, March 2004

Ferguson, JE, and Redish, AD, 'Wireless communication with implanted medical devices using the conductive properties of the body', *Expert Review Medical Devices*, vol. 8(4), pp. 427–433, 2011

McDonald, J et al, 'Integrated Circuits for Implantable Medical Devices', August 2011, retrieved from www.freescale.com/files/32bit/doc/white_paper/ICIMDOVWP.pdf?tid=mMdl?tid=AMdlDR

Soykan, O, Dr, 'Power sources for implantable medical devices', *Medical Device Manufacturing and Technology*, pp. 76–79, June 2002

4.6 Communication

Computer graphics, CAD

CAD drawings allow for the provision of detail previously too complex or time consuming to produce by traditional hand drawing. Standard drawing practice depicts screw threads using parallel lines indicating the diameter, pitch and length of a thread.

Using 3D graphics CAD drawings generate threads that appear in a more realistic fashion simply because the computer can easily and quickly reproduce their likeness. These 3D drawings are produced at the click of a mouse once the initial orthographic drawing has been constructed and dimensioned.

While 3D CAD design software has revolutionised product design, manufacturers still require engineering drawings for production purposes. CAD packages allow for the easy transformation of 3D graphics into detailed workshop drawings with all the attendant documentation.

Advantages of CAD drawings include their ability to be:

- stored in a variety of formats

- corrected or altered very quickly

- created as 2D or 3D representations

- rescaled, zoomed, cropped and so on

- presented as paper printouts, virtual models or rapid prototypes

- electronically distributed for collaboration as part of a group project

- used in conjunction with numerical control machinery for CAD/CAM production.

Disadvantages of CAD drawings include:

- initial cost and upgrading of software

- staff training and high level of skill required

- compatibility between software and hardware

- skills constantly require upgrading as software updates

- steep learning curves associated with early stages of uptake.

The linking of computer-aided design software to computer-aided manufacturing systems has also produced significant benefits including:

- reduced errors and cycle times

- removal of duplication of effort

- improved quality control and decrease labour content.

Computer grahics and graphical design

A range of 2D software packages are available to generate graphic designs. These designs may be developed for use as corporate logos on business cards, letterheads and signage. Linked to 3D printers, routers and printers or plotters even a novice can quickly produce a high quality product.

Australian Standard (AS1100), sectioning and dimensioning

Pictorial drawings such as isometric often do not provide sufficient details of the interior of an object to successfully communicate sufficient information for manufacture. Even the provision of hidden detail in orthographic drawing can overcomplicate already complex drawings. Section planes and additional sectional views allow for a view into the interior of an object. A full section (shown in Figure 4.6.1) is created when a cutting plane 'cuts' an object in half, while a half sectional view is produced by quartering an object. Sectional views use the following guidelines.

- An appropriate section cutting plane line is used.

- Direction of viewing is shown by arrows with large heads.

- Capital letters identify the cutting plane. e.g. AA.

- Section AA or just AA title appears below the sectional view.

- Cross-hatching lines (45°) identify the 'cut' surface.

- Reverse direction hatching is used for adjacent touching components.

- Where more than two adjacent parts touch, the angle of the hatching may be varied to differentiate parts.

A full sectional view produced by cutting plane A-A is shown in Figure 4.6.1.

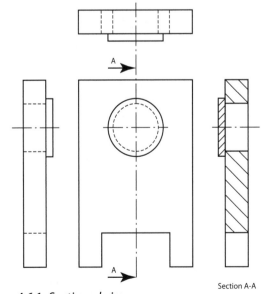

Section A-A

Figure 4.6.1 Sectioned view

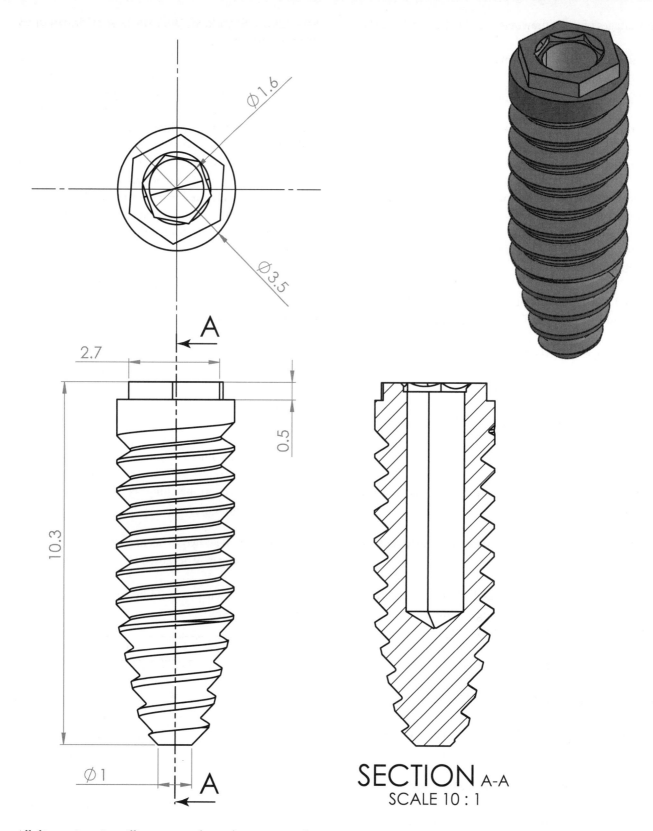

All dimensions in millimeteres unless otherwise stated.

Figure 4.6.2 CAD drawing of dental implant

Report writing and collaborative work practices

Information relating to the nature and range of work done, engineers as managers, ethics related to the profession and community, career prospects and training for the profession are all covered in Section 1.4 of this book.

Notes on collaborative work practices appear in the Communications sections 1.5 and 2.6 of Chapters 1 and 2 respectively.

Sample biomedical engineering report

The following report has been reproduced with the kind permssion of the Henkel Corporation, Rocky Hill, CT, www.henkelna.com. This article was previously published by Scott D Anderson in *Medical Design*, April 2010.

Examining the effect of sterilisation on bulk adhesive properties

Sterilisation can greatly influence the integrity of a medical device, especially those bonded with adhesives. Therefore, it is critical that device manufacturers select the adhesive best suited for the substrate materials, end-use environment and sterilisation technique.

The data shown in Charts 1 and 2 reflect the post-sterilisation performance of three light cure acrylic adhesives used to bond 22-gauge (ga) stainless steel cannulas to either polycarbonate or plasma-treated polypropylene hubs.

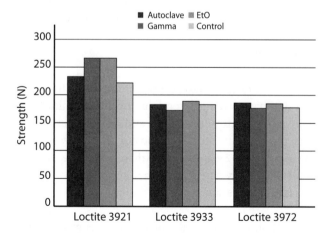

Chart 1 22 ga needle pull strength on polycarbonate

The pull strength data from this study on actual devices shows post-sterilisation performance similar to that of the untreated control group.

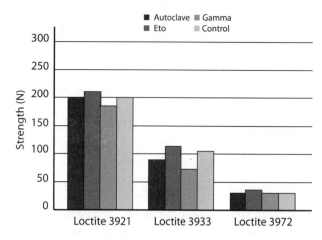

Chart 2 22 ga needle pull strength on treated polyporpylene

Often there is actually an improvement in strength. This improvement may be the result of elevated temperatures enhancing the adhesive's cross-linking reaction, or of annealing that actually relaxes stress on the component.

But what happens when we eliminate both substrates and joint design from the test and look only at the properties of the adhesive itself and how it is affected by sterilisation? To answer this question, let's focus on the performance of typical light cure acrylic and light cure silicone adhesives when exposed to autoclave, ethylene oxide and gamma irradiation sterilisation.

Adhesives studied

This study tested the Loctite® light cure acrylic adhesives referenced in Charts 1 and 2:

3921™, a highly fluorescent, 150 cP (centipoise) adhesive that provides bond strength on dissimilar materials. This material is commonly used in needle bonding applications.

3933™, a 3250 cP adhesive that provides bond strength to polycarbonate and other thermoplastics with minimal stress cracking. This material is typically used for bonding thermoplastic substrates in fluid devices such as housings for filters and fittings.

3972™, a 4500 cP adhesive that provides tack-free curing capabilities at wavelengths greater than 254 (nm), including the visible wavelengths in excess of 405 nm. This material is used in devices where there is significant adhesive exposed in the bond line, for example, in tube fittings where the bond line is not encapsulated between two substrates and a tack-free surface is required to prevent contamination.

CHAPTER 4

These light cure acrylic adhesives were selected primarily due to their glass transition temperature (T$_g$) and their ability to be cured under ultraviolet (UV) and/or visible (Vis) wavelengths. T$_g$ is the temperature at which a substance changes from a glassy solid to a rubbery soft material. Loctite® 3921™ has a T$_g$ of 82 °C, while 3933™ and 3972™ have T$_g$s of 54 °C and 49 °C respectively. Glass transition temperature is critical to the performance of a medical device exposed to sterilisation. An adhesive is far less likely to support a load once its T$_g$ has been exceeded as the material becomes soft and pliable, losing its rigidity and strength. While the adhesive's ability to support a load returns after cooling down, any assembly that is under stress during the sterilisation cycle may fail at sterilisation temperatures. The study also included testing two silicone adhesives formulations. For this, the cure method was the most important performance criteria in the selection process:

5056™, a 2 200 cP light cure silicone, offers superior heat and moisture resistance and bonds well to silicone tubing and polycarbonate or thermoplastic fittings. This traditional light cure adhesive will not cure in areas that are not exposed to light of the appropriate wavelength and intensity during the curing process.

5240™, a 25 000 cP dual cure silicone, cures on exposure to light and moisture and offers high tear strength. The secondary moisture cure mechanism allows the adhesive to cure in shadowed areas where light cannot reach. Both of these adhesives would typically be used for bonding respiratory devices such as masks or breathing circuits, or for assembling components made from silicone substrates.

Test method

Glass transition temperature was not a critical factor in the selection of silicone adhesives as the Tg of silicones is typically in the -40°C range and all of the tested sterilisation methods operated above the T$_g$ of silicones.

For this study, Henkel's lab manufactured bubble-free films from all the test adhesives. These films were made in moulds that allowed light transmission and generated films with consistent thicknesses of 0.8 mm for the light cure acrylics and 2 mm for the silicones.

Post-cure, the adhesive films returned to ambient conditions and were prepared into test samples. The cured light cure acrylic films were machined into tensile bars with dimensions of 150 mm by 6 mm. The elastomeric silicones were punched into dog bone

shapes with dimensions of 25 mm wide at the jaws of a mechanical properties tester and 6 mm wide at the neck and an overall length of 115 mm. This shape allowed the force to be concentrated in the neck area, forcing failure away from the jaws.

Once the specimens were prepared, gamma irradiation, ethylene oxide and autoclave sterilisation processes began. The gamma irradiation took place for 108 minutes between 27.3 kiloGray (kGy) to 30.5 kGy. The ethylene oxide specimens were exposed to sterilant for six hours at 15.2 in Hg absolute at 54.4°C. The autoclave samples were exposed for six minutes to 120°C temperatures at 0.103 megapascal (MPa).

Once the sterilisation processes were completed, the samples were tested in a mechanical properties tester for elastic modulus, tensile strength at break, and elongation at break. Samples were placed in the mechanical properties tester and pulled until they broke. Different measurements were taken for each attribute tested.

- Elastic modulus, for this study, is defined as the ratio of stress over strain. This attribute is more relevant for rigid materials such as light cure acrylics than for flexible materials such as silicones. For this reason, silicones were not included in the modulus testing.

- Tensile strength at break measured the strength of the adhesive in terms of force per unit area. For this study, tensile strength was the point on the stress-strain curve where the adhesive sample failed rather than where the sample yielded.

- Elongation, reported as a percentage, measures how far the adhesive can be stretched prior to breaking.

Study results

The results of this study are represented in Charts 3, 4 and 5. Chart 3 reports modulus results and illustrates that gamma, ethylene oxide, and control results are very consistent. Autoclave exposure, however, reduced the rigidity of 3972 by more than 50%. The end-use application truly determines whether this loss of rigidity is critical for the success of the device.

Chart 4 shows the results of tensile strength at break testing. The tensile strength of Loctite® 3921™ increased after autoclaving while its modulus decreased. The tensile strength of Loctite® 3933™, Loctite® 5240™ and Loctite® 5056™ was very consistent across all sterilisation methods.

190   *Excel* Preliminary Engineering Studies

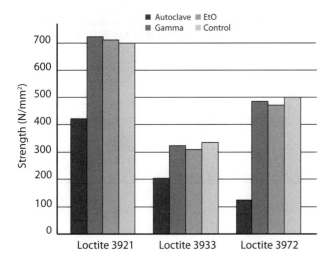

Chart 3 Modulus results

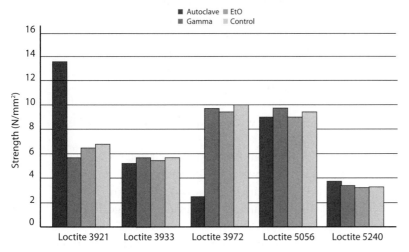

Chart 4 Tensile strength at break

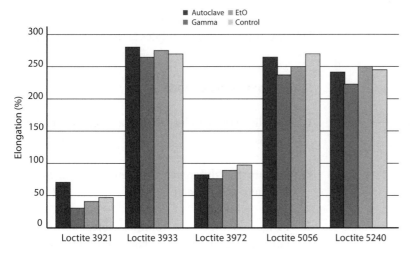

Chart 5 Elongation results

Chart 5 shows the results of elongation testing. After autoclave, the 3921™ exhibited an improved ability to stretch under stress. The remaining adhesives retained their ability to stretch or elongate even after sterilisation, regardless of the sterilisation method employed. Depending on the adhesive chemistry and sterilisation method selected, the study data shows similar performance in all three areas—modulus, elongation and tensile strength—to performance recorded before sterilisation. Put simply, the adhesives tested did not change dramatically as a result of sterilisation.

Conclusion

As a result of this study, engineers designing disposable medical devices should feel confident that the bulk properties of the adhesives will not change significantly when sterilised via ethylene oxide or gamma irradiation. Any changes to the structural integrity of a medical device after sterilisation is related to the interaction of the adhesive and the substrate materials, not to changes to the bulk properties of the adhesive.

Engineers designing non-disposable medical devices should be aware of the difficulties that autoclave presents to adhesives. While the silicones tested in this study performed well under autoclave, designers must understand that this study exposed the adhesives to only one cycle of autoclave sterilisation. A typical non-disposable medical device is exposed to hundreds of autoclave cycles over its usable life, a factor that will undeniably affect the long-term performance of the adhesive.

Regardless of the type of medical device being designed and manufactured, the relationship between the end use of the device, the substrates specified, the adhesive chemistry, and the actual design of the bond joint can all impact the strength of the final assembly, yielding different results for each device. To ensure a robust device design, engineers must thoroughly test the assembly under both manufacturing and sterilisation conditions.

4.7 Sample Preliminary questions and answers

Objective-response questions

1. Which group of materials could be used in surgical instruments today?

   A   PMMA, stainless steel, titanium
   B   UHMWPE, ebony, ivory, PMMA
   C   titanium, Co-Cr alloy, UHMWPE
   D   stainless steel, titanium, Co-Cr alloy

2. A lever with the effort between the fulcrum and the load is a

   A   first-class lever.
   B   first time lever.
   C   third-class lever.
   D   second-class lever.

3. The levers of the human body predominantly act as

   A   magnifiers of force.
   B   magnifiers of effort.
   C   magnifiers of motion.
   D   all of the above.

4. Logic gates

   A   work once only.
   B   invert all decisions.
   C   are the building blocks of digital systems.
   D   produce outputs in a variety of coded formats.

5. Hot isostatic pressing is performed to

   A   repair surface defects.
   B   reduce the size of castings.
   C   improve dimensional tolerances.
   D   improve mechanical properties of castings.

6. Hydroxyaptite is defined as

   A   bioinert.
   B   bioactive.
   C   natural bone.
   D   chemically inert.

7. Calculate the mechanical advantage of the system shown in Figure 4.7.1 given efficiency is 100%.

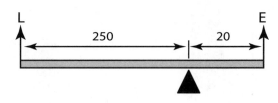

Figure 4.7.1 Mechanical advantage

   A   0.08
   B   8.00
   C   12.5
   D   0.125

8. Active biomedical implants

   A   involve movement.
   B   require a power supply.
   C   are operated by internal batteries.
   D   actively improve bodily functions.

9. Total voltage in a series circuit is equal to

   A   current flowing in the circuit.
   B   the inverse of total resistance.
   C   the sum of all individual resistances.
   D   the sum of the individual voltage drops.

10. A quenched martensitic structure typically exhibits

   A   equiaxed grains.
   B   columnar grains.
   C   a needle-like or acicular structure.
   D   fine grains with precipitates at the grain boundaries.

Short-answer questions

1. Explain why stainless steel has high resistance to corrosion.   (2 marks)

2. Explain the difference between ceramics that are 'bioinert' and 'bioactive'.   (2 marks)

3. Fatigue is the most common form of materials failure. Explain the mechanism of fatigue from initiation to failure.   (2 marks)

Longer-answer questions

1. Compare and contrast the processes of soldering, brazing and welding. (2 marks)

2. Discuss the relative advantages and disadvantages of hot and cold working. (6 marks)

3. Explain how Pasteur's germ theory changed surgical instruments. (3 marks)

4. Determine the calf muscle force that must be exerted to hold the heel in the raised position (Figure 4.7.2) if the ground reaction force (GRF) is 600 N. For the purpose of simplicity, assume the weight of the foot is negligible and all distances represent effective lever arms. (3 marks)

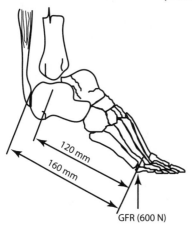

120 mm
160 mm
GFR (600 N)

Figure 4.7.2 Ground force reaction

5. Determine the effective load arm as shown in Figure 4.7.3 when flexing the biceps if the load arm is 150 mm. Illustrate your answer by graphing the angle versus effective lever arm. (4 marks)

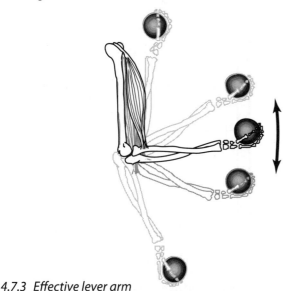

4.7.3 Effective lever arm

Answers to objective-response questions

1. **D** PMMA is a polymer used as a bone cement. Ebony and ivory are no longer used in surgical instruments due to problems with sterilisation. HMWPE is a polymer that has been used to form the cup portion of hip prosthetics.

2. **C** First-class levers and first order levers are the same thing, and have the fulcrum in the middle. Second class levers have the load in the middle. Remember FLE.

3. **C**

4. **C** Logic gates act as digital switches producing a binary output of '0' or '1' working as and when required. Depending on the combinations of logic gates used, various operations can be performed within a circuit. Only some logic gates invert operations.

5. **D**

6. **B** Bioactive is a material similar to the inorganic component of natural bone and therefore compatible with the normal body processes of bone dissolution and growth.

7. **A**
$$MA = \frac{\text{length of effort arm}}{\text{length of load arm}}$$
$$MA = 20 \div 250 = 0.08$$

8. **B**

9. **D**

10. **C**

Answers to short-answer questions

1. A dense tightly adherent layer of chromium oxide forms on the surface, preventing further oxidation.

2. Bioinert ceramics are inert within the body. They do not take part in the body's process of resorption and regrowth. Bioactive ceramics are compatible with the normal body processes of bone dissolution and growth.

3. A fatigue fracture always starts as a small crack which, under repeated application of stress, grows in size. As the crack expands, the load-carrying cross-section of the component is reduced, resulting

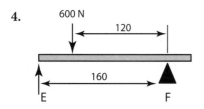

in an increase in stress. Failure occurs progressively over a number of stress cycles taking from several hours to years.

Answers to longer-answer questions

1. Soldering and brazing are similar operations and involve the joining of two or more parts by melting a filler metal with a heat source. The molten filler metal flows into the joint and, on solidifying, holds the parts together. The heat source for soldering is usually a hot 'iron' while brazing is accomplished with the aid of an oxyacetylene torch. The primary difference between the processes is the temperature at which the filler metal solidifies. Soldering uses filler metals with solidification temperatures <500 °C, (e.g. Pb, Sn, Sb etc.), while brazing uses alloys with solidification temperatures >500 °C (e.g. Cu, Ni etc.). Welding is a fusion process where high temperatures melt both the filler rod and the parent material to 'fuse' the materials together and cool in a fashion similar to a casting.

2. Strength, machinability, dimensional accuracy, and surface finish of metals are improved by cold working. Cold work is normally performed at room temperature. There is no oxidation or scaling as seen with hot working. Larger forces are required to perform cold working operations than hot working. Since there is no recrystallisation occurring, metal grains will be significantly distorted, potentially leading to fracture if the ductility of the metal is exceeded. Hot working requires less force to deform metals and may generate favourable directional properties through realignment of fibres.

3. Pasteur's germ theory explained that microscopic organisms (germs) were responsible for many diseases. In an attempt to eliminate infection from germs introduced during surgery, cleaning and sterilisation procedures for surgical instruments were introduced. In order to facilitate cleaning, many instruments were redesigned to allow separation and to eliminate those materials that were not compatible with sterilisation.

4.

Figure 4.7.4 Force diagram

$$\Sigma_{\text{Moments}} = 0$$

$$(\text{effort} \times \text{effort arm}) - (\text{load} \times \text{load arm}) = 0$$

$$(E \times 0.160) - (600 \times 0.120) = 0$$

$$E = 720 \div 0.16 \text{ or } E = 151 \text{ N}$$

5. If the forearm is at an angle of 30° to the horizontal the force diagram will appear as shown in Figure 4.7.5

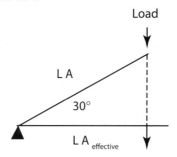

Figure 4.7.5 Effective load arms

The effective load arm will be:

$$\text{LA}_{\text{effective}} = \text{LA} \sin 60° \text{ or LA} \cos 30°$$

Determining the effective load arm in this way for a number of angles allows Table 4.7.6 to be obtained for flexure. A similar data set will be obtained for extension below horizontal.

Angle	0°	30°	45°	60°	75°	90°	120°	135°
LA mm	0	75	106	130	145	150	130	130

Figure 4.7.6 Flexure data

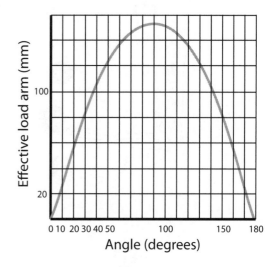

Figure 4.7.7 Plot of effective load arm vs angle

4.8 Glossary

Amorphous	Amorphous materials are usually characterised by certain areas of short-range order. A long-range order, as in crystals, does not exist in amorphous substances. The terms 'amorphous', 'non-crystalline' and 'glassy' are interchangeable.
Antiseptic	Against germs
Aseptic	Without germs
Binary code	Binary code is one based on two states such as 'on' or 'off', 'up' or 'down', 'true' or 'false'. If these two states are represented numerically the two options are the digits '0' or '1'.
Bioactive	Materials that actively promote biological interaction
Biocompatible	Material that is compatible with biological processes
Bioinert	Materials that do not promote or retard biological interaction
Biomedical	Relating to biological and medical systems
Ceramic	A multi-phase material containing phases composed of metals and non-metals, ceramics are typically hard and brittle with good insulating properties.
Composite	Multi-phase materials formed from a combination of materials, which differ in composition or form
Corrosion	An electro-chemical reaction that results in the conversion of metallic materials into oxides, salts or other compounds, metals that undergo corrosion lose strength, ductility and other important mechanical properties
Fulcrum	Point about which a lever arm moves
Glass	Glass is a ceramic produced through the fusing of inorganic materials and cooled to a hard condition without any crystalline structure developing; it is amorphous.
Hydroxyapatite	The principal bone salt $Ca(PO_4)3OH$ which provides the compressive strength of vertebrate bone
Investment casting	Casting process also known as *lost wax casting*
Lever	A simple machine that can be used to magnify effort or motion
Logic gate	Logic gates act as digital switches in which an output of '0' or '1' is produced. Depending on the combinations of logic gates used, various operations can be performed within a circuit.
Nitinol	An alloy of nickel and titanium in almost equal proportions with shape memory properties

Parallel circuit	Parallel circuits form multiple pathways or branches that enable a range of separate paths for current flow.
Passivate	To treat or coat a metal in order to reduce the chemical activity of its surface
PIC	A programmable interface controller (PIC) is a small computer complete with input, output and memory that can be programmed to perform simple tasks.
Plasma spray	A technology used to apply coatings to bio-inserts by spraying powdered particles transformed into plasma, accelerated and deposited in a molten form onto implant surfaces
Prosthesis	A prosthetic device or prosthesis is an artificial part used to replace a damaged or diseased body part.
Resorb	Biological process of dissolving and assimilating tissue such as bone
Scaffold	A temporary structure that allows support for biological growth of bone or tissue
Sepsis	Germs
Series circuit	A simple series connection provides only one pathway for current to flow. Parallel circuits form multiple pathways or branches that enable a range of separate paths for current flow.
Shape memory alloy	Ability of a metal to return to change between two shapes on heating and cooling
Sintering	A heating process used in powder metallurgy, involving the consolidation of metallic powder into a solid compact; temperatures below the melting point of the metal powders are used such that fusion takes place by a process of solid state diffusion
Stainless steel	Iron base alloys of 13–30wt% Cr named for their resistance to discolouration or staining due to corrosion
Titanium	Non-ferrous metal used extensively in industry due to its high resistance to corrosion and good strength-to-weight ratio; these properties along with excellent biocompatibility has seen titanium and its alloys used in biomedical applications
Torque	The moment of a force; a measure of a force's tendency to produce torsion and rotation about an axis.
Transcutaneous charging	Allows for re-charging of implanted devices through the skin without direct contact between the device and the charger
Truth table	Used in digital electronics, a truth table predicts the output of a circuit under all possible combinations of input and output conditions.
Weld decay	A popular term for a defect that may occur as a result of welding stainless steels. The region adjacent to the weld may reach a sufficiently high temperature to precipitate chromium carbides at the grain boundaries. The region adjacent to the grain boundaries are consequently depleted in chromium, resulting in a loss of corrosion resistance.

ENGINEERING STUDIES

Sample Preliminary examination

General Instructions

- Reading time – 5 minutes

- Working time – 3 hours

- Write using black or blue pen. Black pen is preferred.

- Draw diagrams using pencil.

- Calculators may be used.

- You may assume gravity to be 10 m/s^2

- A formulae sheet is provided at the back of this paper.

- Diagrams are not drawn to scale.

Total marks – 100

> Section I

20 marks

- Attempt Questions 1–20.

- Allow about 30 minutes for this section.

> Section II

80 marks

- Attempt Questions 21–27.

- Allow about 2 hours and 30 minutes for this section.

Section I

20 marks
Attempt Questions 1–20.
Allow about 30 minutes for this section.

Circle the letter corresponding to the correct response.

1. Concurrent vector forces act

A   parallel to each other.
B   through the same point.
C   within the same time frame.
D   along the same line of action.

2. Secondary bonds result from

A   intermolecular dipole attraction.
B   sharing of electrons in the outer shell.
C   an electron cloud or gas of valence electrons.
D   the loss or gain of an electron in the outer shell.

3. Polymeric structures may be defined as

A   hard, tough, elastic, ductile.
B   branched, linear, network or cross-linked.
C   thermosetting, devitrified, repetitive and ionic.
D   thermosoftening, thermosetting, amorphous, conductors.

4. Identify the structure from those shown below that represents a steel beyond the eutectoid point (0.83% C).

A   B   C   D

5. In the front view of a multi-view orthogonal drawing, a horizontal surface will appear as

A   a point.
B   an ellipse.
C   a normal line.
D   a foreshortened surface.

6. An object is propelled along a straight-line path by a force. If the net force were doubled, its acceleration would

A   double.
B   be halved.
C   be quadrupled.
D   stay the same.

7. The type of stainless steel formed is determined by the interplay between

A   iron and nickel.
B   iron and chromium.
C   nickel and chromium.
D   ferrite and austenite stabilising elements.

8. Calculate the strain in a 35 mm long, 1.2 mm^2 wire with a Young's modulus of 90 GPa when it is loaded to 50 N.

A 0.463×10^{-3}
B   0.016
C   41.67
D   42

9. Given that orthographic drawings are created in 3rd angle projection, identify the correct top and front views of the isometric drawing shown below.

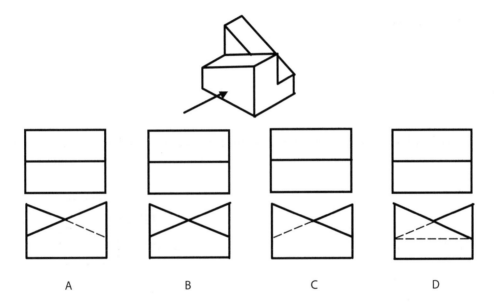

A   B   C   D

10. Physical qualities determining mould material in casting operations is decided by

A   mould material costs.
B   component size and number of mould runners.
C   heating method of cast material and mould cavity size.
D   material casting temperatures and mould reusability requirements.

11. An example of kinetic energy is

A   a battery.
B   a wound spring.
C   a car driving at a constant velocity.
D   an elevator at the top of a shaft ready to descend.

12. In conventional current

A   the flow is from the positive terminal to the negative terminal.
B   the flow is the same as true current flow.
C   the flow is from the negative terminal to the positive terminal.
D   protons move as opposed to electrons.

13. Which one of the following types of stress-strain relationship best describes the behavior of brittle materials such as ceramics?

A   ductile
B   elastic
C   plastic
D   tough

14. A unique property of cast iron is its

A   stiffness.
B   brittleness.
C   high hardness.
D   damping capacity.

15. A truck travelling at a constant velocity suddenly brakes. The force on a box (at the point of moving), sitting in the truck back is

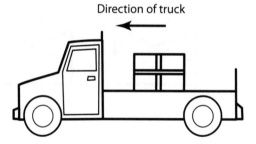

Direction of truck

A   zero if no movement of the box.
B $F = \mu_s N$ forwards in the truck.
C $F = \mu_s N$ towards the back of the truck.
D   greater than $F = \mu_s N$ in the original direction of the truck.

16. Allotropic materials

A   exhibit the same strength properties in all directions.
B   retain their structural form over a range of temperatures.
C   exist in different structural forms at different temperatures.
D   are materials in which a process, such as a chemical reaction, proceed at the same rate, regardless of direction.

17. Third-class levers

A   offer a mechanical advantage.
B   have an input effort that is lower than the output load.
C   have the fulcrum placed between the load and the effort.
D   move the load (or load arm) a greater than the distance moved by the effort.

18. Which of the vectors in the force diagram represents a resultant?

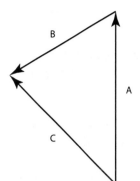

A   A and B
B   C and A
C   only vector C
D   A, B and C

19. Engineers should follow the appropriate professional code of ethics because

A   the public will trust engineers more.
B   it will help in avoiding legal problems, such as getting sued.
C   it raises the image of the profession and therefore engineer's pay.
D   it provides a clear definition of an engineer's responsibilities and what the public has a right to expect.

20. A basic electric circuit is composed of

A   a switch, a battery and a copper wire.
B   a load, a resistor and a conductive path for current to flow.
C   a voltage source, a load and a conductive path for current to flow.
D   a voltage source, a conductive path for current to flow and a battery.

Section II

80 marks
Attempt Questions 21–27.
Allow about 2 hours and 30 minutes for this section.

Answer the questions in the spaces provided. These spaces provide guidance for the expected length of response.

Question 21 (10 marks)

(a) Braking systems can have environmental and medical repercussions. Discuss how each of these   **3**
factors is a consideration for materials selection.

Environmental considerations:

_____

_____

_____

Medical considerations:

_____

_____

_____

(b) As transport systems evolved from horse-drawn carts to internal combustion engine driven vehicles,   **2**
why was it imperative that braking systems improve?

_____

_____

(c) Explain how technological advances such as hydraulic systems improved braking.   **3**

_____

_____

_____

(d) Explain how modern tecchnological systems such as regenerative braking reduce vehicle   **2**
environmental impacts.

_____

_____

Section II (continued)

Question 22 (12 marks)

(a) A box of brake parts is transported as shown. Determine the pressure in the 125 mm diameter hydraulic cylinder supporting the boom shown below if the crate has a mass of 200 kg (ignore the mass of the supporting cable). **3**

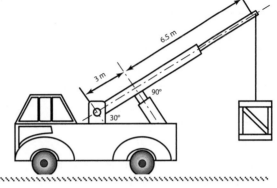

_____

_____

_____

_____

_____

(b) Calculate the shear force required to punch out the brake plate steel blank shown below given: the perimeter of the blank is 475 mm, the holes are each 15 mm in diameter, the plate is 8 mm thick and the ultimate shear strength of the plate is 400 MPa. **3**

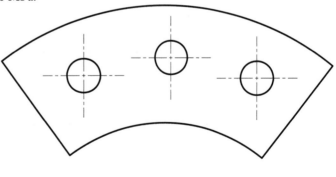

_____

_____

_____

_____

_____

Question 22 (continued)

(c) Oil is often chosen for use as a hydraulic fluid. Outline TWO reasons for this choice.   2

_____

_____

_____

_____

_____

_____

(d) Tension springs for brakes are made from 0.8% carbon steel. Their high yield strength is obtained   2
from heat treatment. Describe this heat treatment process.

_____

_____

_____

_____

(e) Many composites are comprised of a matrix and fibres. Describe the functions of these components   2
within a composite material.

_____

_____

_____

_____

Section II (continued)

Question 23   (12 marks)

Disposable scalpels such as the one shown below are often made of stainless steel. In this situation, the stainless steel is is only 0.5 mm thick.

(a) Complete the top view of the scalpel in the space below and correctly dimension the thickness of the blade.   **6**

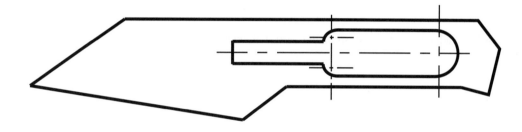

Question 23 (continued)

(b) The internal mounting section of the scalpel occasionally fails at the points indicated. How does   **2**
the design of the object contribute to its failure?

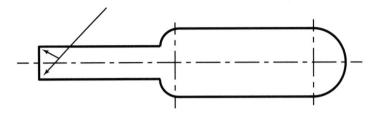

_____

_____

_____

(c) In the space below sketch an improved design that would alleviate the problem identified above.   **1**

(d) Early scalpels used by the Egyptians were made of obsidian. Identify TWO reasons why obsidian   **3**
was used in the past and ONE resaon why obsidian has been replaced today.

_____

_____

_____

_____

_____

Section II (continued)

Question 24   (12 marks)

(a) The components of an electric iron include a body, sole plate, water tank, power cable, plug and various internal components (including electrical insulators). Complete the table below (the 'plug casing' is filled out as an example).   **6**

Part	Specific material	Manufacturing method	Forming property	Service property
Plug casing	Nylon	Injection moulded	May be liquefied to allow injection	Electrical and heat insulator
Sole plate		Cast then machined	Castability	
Water tank	Polyethylene			Water-resistant Chemical-resistant Transparent
Ceramic insulator	Aluminium oxide (Al_2O_3)		Vitrifies on firing forming glassy matrix	

(b) Which of the molecular structures shown below best reflects the material chosen for the water tank? Justify your choice.   **2**

A   B   C

_____

_____

_____

_____

Question 24 (continued)

(c) A wing nut on a domestic lawnmower holds a throttle cable in place. If the nut is tightened clockwise to a torque of 1.2 Nm and the nut has the dimensions shown, sketch the force-couple required to loosen the nut. Ignore friction.

2

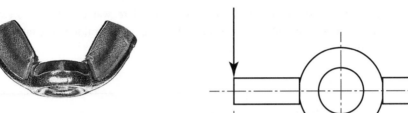

(d) Identify a protective covering for the throttle cable and explain how it may be applied.

2

_____

_____

_____

_____

_____

_____

Section II (continued)

Question 25 (12 marks)

(a) Determine how much your leg shortens when you stand up, if the supporting bone has a Young's modulus of 16.8 GPa. Assume a bone area of 300 mm^2, length 1.26 m and body mass of 58.5 kg.   **4**

(b) The crush strength of teeth varies depending on the tooth in question (134, 195 and 277 Mpa). Using the tooth strength data provided, how many of the teeth could be crushed if the effort applied to the forceps handles was as high as 550 Newtons. Assume the pliers are 100% efficient and a tooth area of 4 mm × 4 mm.   **4**

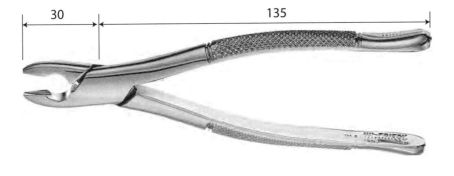

(c) Describe FOUR steps in the process of investment casting a hip replacement.   **4**

Section II (continued)

Question 26   (12 marks)

(a) Calculate the force in the brake cable shown when a 47 N force is applied to the hand brake lever.   **2**

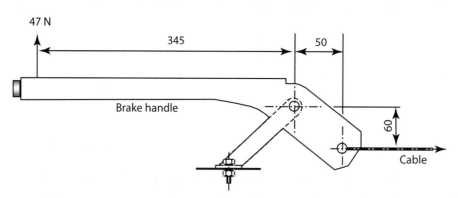

47 N

345

50

Brake handle

60

Cable

_____

_____

_____

(b) In the disc brake illustrated below, the coefficient between the brake pads and the disc is 0.4 and the effective radius of the brake pads is 100 mm. If the disc is travelling at 3 000 rpm and the force on each pad is 100 N, calculate the moment resisting rotation of the disc.   **2**

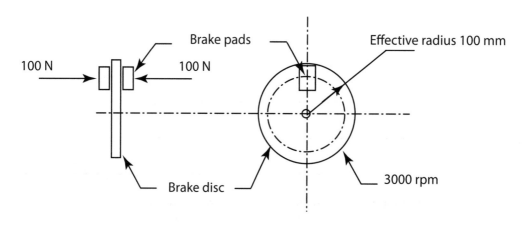

100 N

Brake pads

100 N

Effective radius 100 mm

Brake disc

3000 rpm

_____

_____

_____

(c) If the disc in the brake system described above makes 20 revolutions before coming to rest, calculate the energy absorbed by the pads while the disc is brought to a stop.

3

_____

_____

_____

_____

(d) Describe how parking brake cables are manufactured.

3

_____

_____

_____

_____

(e) Explain how design features incorporated into brake discs help dissipate excess heat.

2

_____

_____

_____

_____

Section II (continued)

Question 27 **(10 marks)**

(a) The CAD drawing of a dental implant shows a top view, a rendered front view and an isometric of the component. Complete the right side view as a full section considering that the bored hole in the centre only penetrates approximately halfway down. Construct your sketch using AS1100 standards. **6**

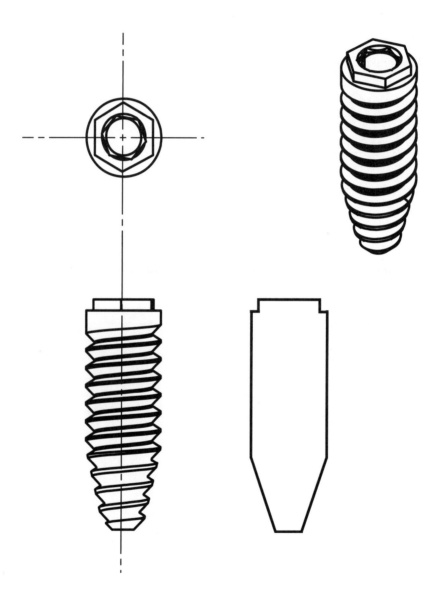

Question 27 (continued)

(b) Complete the table for the dental implant drawing shown on the previous page.   2

Name a suitable metal for the implant	
Name TWO pieces of information that the full section reveals	

(c) Corrosion is an important factor in bio-implants. Describe the mechanism of passivation and   2 how it protects specific materials.

_____

_____

_____

_____

End of paper

FORMULAE SHEET

Force, Moments

$F = ma$; $M = Fd$

If a body is in equilibrium, then $\Sigma F_x = 0$; $\Sigma F_y = 0$; $\Sigma M = 0$

Friction

$F = \mu N$; $\mu = \tan\phi$

Energy, Work, Power

$KE = \frac{1}{2}mv^2$; $PE = mgh$; $W = Fs = \Delta PE + \Delta KE$; $P = \dfrac{W}{t}$; $P = \dfrac{Fs}{t}$

Pressure

$P = \dfrac{F}{A}$; $P = P_o + \rho gh$

Stress and Strain

$\sigma = \dfrac{F}{A}$; $\varepsilon = \dfrac{e}{L}$; $E = \dfrac{\sigma}{\varepsilon}$; $\sigma = \dfrac{My}{I}$

$\sigma_{allowable} = \dfrac{\sigma_{yield}}{F \text{ of } S}$ (Ductile) ; $\sigma_{allowable} = \dfrac{\sigma_{UTS}}{F \text{ of } S}$ (Brittle)

Machines

$MA = \dfrac{L}{E}$; $VR = \dfrac{d_E}{d_L}$; $\eta = \dfrac{MA}{VR}$

Digital Electronics

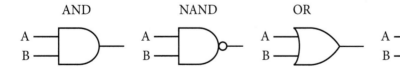

| AND | NAND | OR | NOR |

Electricity, Electronics

$E = IR$; $P = I^2R$

Series $R_t = R_1 + R_2 + R_3 + R_4 + \ldots R_n$

Parallel $\dfrac{1}{R_t} = \dfrac{1}{R_1} + \dfrac{1}{R_2} + \dfrac{1}{R_3} + \dfrac{1}{R_4} + \ldots \dfrac{1}{R_n}$

Sample Preliminary examination answers

Section I answers

(20 marks)

Questions 1–20

1.	B	11.	C
2.	A	12.	A
3.	B	13.	B
4.	B	14.	D
5.	C	15.	C
6.	A	16.	C
7.	D	17.	D
8.	A	18.	C
9.	A	19.	D
10.	D	20.	C

Section II answers

(80 marks)

Question 21 (10 marks)

(a) Environmental considerations:
Copper-containing dust entering the environment can find its way into the soil and water table either via stormwater or airborne particle deposition.

Mercury switches have been phased out from ABS systems due to their persistence in the environment and potential risks to contaminating people, land animals and marine life.

Medical considerations:
Workers in companies using raw materials or products containing asbestos inhale fibres suspended in the air, thus jeopardising their health, and may carry fibres home on their clothing to contaminate household environments.

Fibres generated as part of the braking process from asbestos-based brake pads can lodge in the lungs and induce adverse respiratory conditions such as mesothelioma (cancer of the thin membrane that surrounds the lung and other internal organs).

Breathing of dust particles (such as those produced from copper-based pads during braking) has been known to cause disruption of the body's normal enzymatic activity.

(b) Larger, more powerful and faster vehicles required better braking systems to stop vehicles predictably, reliably, effectively and safely.

(c) Hydraulic systems improved braking via:
- reducing overall weight
- increasing values for mechanical advantage
- better, more even distribution of force to each brake surface
- improved response times, and a better transfer of energy between the driver's foot and the brake
- a greater freedom of design considering flexible hydraulic lines did not need to be mounted on rigid mountings.

(d) Vehicle environmental impacts are:
- reduced vehicle emissions
- improved fuel economy
- extended battery pack life on hybrid vehicles.

Question 22   (10 marks)

(a) To find F in the hydraulic ram use lever arms.

Force from crate = 200 × 10

$$= 2 \times 10^3 \text{ N} \quad = 2 \text{ kN}$$

$$3 \times F = 2 \text{ kN} \times 9.5 \cos 30$$

$$F = 5.48 \text{ kN}$$

Note that because the load was at an angle the effective lever arm was calculated for the crate.

$$\text{area} = \pi \times d^2 \div 4$$

$$= \pi \times 15\,625 \div 4 = 1\,2271.8 \text{ mm}^2$$

Pressure in the cylinder = load /area

$$= 5.48 \times 10^3 \div 1\,2271.8$$

$$= 0.44 \text{ N/mm}^2 \text{ or } 0.44 \text{ MPa}$$

(b) Area under shear = $[475 + 3(\Pi\, d)] \times 8$

$$= [475 + (3 \times 15\, \Pi\,)] \times 8$$

$$= (475 + 141.37) \times 8$$

$$= 616.37 \times 8$$

$$= 4930.97 \text{ mm}^2$$

$$\text{Stress} = \frac{\text{Force}}{\text{area}}$$

Shear force = Stress × area

$$= 400 \times 4\,930.97$$

$$= 1,972,389.342 \text{ N or } 1.97 \text{ MN}$$

(c) Any TWO of:

- little or no compressibility of the fluid supports even transmission of force in all directions
- 'slippery' nature reduces friction and wear
- non-corrosive properties preserves system components
- ability to operate over a range of temperatures.

(d) Heat to 770 °C–800 °C. Quench in oil to harden. Reheat to 200 °C–400 °C according to temper desired and cool slowly.

(e) The matrix acts as a binder to hold and suspend the fibres. The matrix transfers loads to fibres while at the same time protecting them from abrasion and exposure to the environment.

The fibres are dispersed throughout the binder and are used to support loads. Different configurations and types of fibres provide specific properties.

Question 23 (12 marks)

(a)

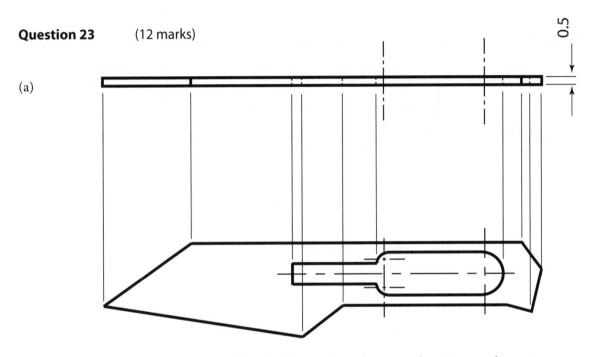

Projection position length, outlines, hidden detail, center line, dimension lines/arrows, dimension

(b) The sharp corners act as stress raisers concentrating and focusing stresses at the corner where cracks are often first initiated.

(c) Curves replace sharp corners.

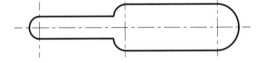

(d) Advantages to ancient cultures include readily available raw material, non-porous volcanic glass, easily cleaned, easily obtained sharp edge using tools and technologies available at the time.

Reasons for replacement with modern alternatives include obsidian can be brittle, no concerns about flaws in natural materials, mass production of individually sterilised and packaged sharp and hard stainless steel blades.

Question 24   (12 marks)

(a)

Part	Specific material	Manufacturing method	Forming property	Service property
Plug casing	Nylon	Injection moulded	May be liquefied to allow injection	Electrical and heat insulator
Sole plate	**Stainless steel or aluminium alloy**	Cast then machined	Castability	**Corrosion-resistant or conductor of heat**
Water tank	Polyethylene	**Blow moulding**	**Pliant over a range of temperartures**	Water-resistant Chemical-resistant Transparent
Ceramic insulator	Aluminium oxide (Al_2O_3)	**Cast then fired**	Vitrifies on firing forming glassy matrix	**Electrical insulator**

(b) Polyethylene—Structure A represents a linear thermosoftening polymer suitable for blow moulding.

B is incorrect because it shows cross linking while C shows a branched structure, both of which are unsuitable for blow moulding.

(c)

d = 0.016 m $M = F \times d$

M = 1.2 Nm $F = \dfrac{M}{d}$

$= \dfrac{1.2}{0.016}$

$= 75$ N

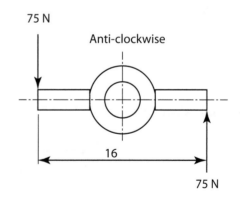

(d) The cable may be passed through an extrusion die where a protective coating of heated PVC covers the cable.

Question 25   (12 marks)

(a) Load $= 58.5 \times 10$ N   Convert all measurements to mm

Stress $(\sigma) =$ load/area
$$= 585 \div 300$$
$$= 1.95 \text{ N/mm}^2$$
$$= 1.95 \text{ MPa}$$

Young's modulus $(E) =$ stress $\div$ strain

strain $=$ stress $\div$ E
$$= 1.95 \div (16.8 \times 10^3)$$
$$= 0.116 \times 10^{-3}$$

strain $(\varepsilon) = \Delta l / l_o$

Therefore,
$$\Delta l / l_o = 0.116 \times 10^{-3}$$
$$\Delta l = 1.26 \times 10^3 \times 0.116 \times 10^{-3}$$
$$= 0.146 \text{ mm}$$

(b) Force generated at tooth: $F_E \times D_E = F_L \times D_L$

$$550 \times 135 = F_L \times 30$$

$$F_L = \frac{550 \times 135}{30}$$

$$F_L = 2\,475 \text{ N}$$

Compressive stress at tooth   Stress $= \dfrac{\text{load}}{\text{area}}$ (area of 4 mm × 4 mm assumed)

$$= \frac{2475}{16}$$

$$= 154.7 \text{ MPa}$$

Previous crush strength data for teeth of 134, 195 and 277 MPa shows that with the calculation above it is possible to crush at least one of these teeth.

(c) A permanent mould or die (often made of metal) is used to produce an expendable wax pattern.

The wax pattern is subsequently dipped into a series of ceramic slurries, gradually building up a outer casing.

After setting, the mould is gently heated to melt the wax pattern, leaving a smooth mould cavity behind.

In the final stage of production, metal is cast into the mould to form the part.

Question 26   (12 marks)

(a) $F_1 \times d_1 = F_2 \times d_2$

$47 \times 345 = F_2 \times 60$

$F_2 = \dfrac{47 \times 345}{60}$

$= 270.25$ N

(b) $F_R = \mu N$

$= 0.4 \times 100$

$= 40$ N force

Resisting moment $= (40 \times 0.100) \times 2$ pads

Resisting moment $= 4$ Nm $\times 2 = 8$ Nm

(c)   Energy $=$ ability to do work (W).

$W = Fs$

$= F \,(\pi \times d \times \text{revolutions})$

$= 100 \,(\pi \times 0.2 \times 20) \times 2$ pads

$= 2\,513.27$ J

$= 2.5$ kJ

(d) Individual strands of high carbon steel (0.7%C–0.8%C) are cold drawn through a series of dies until the desired diameter is achieved. The heavily cold worked strands are then twisted together to form a multi-stranded cable.

(e) Perforations: drilled or slotted brake discs increase surface area, allowing increased airflow to take heat away from the disc, thus improving performance, reducing wear and maintaining dimensional stability.

Question 27   (10 marks)

(a)

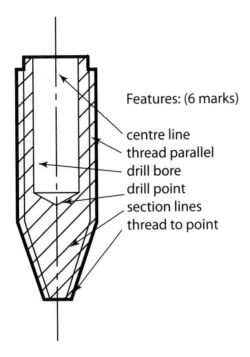

Features: (6 marks)

centre line
thread parallel
drill bore
drill point
section lines
thread to point

(b)

Name a suitable metal for the implant	Titanium, stainless steel
Name TWO pieces of information that the full section reveals	Width and depth of drill penetration, thread pitch, drill point cavity

(c) Corrosion rate depends on the reactivity of the material in the environment. Porous, loosely adhering oxides allow continued corrosion by either allowing corrosion through the oxide or by loss of the oxide, exposing the surface to further attack. In biomedical engineering materials exhibiting passivation include titanium and stainless steel. The rate at which a dense, tightly adherent protective oxide is formed at the surface determines how well a metal surface is protected from continuing attack.

INDEX

F

G

H

I

K

L

M

N

W

weld decay 173, 196

welding 37, 44–46, 84, 164–165, 173, 193–194, 196

wood 32, 40, 48, 56–57, 107, 126, 131, 136, 148–149, 151, 153

work hardening 25, 35, 78–79, 101–103, 105, 129, 168, 171

X

X-ray 41, 86, 145–146, 152

Y

yield point 132, 135, 137, 141, 168–169

Young's modulus 25, 116, 119, 137, 141, 169, 178

Z

zirconia 170, 180, 182

NOTES